The Dynamics of Global Economic Governance

The Dynamics of Global Economic Governance

The Financial Crisis, the OECD and the Politics of International Tax Cooperation

Richard Eccleston

Associate Professor, University of Tasmania, Australia

Edward Elgar

Cheltenham, UK • Northampton, MA, USA

Published by
Edward Elgar Publishing Limited
The Lypiatts
15 Lansdown Road
Cheltenham
Glos GL50 2JA
UK

Edward Elgar Publishing, Inc.
William Pratt House
9 Dewey Court
Northampton
Massachusetts 01060
USA

A catalogue record for this book
is available from the British Library

Library of Congress Control Number: 2012943744

ISBN 978 1 84980 279 6 (cased)

Typeset by Servis Filmsetting Ltd, Stockport, Cheshire
Printed and bound by MPG Books Group, UK

Contents

Acknowledgements

Writing this book and trying to make sense of the financial crisis and its many and varied impacts on international economic relations has been quite a journey and I have accumulated a number of debts, both personal and professional along the way.

Firstly the project would not have been possible without strategic funding from the University of Tasmania and the Australian Research Council (Discovery Project 1095946). I am also indebted to the 40 or more national tax officials, business and NGO representatives as well as OECD and UN staff who were willing to discuss developments in the international tax regime. In order to elicit frank and at times critical perspectives on politically sensitive aspects of international taxation these interviews were conducted on a non-attributable basis. So while interviewees are not acknowledged by name in the pages that follow, I am very grateful for your time and contributions.

The book and broader project has benefited from feedback from numerous colleagues and seminars and workshops held in Australia, the United States and the United Kingdom. Specific thanks go to colleagues at the University of Tasmania including Aynsley Kellow, Peter Carroll, Hannah Murphy, Matt Sussex and Matt Killingsworth. I would also like to thank Tim Woolley for his research assistance. More generally I would like to thank Jason Sharman, Stephen Bell, John Ravenhill, Andy Hindmoor, Wes Widmaier, Shahar Hameiri, Dale Pinto, John Passant, Adrian Sawyer, Len Seabrooke, Sol Picciotto, David Spencer, Tony Porter, Rod Rhodes, Oran Young and Bob Reinalda for their various contributions to my thinking large and small. I owe a particular debt to Richard Woodward from the University of Hull for providing detailed comments on the manuscript. While the analysis that follows has benefited greatly from these many and varied contributions I naturally assume responsibility for any errors or omissions.

On the production front, I can't speak highly enough of Laura Seward, Jenny Wilcox, Emma Gribbon, Barbara Slater and their colleagues at Edward Elgar for their patience and support and for providing timely and professional editorial assistance.

Finally, I owe a great deal to my friends and family for their unwavering support. Special thanks go to my wife Claire, both for her love and under-standing and for shouldering more than her fair share of responsibility for caring for our three young sons. I would also like to acknowledge my deep appreciation for the assistance Claire's parents (Heather and Tony) have provided for our family, especially when I have been abroad conducting research for this project.

I would like to dedicate this book to our three little boys, Sam, Nicholas and Benjamin as well as to the memory of my late mother Diane. I only hope that we can succeed in providing our children with the love and support that I enjoyed as a child.

RICHARD ECCLESTON
HOBART
AUGUST 2012

Introduction: the financial crisis and the politics of international tax cooperation

The ongoing financial crisis, which first disrupted world markets in early 2008, is now entering its fifth year, and the outlook for the global economy remains as fragile as ever. Despite the initial success of the policy responses to the crisis devised by G20 leaders, the tepid recovery of 2009 and 2010 has waned as unprecedented levels of sovereign debt have triggered renewed financial instability in the eurozone and beyond. The political and economic malaise which continues to threaten the global economy has many dimensions. Through a detailed analysis of one aspect of the regulatory response to the financial crisis – international tax cooperation – this book examines the ways in which the ongoing crisis has influenced patterns of international economic cooperation and assesses the prospects of providing effective global governance. In addressing these issues this book aims to shed light on what is emerging as one of the critical questions of our age: Does the international system have the political capacity to devise and implement an effective governance response to the grave challenges currently facing the global economy?

The analysis that follows focuses on one dimension of the international policy response to the financial crisis – albeit a critically important one. The detailed analysis of the politics of international tax cooperation presented in this book is motivated by three sets of considerations. First, improved international tax cooperation in general and increased tax transparency and information exchange in particular promise to enhance the capacity of national governments to tax the offshore assets of resident individuals and companies. Even before the onset of the financial crisis international tax evasion was regarded as a significant and growing problem. Estimates vary, but there is a rough consensus that governments may lose as much as $US300 billion per annum through international tax evasion (Palan et al. 2010, 63; Hollingshead 2010). The threat of international tax evasion has long been a concern to relatively high-tax European welfare states, but as the financial crisis has evolved into a severe sovereign debt crisis the goal of improving international tax enforcement and compliance now enjoys broad-based support.

International taxation is also an important case study because of the nature of the governance problem at the heart of tax cooperation and the institutional structure of the international tax regime. International tax cooperation represents a critical test of governance capacity in the aftermath of the financial crisis because despite the growing resolve among world leaders to address the problem, the reality is that reaching and enforcing international tax agreements is notoriously difficult. This is because national governments (even within the European Union) fiercely defend their sovereign right to tax and spend in accordance with domestic political imperatives. Moreover, while there is a consensus that enhanced international tax cooperation would yield global welfare benefits, there are also powerful economic incentives for individual countries to defect from any agreement. As will be explained in greater detail in Chapter 2, international tax cooperation represents a *collaboration problem*; a problem that is traditionally difficult to resolve without robust enforcement procedures that can be imposed on potential defectors. Despite the governance challenges involved, the importance of an effective international tax regime for global commerce has led to the formation of a complex legal, diplomatic and organisational apparatus which aims to promote international tax cooperation. Given this level of institutionalisation this study presents an opportunity to assess the ability of international regimes to promote cooperation in relation to contested collaboration problems. In short, the international tax arena can yield important lessons concerning global economic governance in the twenty-first century.

Finally, the case of international tax cooperation has been widely lauded as one of the more successful examples of international cooperation and regulatory reform arising from the financial crisis. Keen to highlight their diplomatic achievements, world leaders and senior tax officials argue that more international tax agreements were delivered in the 10 months following the G20's endorsement of the OECD's standard for tax information exchange in early 2009 than was achieved in the preceding 10 years (Gurria 2009). The contrast between this apparent success in relation to international taxation cooperation compared to other regulatory arenas, where progress has been more problematic, raises a number of questions. Was cooperation enhanced by an existing policy consensus, or can the process be explained in terms of strategies and diplomatic efforts employed by the organisations and actors at the heart of the regime? Or were the changing economic incentives and new ideas emerging from the crisis important drivers of regime change and cooperation? Finally, how did changing domestic political factors influence the policy preferences of key states in the international tax regime? By systematically exploring these questions this book will evaluate the complex ways in which the financial crisis shaped the international reform agenda and the political and economic context in which international tax cooperation occurs. On a less sanguine note, the book concludes by arguing that despite the progress that has been made in terms of brokering international tax agreements, very significant barriers to effective implementation and ongoing compliance remain, threatening the sustainability of the regime. This more pessimistic assessment concerning the effectiveness of the regime poses fundamental questions about the prospects of achieving effective global economic governance in the aftermath of the financial crisis.

In order to explore these themes the book presents a historical account of the evolution of the international tax regime, or 'the sets of rules and decision-making procedures that give rise to social practices and assign roles to participants and govern their interactions' in the international tax arena (Young 1999, 5). Within this broad field of enquiry there is a particular emphasis on attempts to broker international agreements to restrict international tax evasion or the unlawful concealment of income and assets in order to avoid tax obligations, although it must also be noted that in practice this distinction between legal tax avoidance and illegal tax evasion is subject to the vagaries of legal interpretation (Picciotto 2011, 226). This historical approach is necessary because established practices, ideas and institutions provide both the context in which contemporary governance problems are defined and the strategies and resources that can be drawn upon in order to solve them. This longitudinal research strategy is also necessary in order to assess regime dynamics, or the ways in which patterns of international cooperation vary over time and the political and economic causes of such changes.

In addition to providing a historical account of the evolution of international tax cooperation in general and of tax information exchange in particular, the analysis that follows is designed to enhance our theoretical understanding of the dynamics of international regime change and the role of the financial crisis in shaping patterns of international tax cooperation. As will be outlined in greater detail in Chapter 2, there is an extensive and diverse literature encompassing both rationalist and sociological traditions on the politics of international cooperation. A common theme in the most recent contributions to this scholarship is the need for empirically grounded 'synthetic interpretations of change' which analyse the diverse factors influencing the nature and effectiveness of international agreements (Keohane 2009, 40). Reflecting this theoretical ambition, Chapters 3 to 6 are designed to assess the relative importance of material, institutional, ideational and domestic political variables in shaping patterns of cooperation in the international tax arena.

THE REFORM AGENDA

International taxation is mind bogglingly complex. Basic principles concerning which jurisdiction has the right to tax an international transaction
may be relatively straightforward, but the complexity of global commerce
combined with years of entrepreneurial (and increasingly aggressive) tax
planning have spawned complex provisions concerning all manner of
specialist topics from 'thin capitalisation' to 'transfer pricing', and from
'permanent establishment' to 'controlled foreign corporations'. While
technical debates concerning each of these regulatory issues are important,
in public debate at least they have been eclipsed by the growing political
controversy concerning tax transparency and information exchange. As
is explained in greater detail in the next chapter, the most egregious and
common cases of international tax evasion involve the deliberate non-
disclosure of assets and investments concealed in what are commonly
described as 'tax havens' or 'secrecy jurisdictions'. The reform agenda
that has dominated the international tax policy debate since the mid-1990s
concerns creating a regime to promote tax transparency by establishing procedures for tax and financial information exchange between tax
authorities with a view to creating an environment in which governments
can accurately determine their residents' worldwide income, including
funds held offshore. Few would argue that reaching agreement on and
implementing an effective regime for tax information exchange would
resolve all of the challenges and controversies associated with international tax avoidance and competition, but most concur that such an agreement would represent unprecedented progress towards the broader goal
of creating an efficient, equitable and sustainable framework for taxing
capital income. Given the prominence of the political debate associated
with tax information exchange and the potential impact it could have on
international tax evasion, this book focuses on the politics of the international tax transparency regime.

THE POLITICS OF INTERNATIONAL TAX
COOPERATION

Taxation is best regarded as a necessary evil. Tax revenue may be the
financial lifeblood of the modern state yet even in the face of spiralling
budget deficits, governments the world over find it increasingly difficult
to make a political or economic case to increase taxation (Sachs 2011;
Martin 2009). The increasingly problematic nature of the fiscal contract
may be most apparent in the domestic context but it applies equally to

international taxation. At this level governments want to maximise their tax take without compromising their ability to attract mobile international investment (Webb 2004). This basic rationale has informed many strategies, from the creation of preferential tax regimes, such as that introduced in Ireland in the late 1990s to attract investment into strategic industries, to the more general trend towards taxing mobile capital more generously than labour income or consumption (Blue 2000). The same logic explains the growth of tax havens, which in a general sense can be defined as jurisdictions whose 'laws and other measures can be used to evade or avoid the tax laws or regulations of other jurisdictions' (TJN 2007). This general definition provides a useful foundation for the analysis that follows, but given our interest in tax transparency, this book focuses on the closely related concept of a 'secrecy jurisdiction', or 'a state, dependency or other form of government which is either unable to obtain, unwilling to hold, or reluctant to share tax and financial information in accordance with accepted international practices and agreements' (OECD 2000). Whereas some jurisdictions may have historically been defined as tax havens because they impose low or non-existent taxation, or perhaps because they offered preferential tax rates to foreign investors, our concern is with the financial secrecy that is the root cause of international tax evasion.

This subtle distinction between a secrecy jurisdiction and a tax haven is also important because, as the analysis presented in this book will highlight, some wealthy high-tax states that would not traditionally be categorised as tax havens may conceal the identities of offshore investors in order to attract foreign capital. In short, both traditional tax havens and wealthy industrialised states have used tax and financial secrecy to promote foreign investment. Finally, while the definition of secrecy jurisdictions provided above is central to the analysis below, it is important to note there is an ongoing debate concerning what constitutes accepted 'international practice' given that no jurisdiction wants to be accused of being in breach of accepted international standards. This debate over establishing an appropriate standard for tax information exchange and the process for assessing whether jurisdictions conform with this standard is a central focus of the second half of this book.

In broad terms secrecy jurisdictions represent a global governance problem because they promote their tax and financial opacity to attract savings from wealthy foreign investors eager to evade tax obligations in their country of residence. In the case of traditional tax havens, such as the Cayman Islands, Luxembourg or Jersey, with their low tax rates and finance oriented economies, tax secrecy has served as a catalyst for the creation of a relatively large financial services sector that stands as the cornerstone of the local economy. Tax havens that follow this development strategy soon become politically and economically dependent on financial services and are naturally resistant to any proposal to enhance tax transparency given the fundamental threat it poses to their established business models. Less well understood is the fact that large developed economies which host significant financial centres also face similar incentives but act in a slightly different way given their twin goals of maximising revenue to fund their large government sector *and* their desire to attract mobile capital. In order to pursue these competing policy goals developed countries may promote a regime for enhancing tax transparency in order to ensure their citizens pay tax on their offshore investments while subtly trying to protect foreigners who invest in their economy from the provisions of the same regime (Picciotto 2011; Sharman 2006). In short, the desire simultaneously to maximise tax revenues while remaining attractive to foreign investment has led major states in the international tax regime to act hypocritically.

This dynamic can broadly explain the politics of international tax cooperation in recent decades. States that have lost significant revenue to international evasion have periodically proposed the creation of a more robust regime for tax information exchange, while those which stand to lose have resisted reform. Switzerland's response to the OECD's Harmful Tax Competition (HTC) project launched in 1998 (described in Chapter 3) perhaps provides the clearest and most significant example of this strategy. Rather than oppose the initiative directly, the Swiss government simply refused to participate in the regime and remained exempt from its provisions under the OECD's 'mutual agreement' procedures. This diplomatic tactic ultimately undermined the political legitimacy of the HTC project, but in the short term it ensured that Switzerland avoided scrutiny while non-OECD secrecy jurisdictions, many of whom competed with Swiss banks to attract funds, were subjected to the emerging tax transparency regime. This broad depiction of the politics of international tax cooperation (or lack thereof), with its emphasis on instrumentalism and competing state interests is broadly consistent with realist explanations of international relations and the belief that international cooperation will only exist to the extent that it is consistent with the interests of the key states in the international regime. There may be an element of truth in this stylised account, but as the empirical analysis presented in the following chapters will demonstrate, the reality is more nuanced and complex.

This book argues that effective international tax cooperation is critically dependent on the support of key states in the international tax regime. However, at an empirical level it also notes that support for cooperation between leading states in the regime has fluctuated in recent years. This evidence suggests that the policy preferences of key actors in the international tax regime, such as the United States, are defined by complex combinations of strategic, institutional and domestic political considerations. In order to analyse these processes the study adopts a grounded, inductive approach to assess the influence of key variables – including economic factors, domestic politics and international organisations – on shaping the international tax policy preferences of key states in the regime.

A second set of considerations that contributes to the complexity of international tax cooperation relates to the growing role of non-governmental actors in the international tax arena. Central in this regard are the political and commercial interests and strategies of the international banks and financial services providers that the regime is attempting to regulate. Here too the political landscape is characterised by complexity, with corporate actors promoting a range of policy positions from compliance to defiance depending on the scope of their operations and their outlook in relation to the likely effectiveness of the regime. All credible commentary on the politics of international taxation concedes that financial interests dominate the policy debate with all states acutely aware of the potential impact of regulatory changes on patterns of international investment. Financial interests may dominate, but since the onset of the financial crisis they are no longer the sole voice in the policy debate, with 'tax justice' NGOs, many of which are organised internationally, increasingly asserting themselves and successfully promoting the cause of tax transparency on the mainstream political agenda. In light of these important developments this book will assess the impact of non-state actors on international tax cooperation at both the international and domestic levels.

Finally, the analysis presented below is sensitive to the fact that the international tax arena is highly institutionalised. Indeed international organisations have played a prominent role in negotiating and promoting international tax standards since the League of Nations established a Fiscal Committee in the late 1920s (Picciotto 1992, ch.1), while tax matters have been a major focus on the OECD's agenda since its creation in 1961 (Carroll and Kellow 2011). The fact that the international tax arena is so deeply institutionalised provides an opportunity to assess the independent role of international organisations such as the OECD in promoting international tax cooperation. To this extent the book argues that while there is limited evidence of international organisations shaping national policy preferences through a process of institutional socialisation (Finnemore 1996; Checkel 2005), at the height of the crisis the OECD did play an important agenda-setting role in promoting international tax cooperation at successive G20 leaders' meetings.

Above all else this book seeks to describe and analyse the complex ways in which the financial crisis has transformed the politics of international tax cooperation. To this extent the financial crisis should be regarded as the changing context in which international cooperation has occurred rather than being an independent variable which can of itself explain the progress that has been made towards creating an effective regime for tax information exchange. The financial crisis may have been a profound catalyst for change in the international tax arena but the reform process described below has been heavily mediated by pre-existing agendas, institutions and actors. As Streeck and Thelen (2005) have argued, the governance response to the financial crisis can be characterised by continuity as well as change.

THE FINANCIAL CRISIS AND THE DYNAMICS OF INTERNATIONAL TAX COOPERATION: A SUMMARY

This book has two related objectives. The first is to explain the significant developments in the international tax regime that have occurred since 2009 and the role of the financial crisis in this process. Second the book offers tentative conclusions concerning the likely effectiveness of the regime and whether recent progress that has been made concerning international tax cooperation is cause for more general optimism in relation to establishing effective global economic governance in the aftermath of the financial crisis. Given these tasks Chapter 1 begins with an empirical overview of the nature of international taxation and the governance problems associated with it. This chapter notes that while there is a good deal of ambiguity and contestation about how to define and measure international tax evasion, there is a growing consensus that it is a significant and growing problem with profound implications for the financial sustainability of developed and developing economies alike. Having provided this broad context the chapter concludes by documenting some of the main tax avoidance and evasion strategies and the ways in which they are facilitated by lax regulation and a lack of transparency in secrecy jurisdictions.

Chapter 2 provides the theoretical foundations for the analysis that follows. Having provided a synoptic survey of the extant literature on international cooperation the chapter highlights the need to adopt a historically grounded research method that can give due consideration to the complex range of factors which influenced recent developments in the international tax regime. This account goes beyond a traditional narrative in that the analysis is designed to provide insights into the competing explanations of international regime change in the extant literature. In this sense the study aims to provide an empirically grounded explanation of regime change which is both animated by and contributes to existing theoretical debates on international cooperation.

Having outlined the research method employed in the study Chapters 3 to 6 provide a detailed empirical account of recent developments in the international tax regime. Chapter 3 traces the historical development of the international tax regime from its early twentieth-century origins through to the recent period of rapid change in the immediate aftermath of the financial crisis. A central goal of this chapter is to explain the factors which led to the failure of the OECD's first attempt, in the form of the Harmful Tax Competition (HTC) initiative, to create an international tax information exchange regime. After documenting the declining political commitment to the HTC initiative in the early 2000s Chapter 4 explains how the financial crisis resulted in renewed and unprecedented enthusiasm for international tax cooperation. Yet rather than being a natural and inevitable response to the financial crisis, the chapter argues that the G20's endorsement of the OECD's tax transparency regime was a product of deliberate and effective advocacy on the part of the OECD which was able to exploit world leaders' acute need to identify coherent and credible policy responses to an unprecedented situation. Having highlighted the OECD's important agenda-setting role the remainder of the chapter describes the subsequent creation of the Global Forum on Transparency and Exchange of Information for Tax Purposes and the new-found political enthusiasm for all manner of jurisdictions to participate in the Global Forum process.

The dramatic developments at the international level described in Chapter 4 may have grabbed headlines, but a central theme of the book is that patterns of international tax cooperation are profoundly influenced by domestic political and economic considerations. Reflecting this theme, Chapter 5 focuses on the domestic politics of international tax cooperation in the United States and Switzerland, two of the most significant states in the international tax regime. The chapter highlights how the financial crisis not only shaped the international political agenda but also had a profound impact on the domestic politics of international taxation. In the United States the onset of the financial crisis increased domestic political support for offshore tax initiatives, such as the Stop Tax Haven Abuse Act 2006, which preceded the crisis, while the dramatic escalation in government debt resulting from the crisis has motivated all sides of American politics to support policies aimed at enhancing tax enforcement and compliance. In Switzerland, the combined effect of the financial crisis and international tax evasion scandals involving large Swiss investment banks such as UBS has been to undermine the legitimacy of the Swiss government's otherwise stoic defence of bank secrecy. While the all-powerful banking industry remains opposed to tax and financial transparency there is growing recognition that the pre-crisis regime is politically unsustainable.

The analysis in Chapter 6 focuses on the implementation of tax information exchange agreements entered into at the height of the crisis. The chapter argues that the effectiveness of the entire regime is critically dependent on robust compliance given that states frequently fail fully to honour their international tax obligations. Notwithstanding these concerns the evidence suggests that the revised Global Forum, with its broad membership and enhanced peer review regime has made a positive contribution to compliance behaviour. Despite this progress many fundamental challenges remain, and with only one quarter of the Global Forum's members having been subjected to a complete 'phase two' review, it is too soon to draw definitive conclusions about the success of the regime. More importantly, Chapter 6 highlights the critical distinction between regime compliance (whether a jurisdiction meets its international obligations) and the more problematic issue of regime effectiveness (whether the regime successfully addresses the policy problem it was designed to solve). Unfortunately, on the question of regime effectiveness there is much less cause for optimism. A central concern here is that the OECD standard for tax information exchange on request, which was endorsed by the G20 in 2009 and has been the focus of the Global Forum's subsequent work, may be ineffective in detecting and deterring international tax evasion. This has been the main criticism of tax justice NGOs who highlight the 'creeping futility' associated with promoting what they regard as a flawed standard for tax information exchange (Meinzer 2012). While few disagree that automatic information exchange of tax and financial information between tax authorities would be a highly desirable and potent weapon in the fight against international tax evasion, the chapter argues that if key states in the regime maintain their resolve to tackle international tax evasion then the standard currently being promoted by the Global Forum may be an intermediate step on the path to broad-based automatic information exchange. The OECD's July 2012 report on developing and implementing automatic information exchange represents progress towards this goal, but success is far from assured. The history of international tax cooperation is one of variable political commitment with periods of firm resolve interspersed with years of complacency and neglect. Ultimately the future of international tax cooperation is critically linked to broader developments in the international political economy and whether the progress that was made in terms of promoting international economic cooperation at the height of the financial crisis can be institutionalised and consolidated.

BEYOND THE FINANCIAL CRISIS: REGIME SUSTAINABILITY AND THE FUTURE OF GLOBAL ECONOMIC GOVERNANCE

The future of international tax cooperation is inextricably linked to broader developments in global economic governance and the critical question of whether the international community is capable of developing and sustaining collective responses to the challenges facing the global economy in the aftermath of the financial crisis. Given the governance challenges associated with international tax cooperation, and the ever present economic incentives for secrecy jurisdictions to defect from commitments to exchange tax information, the sustainability of the international tax regime is highly dependent on effective global institutions and leadership. Unfortunately the institutional architecture of the global economic system remains in a state of flux and, as a consequence, the outlook for effective global economic governance remains uncertain. On a positive note, as is described in Chapter 4, the acute threat of global financial calamity which prevailed in 2008 and 2009 did prompt unprecedented international economic cooperation. However, as the financial crisis has evolved, and the political priorities of world leaders have gradually shifted from promoting international cooperation and solidarity to managing crisis-induced domestic political imperatives and pressures, the spirit of international economic cooperation has gradually waned. Even the G20 Leaders' Forum, which is widely regarded as the most significant institutional response to the crisis is being subjected to growing criticism for being unrepresentative and increasingly divided (Vestergaard 2011; Wade 2011). Similar political dynamics can also be observed within the eurozone, as a spirit of solidarity has given way to conflict over the terms of financial bailouts and who should fund them.

Arguably the root cause of the nascent mercantilism emerging in the global economy is a lack of leadership in the international system. Liberal international relations scholars have rightly argued that hegemonic groups can use international institutions to provide effective international leadership, but the reality of the post-financial crisis world order is that existing international economic institutions are struggling to adapt to the new political and economic reality, with commentators such as Jeffrey Sachs arguing that the financial crisis and its aftermath highlight the lack of transatlantic leadership (Sachs 2011). The financial crisis may have increased the relative economic power of China and the other so-called BRIC economies (those of Brazil, Russia and India as well as China) but it is equally apparent that the global economy is entering a significant period of transition. As Robert Wade (2011, 347) has argued

The United States remains the dominant state, and the G7 states together continue to exercise primacy, but now more fearfully and defensively. China is split between asserting itself as 'the wave of the future' and defending itself as too poor to take on global responsibilities (it is roughly 100th in the per capita income hierarchy). The combination of G7 defensiveness and emerging states' jealous guarding of sovereignty produces a spirit of Westphalian assertion in international fora, or 'every state for itself.'

As will be revealed in subsequent chapters these broader political dynamics are evident in the international tax regime. The push to enhance tax transparency has been very much a transatlantic project, with periodic interventions from China, India and other emerging economic powers. The Global Forum may have made real progress in allowing non-OECD states to participate in the international tax regime but it is important to acknowledge the fundamental difference between participation and tacit consent and providing diplomatic and financial leadership. In this sense the politics of international tax cooperation is symptomatic of the broader challenges associated with governing the global economy in the aftermath of the financial crisis, with the extent and nature of international cooperation increasingly dependent on the foreign economic policy priorities of China and other emerging powers.

REFERENCES

Blue, J. (2000) 'The Celtic Tiger Roars Defiantly: Corporation Tax in Ireland and Competition within the European Union', *Duke Journal of Comparative and International Law*, **10**, 443–67

Carroll, Peter and Aynsley Kellow (2011) *OECD: A Study of Organisational Adaptation*, Cheltenham, UK and Northampton, MA, USA: Edward Elgar.

Checkel, Jeffrey T. (2005) 'International Institutions and Socialization in Europe: Introduction and Framework', *International Organization*, **59** (4), 801–26.

Finnemore, Martha (1996) *National Interests in International Society*, Ithaca, NY: Cornell University Press.

Gurría, Angel (2009) 'Remarks by Angel Gurría at the Global Forum on Transparency and Exchange of Information', available at: http://www.oecd. org/document/7/0,3746,en_2649_33767_43596999_1_1_1_1,00.html (accessed November 2011).

Hollingshead, Ann (2010) *Privately Held, Non-Resident Deposits in Secrecy Jurisdictions*, Global Financial Integrity, available at: http://www.gfinteg rity.org/storage/gfip/documents/reports/gfi_privatelyheld_web.pdf (accessed November 2011).

Keohane, Robert (2009) 'The Old International Political Economy and the New', *Review of International Political Economy*, **16** (1), 34–46.

Martin, Isaac (ed.) (2009) *The New Fiscal Sociology: Taxation in Comparative and Historical Perspective*, Cambridge: Cambridge University Press.

Meinzer, Markus (2012) 'The Creeping Futility of the Global Forum's Peer Reviews', *Tax Justice Network Tax Justice Briefing – March 2012*, available at: http://www.taxjustice.net/cms/upload/GlobalForum2012-TJN-Briefing.pdf (accessed March 2012).
OECD (2000) *Improving Access to Bank Information for Tax Purposes*, available at: http://www.oecd.org/dataoecd/3/7/2497487.pdf (accessed June 2011).
Palan, Ronen, Richard Murphy and Christian Chavagneux (2010) *Tax Havens: How Globalization Really Works*, Ithaca, NY: Cornell University Press.
Picciotto, Sol (1992) *International Business Taxation: A Study in the Internationalization of Business Regulation*, London: Weidenfeld and Nicolson.
Picciotto, Sol (2011) *Regulating Global Corporate Capitalism*, Cambridge: Cambridge University Press.
Sachs, Jeffrey (2011) 'Tripped up by Globalisation', *Financial Times*, 18 August.
Sharman, Jason (2006) *Havens in the Storm*, Ithaca: Cornell University Press.
Streeck, Wolfgang and Kathleen Thelen (2005) *Beyond Continuity: Institutional Change in Advanced Political Economies*, Oxford: Oxford University Press.
Tax Justice Network (2007) 'Identifying Tax Havens and Offshore Finance Centres', Tax Justice Network Briefing Paper, available at: http://www.taxjustice.net/cms/upload/pdf/Identifying_Tax_Havens_Jul_07.pdf (accessed July 2012).
Vestergaard, Jakob (2011) 'The G20 and Beyond: Towards Effective Global Economic Governance', *Danish Institute for International Studies*, available at: http://www.diis.dk/graphics/publications/reports2011/rp2011-04-g20-and-beyond_web.pdf (accessed January 2012).
Wade, Robert (2011) 'Emerging World Order? From Multipolarity to Multilateralism in the G20, the World Bank, and the IMF', *Politics and Society*, **39** (3), 347–78.
Webb, Michael (2004) 'Defining the Boundaries of Legitimate State Practice: Norms, Transnational Actors and the OECD's project on Harmful Tax Competition', *Review of International Political Economy*, 11, 37–58.
Young, Oran R. (1999) *Governance in World Affairs*, Ithaca: Cornell University Press.

1. Governing international taxation: problems and challenges

In their seminal work on the impact of economic integration Keohane and Nye (1977) argued that a condition of *complex interdependence* characterised world affairs. States may have retained formal sovereignty and remain key actors in the global economy and world politics, but with the rapid internationalisation of markets, systems of production and corporations, the political authority of states is either being challenged or is in decline. In the absence of formal political authority above the level of the state, and given the inherently anarchical nature of the international system, effective governance in a 'globalised' world requires institutions and practices capable of enhancing and sustaining cooperation and providing order in international economic relations.

Nowhere is this need for effective global governance based on co-operation and shared decision-making more apparent than in relation to international taxation issues. Even within the European Union, and despite calls for closer fiscal integration dating back to the 1960s, there has been a distinctive lack of supranationalism as states have been extremely reluctant to cede their sovereign authority in relation to managing their domestic tax affairs (Cohen 1977; Radaelli and Kraemer 2008). In an era of transnational production and global capital markets national tax systems are highly interdependent – changing tax policies and practices in one country can have profound impacts on the tax systems of their neighbours. The extent of this interdependence has led commentators such as Radaelli (1997, 176) to conclude that 'international taxation is a governance problem in search of institutionalization'. What is required is an international commitment to efficient and robust arrangements for the taxation and distribution of revenue from international business transactions.

The goal of this chapter is to outline the nature and extent of the governance problems surrounding international taxation. After a theoretical discussion concerning the allocation of the tax base from international business and investment the analysis focuses on the three greatest challenges associated with international tax regulation, namely international tax evasion, avoidance and competition. While all three dimensions of international taxation pose both normative questions and governance challenges, our emphasis will be on the most pressing problems associated with international tax evasion, or the illegal non-disclosure of income or profits in order to reduce or eliminate tax obligations (Picciotto 2011, 226). This specific focus on evasion is motivated by the fact that recent efforts to improve tax transparency have been primarily concerned with reducing evasion. Improved tax transparency combined with less ambiguous 'country by country' corporate reporting will shed more light on international avoidance strategies and the real costs and benefits of international tax competition. Despite this broader agenda the political reality is that the short-term regulatory focus is on improved tax transparency. While this agenda only represents one aspect of the governance problems associated with international taxation, it is an important one and could prove to be a decisive battle in a wider war against tax evasion; success would thus represent significant progress towards the broader goal of establishing a more equitable and sustainable international tax regime. Certainly most commentators agree that if a comprehensive and effective system of tax information exchange could be established then this would be a very important first step in enabling national governments to effectively tax the worldwide income of resident individuals and firms (Tanzi 1995, ch. 6).

Before embarking on an analysis of the international tax regime and recent efforts to improve tax transparency it is first necessary to further elaborate and clarify the terminology that will be used throughout the book. Much debate and indeed a good deal of consternation has been generated by the question of what constitutes legitimate and appropriate international tax policy and the semantic but still significant issue of how to describe jurisdictions that fail to conform with accepted international norms or standards. The term 'tax haven' is widely used in public debate and journalistic accounts of international tax issues. Beyond its pejorative connotations, the term is also burdened by a good deal of conceptual ambiguity. For example, should a tax haven be defined based on low or negligible tax rates alone (as has traditionally been the case), or should such an assessment be made based on whether a jurisdiction holds and is willing to exchange both tax and other relevant financial information with other tax authorities? Under what conditions should a jurisdiction provide tax residency to a foreign entity? Should such status only be granted to firms who undertake substantial economic activity, or can residency be granted to any entity for a nominal fee? These and related questions highlight the complex conceptual issues in relation to defining a 'tax haven'.

Rather than engaging directly with debates concerning tax competition and legal tax avoidance and tax planning (although these are significant issues), the analysis presented in this book focuses more specifically on how a lack of transparency contributes to the problem of international tax evasion. Given this emphasis on transparency and information exchange the analysis that follows uses the term 'secrecy jurisdiction' to describe states, dependencies and other forms of government that are either unable to obtain, are unwilling to hold, or are reluctant to share tax and financial information with other governments in accordance with accepted international practices and agreements. Despite this clear focus on transparency, it is also important to note that there is no clear or accepted understanding of what constitutes a 'secrecy jurisdiction' because what is regarded as being 'acceptable international practice' varies over time and because, at a technical level, transparency has many different dimensions. Instead, as the Tax Justice Network have argued, tax and financial secrecy should be regarded as occupying a spectrum – as a relative concept rather than being an absolute (Tax Justice Network 2009). Whether a specific state or territory can credibly be described as a 'secrecy jurisdiction' is ultimately open to interpretation and the debate over establishing an appropriate standard for tax information exchange and the process for assessing whether jurisdictions conform with this standard is a central focus in subsequent chapters.

Closely related to secrecy jurisdictions are Offshore Financial Centres (OFCs), which can be classified as jurisdictions which act as hubs for foreign investment and the provision of international financial services to non-residents (IMF 2000; Zorome 2007). While it can credibly be argued that many OFCs have and perhaps continue to be secrecy jurisdictions, it is also possible that OFCs are transparent and well governed and attract foreign capital due to the quality of their services, regulation, security and proximity to other markets and commercial centres. Indeed the broad goal of the tax transparency regime that has evolved since 2009 is to encourage secrecy jurisdictions to make the transition to becoming transparent and legitimate OFCs.

Having provided an overview of the international tax regime and the critical role of information exchange in combating international tax evasion this chapter presents an empirical account of the problem by explaining how secrecy jurisdictions have been used to evade tax and to obscure evidence concerning the extent of the problem. This analysis highlights the fact that secrecy jurisdictions not only have financial incentives to undermine attempts to enhance tax transparency, but they are aided in this task by innovative financial service providers keen to attract business by staying one step ahead of national and international regulators.

THE CHALLENGE OF INTERNATIONAL TAXATION

Tax is almost as old as government and the evolution of tax systems is both a cause and consequence of the modern state (Martin et al. 2009). International taxation also has a long history and can be traced back to the origins of trade itself. For a combination of strategic, political and pragmatic reasons imposing tariffs or import duties has been the preferred mode of taxation for much of the history of the modern state (Tanzi 1987). Governments may have been able to tax merchants at key ports and markets, but the evolution of international banking and the modern corporation in the eighteenth and nineteenth centuries posed a new range of issues for tax authorities.

Until the nineteenth century there was a clear, albeit contested, fiscal contract between the citizens and the state. A government would impose a tax on its citizens (or perhaps a merchant seeking access to the domestic market) in return for the provision of state services. But the rapid growth in trade and international commerce in the nineteenth century challenged many of the assumptions of domestic taxation. Should a trading firm based in the United Kingdom which predominantly raised capital from British investors yet conducted most of its business offshore pay tax to the colonial administration in, say, India or to the United Kingdom? Should the profits of this extremely successful enterprise be shared between the two jurisdictions? If so, how should the tax base be allocated between jurisdictions and how should any resulting tax agreement be administered? Reflecting imperial interests, corporate income was only taxed in the hands of shareholders until the late nineteenth century, but with the creation of a separate corporate income tax came the issue of double taxation and a clear need for international tax regulation.

If expanding international trade highlighted the need for a coherent system of international taxation the growth of the modern corporation and international finance in the final years of the nineteenth century created the potential for international tax evasion and avoidance. The modern corporation has its origins in the early seventeenth century with the creation of the British and Dutch East India companies in 1601 and 1602 respectively. However, after the speculative excesses of the South Sea Bubble of 1720 in particular, the formation and management of so-called charter companies was closely regulated by the state (Dale et al. 2005). The proliferation of corporations only began in earnest in the mid-nineteenth century when general acts of incorporation were passed in both the United States and the United Kingdom (Braithwaite and Drahos 2000, ch. 9). As the industrial revolution took hold on both sides of the Atlantic and the American West was gradually opened to development, corporate entities became an important means of raising capital. As the popularity of corporate entities grew, so too did regulatory competition between jurisdictions to host these new firms. The American state of New Jersey led the way with new liberal incorporation laws in 1875 and successfully lured firms from neighbouring New York and Massachusetts (Palan et al. 2010, 110). Lax corporate governance regimes in isolation do not affect international taxation, but when combined with a series of legal cases granting corporations the status of a legal 'person' in the late nineteenth and early twentieth centuries, the governance of international taxation became intertwined with effective and transparent corporate governance standards.

At the heart of the nexus between corporate governance and international taxation is the fact that once corporations are regarded as separate legal entities both companies and their shareholders can be subject to taxation. As the wealth of corporations grew governments naturally had political and financial incentives to tax them directly – the corporate income tax was born. The development of the modern corporation as a separate legal entity and the associated development of corporate taxation raise a number of regulatory issues concerning both *double taxation* and the more insidious phenomenon of *double non-taxation.*

Double Taxation: An Overview

In an international regime built on the principle of preserving sovereignty, as is the case with taxation, the fundamental governance problem concerns which state has the right to tax the profits or income derived from international business (Graetz and O'Hearn 1997). Indeed many commentators correctly point out that the very notion of 'international taxation' as a concept is misleading when the real issue is the application of domestic tax systems to international business transactions (Arnold and McIntyre 2002, 2–3). In technical terms the challenge is to develop a fair and efficient way to allocate the international tax base between sovereign states. The widely held economic ideal is that of tax neutrality whereby international investment decisions are not influenced by tax considerations. Because this theoretical ideal of international tax neutrality is elusive, the most practical approach is to tax international transactions according to either the *source* or *residency* principle. Under the residency principle individuals and firms based within a jurisdiction are taxed as residents by their home government on their worldwide income irrespective of where it is earned. Under the alternative source principle, firms and individuals are taxed on their income in the jurisdiction in which it was earned. Each approach offers a sound theoretical basis on which to establish an international tax regime, but in reality there is a real prospect of distributional conflicts between states over the control of the international tax base.

Take the hypothetical (although common) example of a developing country whose growing export sector is reliant on foreign direct investment. Such a country would benefit greatly from a source-based regime as it could tax profits from onshore production. In contrast our hypothetical country would suffer under a residence-based system because profits would be repatriated to investing countries before being taxed. As we shall see in the following chapter, these tensions have given rise to a complex web of Double Tax Agreements (DTAs) which attempt to '[d]isentangle national jurisdiction to tax by allocating the international tax base to the residence and source countries involved' (Rixen 2008, 63). This uncertainty regarding the allocation of the tax base combined with most states' desire to maximise revenue increases the risk of double taxation. This occurs when two or more overlapping jurisdictions each attempt to tax an international transaction (Picciotto 2011, 216–26). While the risk of double taxation is real, a mitigating factor over the course of the twentieth century has been the ability of international investors and Multinational Corporations (MNCs) to successfully lobby governments to establish DTAs which limit double taxation. Indeed, with the advent of increased capital mobility, financial deregulation and transnational production associated with economic globalisation, competitive pressures to attract investment have enhanced the political power of investors relative to national governments, leading to more intense tax competition and the related problem of double non-taxation.

In practice most DTAs use a combination of the source and residency approaches. As a general principle, active business or corporate income is taxed at the source while investment income is taxed in the country of residence, with the latter having become more important as international capital markets have expanded in recent years. When the tax rate in the source country is lower than in the residency jurisdiction (as is often the case with foreign investment from the developed world) countries such as the United States use a residency-based approach to tax offshore corporate income, but apply a system of tax credits to ensure that investors can deduct tax paid offshore against their domestic liability. Another variation is that governments often impose a withholding tax on the passive earnings of foreign investors, thus deviating from the residence approach. In practice this means that the tax base is shared between the two countries concerned. The issues associated with effectively taxing offshore capital investments are a central theme of this book because as Rixen notes (2008, 61) '[v]ery often tax authorities have to rely on the reports of taxpayers themselves, who have an economic incentive to under-report their true income. Because of this the enforcement of resident taxation relies on the intense exchange of information between tax authorities.' This gives rise to the increasingly significant risk of double non-taxation, or the situation where international businesses or investors are able to exploit anomalies (sometimes unintended, sometimes deliberate) in DTAs and other unilateral provisions to minimise or defer tax obligations. This type of lawful tax minimisation which 'revolves around either the transfer of revenue to a lower taxed person (or entity) or of expenses to one who is more highly taxed; or the manipulation of transactions so that the benefit is received in a form that attracts less tax' (Picciotto 1992, 85) is generally referred to as international tax avoidance. In contrast resident investors who fail to declare their offshore investment income to tax authorities typify illegal international tax evasion. While this demarcation between legal and illegal international tax affairs seems clear cut in theory, the complex reality of international tax leaves many shades of grey (Picciotto 2011, 226). As the former British Chancellor of the Exchequer Denis Healy once quipped 'The difference between tax avoidance and tax evasion is the thickness of a prison wall' (*The Economist* 2006).

Prior to assessing some of the most common strategies for international tax evasion as well as its growth and impact, it is first necessary to outline the factors which have shaped the broad regulatory context in which international taxation occurs. The critical relationship here is how the rise of the modern corporation and developments in international banking and finance have created what Ronen Palan (2003) describes as an 'offshore world' which has profound implications for international taxation.

Corporate Governance

The nature and proliferation of corporate entities have had a profound impact on international tax governance. As noted above, the precise definition of what constitutes a secrecy jurisdiction remains elusive, yet most scholars highlight the clear link between poor corporate governance standards and a lack of tax transparency. For example the OECD's agenda-setting 1998 report *Harmful Tax Competition: An Emerging Issue* highlighted how secrecy jurisdictions use lax corporate governance provisions to ensure that both the managers and beneficial owners of accounts and entities enjoy effective secrecy (OECD 1998; Palan et al. 2010, 93). Moreover successful secrecy jurisdictions have regulatory frameworks 'designed to promote the rapid creation and cost effective administration of off-shore corporations and associated entities' (OECD 1998, 22). These findings highlight the interconnected nature of corporate governance, financial regulation and innovation and international tax regulation. The central role of various corporate entities, as discussed below, in international tax planning is the product of their historical treatment in DTAs as well as the impact of more recent unilateral anti-avoidance provisions.

The fact that corporate income is taxed in the country of source provides a strong incentive for corporations to establish operations in low-tax jurisdictions. While this is true of physical production it is especially the case for operations dealing with intangible financial, management, legal and marketing services. The potential tax advantages of establishing a corporate subsidiary in a low-tax offshore jurisdiction are greatly enhanced by the tax treatment of consolidated companies (Stewart 2005). For the purposes of financial reporting most MNCs report one set of consolidated accounts, which gives the impression of being one multinational entity (Palan et al. 2010, 84). Legally and for taxation purposes the vast majority of MNCs actually consist of a complex web of subsidiary and holding companies domiciled across a vast array of countries. In late 2008 the United States Government Accountability Office found that this type of structure was used by the vast majority of major American firms, with 83 of the nation's largest firms operating one or more subsidiaries in tax haven jurisdictions (GAO 2008, 4). Such a structure offers a number of tax advantages for MNCs including the potential to 'book' profitable transactions offshore (subject to transfer pricing regulations) and the ability to retain and reinvest profits in low-tax jurisdictions deferring the need to repatriate profits to parent companies. Perhaps the best evidence of the extent to which corporate structures are used to manage risk and minimise taxation has been the exponential growth of listed entities in OFCs in recent years, with a 2008 US State Department Report (cited in Palan et al. 2010, 57) finding that the British Virgin Islands (population 22 000) hosts over 800 000 International Business Corporations (defined below), while the Central American state of Panama is home to over 300 000 such entities. Yet these companies are largely fictitious, having been created for regulatory advantage rather than to undertake real economic activity.

If anything the relationship between corporate governance standards and international tax 'planning' opportunities has become stronger in recent years as tax authorities in the developed world have responded to the use of offshore entities to minimise tax liabilities. The US government set the ball rolling in the 1960s with anti-avoidance provisions against Controlled Foreign Companies (CFCs). CFCs are defined as wholly owned subsidiaries located in OFCs which are involved in little if any real economic activity. The broad aim of CFC legislation is to treat such entities as if they were located in the same jurisdiction as the parent company thus eliminating any tax advantage. While CFCs laws have enjoyed a degree of success, as we shall see below, innovative secrecy jurisdictions have responded to the threat by developing new entity structures, such as International Business Corporations, Exempt Corporations and Special Investment Vehicles, to exploit loopholes in CFC laws and to provide opportunities for more blatant tax evasion by limiting the ability of tax authorities outside the secrecy jurisdiction to establish the beneficial ownership and financial activities of these structures.

Banking

Banking and the dramatic intensification of international finance is the third key factor that has shaped the broad institutional context in which international tax regulation has occurred. We have noted that as the mobility of capital and the volume of international business transactions increase, so to do the regulatory challenges associated with the prevailing state-based regimes for governing international taxation. Nowhere is this relationship more apparent than with banking and related financial services where earning passive income from investment takes place independently of geographical constraints. When combined with the fact that passive investment income is generally taxed in the country of residence, opportunistic jurisdictions have the potential to attract investment capital by offering bank secrecy without undermining their own tax base. As will be discussed in detail in Chapter 2, the issue of bank secrecy poses acute challenges for global governance because it creates the potential for secrecy jurisdictions to secure a financial advantage at the expense of the investor's country of residence for tax purposes, exactly the circumstances under which beggar-thy-neighbour policies flourish. Not only does this have the potential to create distributional conflicts between states, but many public finance economists argue that this exploitation of low-tax secrecy jurisdictions has a negative net impact on economic welfare (Tanzi 1995; OECD 1998).

Wealthy private clients have made extensive use of bank secrecy provisions in Switzerland, Luxembourg, the Channel Islands and the Bahamas since the 1930s, but it was not until the 1960s that 'offshore banking' became a pervasive investment strategy (Picciotto 1992, ch. 6). The growth in offshore financial centres is a direct consequence of the rise of the so-called 'Eurodollar' market in the 1960s (Palan 2003, ch. 3). Like so many financial innovations the Eurodollar market was an unintended consequence of the extremely tight capital controls central to the post-war Bretton Woods regime. While extremely complex, the essence of the Eurodollar market was to conduct financial transactions in currency foreign to the country where the given transaction took place as a strategy for avoiding a host of restrictions on domestic lending to foreign borrowers. The important implication of the Eurodollar market and its rapid expansion from a mere US$3 billion in 1960 to US$1trillion in 1980 (Strange 1988, 105; O'Brien and Williams 2010, 229) was that it encouraged nationally oriented banks to establish offshore branches to exploit this lightly regulated and rapidly expanding market. Established regulators in major financial centres such as London and the United States have remained reluctant to impose tougher prudential standards on offshore centres because of their sym-biotic relationship with domestic, or 'on-shore' banking operations, and the risk that more onerous regulation may drive banking operations from semi-regulated jurisdictions such as the Channel Islands and the Cayman Islands to fully fledged 'havens' (Picciotto 1992, 123). The use of offshore centres as legal bases for the provision of international finance has intensi-fied in recent years with specific jurisdictions establishing specialist niches within the broader sector. The Cayman Islands has become the centre of the global hedge fund industry with an estimated 80 per cent of the world's funds registered in the tiny British Overseas Territory (Moya 2009), while Bermuda and Guernsey specialise in reinsurance services and the British Virgin Islands and Panama specialise in the registration of Special Purpose Entities (SPEs) (Palan et al. 2010, ch. 2).

Tax minimisation may not have been a central factor in the creation of offshore finance but tax advantages remain an important considera-tion for most OFCs (Zorome 2007). When combined with the prevailing state-based structure of the international tax regime the 'offshore world' has major implications for the way in which capital is taxed and for the integrity of first world tax systems – issues that have come into sharp relief in the context of the financial crisis.

INTERNATIONAL TAX EVASION: STRATEGIES AND SIGNIFICANCE

There may be a good deal of debate about the extent and cost of inter-national tax evasion, but we can be reasonably certain that international tax planning in all its guises has increased significantly in recent decades (Gravelle 2009). The combination of financial liberalisation, innovative financial entrepreneurs, improved communications and transport technol-ogy, together with a growing array of international business models and strategies has created an environment in which the cost of international tax planning has fallen dramatically. On the supply side, as a consequence of the growing demand for international tax services, small states have engaged in a development strategy designed to exploit their tax sovereignty by implementing tax, corporate governance and banking laws designed to attract mobile investment (Sharman and Mistry 2008). While a good deal of this activity is lawful (although not necessarily desirable) international tax avoidance or 'planning', the problem of illegal international tax evasion whereby individuals and firms deliberately conceal income and assets from tax authorities persists (Sharman 2010, 12). Indeed, as governments have increased unilateral anti-avoidance measures such as CFC and transfer pricing provisions designed to limit the use of shell or 'post-box' companies, international tax advisers have responded by devising new entity structures designed either to circumvent anti-avoidance provisions or to conceal the owner or financial beneficiary of the asset in question. In order better to understand the use of secrecy jurisdictions in illegal international tax planning it is necessary to examine some of the most common strategies used to evade taxation.

International tax planning strategies have become increasingly complex in recent years. Indeed the lack of disclosure concerning the structure, activities and ownership of many companies, trusts and other entities in secrecy jurisdictions is such that tax authorities in advanced economies are all too often unaware of the nature and scope of the issues they are trying to regulate. This has led innovative regulators to work with the suppliers of international tax services to gain a better understanding of the industry they are trying to regulate (Braithwaite 2001).

Despite this complexity, secrecy jurisdictions facilitate international tax evasion by exploiting two important institutional features of international tax law as it has evolved over the course of the twentieth century. The first is that legal transactions associated with economic exchange can occur in a jurisdiction other than that in which the economic activity physically takes place or where the actors in the transaction reside for tax purposes (Palan et al. 2010, 81; Sharman 2010). Indeed, scholars such as Palan et al. (2010, 81) argue that the key characteristic of a secrecy jurisdiction is a state which 'creates legal instruments by which individuals and companies can reduce, or completely sever, their "connecting factor" to their country of origin'. When combined with the sovereignty-preserving nature of the international tax regime – the second institutional feature exploited in this context – and the relatively unchallenged right of states to establish domestic tax policies as they see fit, conditions are ripe for both international tax planning and more blatant evasion in all of its guises to flourish. To be sure, most of the sophisticated international tax schemes designed by lawyers and accountants constitute legal tax mitigation, while another sizeable portion occupy the considerable grey area where their legality is contested, with assessments of 'tax risk' now dominating discussions in boardrooms and corporate tax departments the world over. Yet our focus is on what are arguably the more egregious cases of illegal tax evasion where schemes are devised and strategies adopted to deliberately conceal income and assets from tax authorities. Indeed one of the inevitable ironies of the international campaign to minimise both international tax avoidance and evasion over the last decade is that practices that were previously legal or at least contestable have been outlawed, potentially increasing illegal evasion. The following section describes the basic techniques used by wealthy individuals and corporations to evade taxation and evaluates their extent and significance.

Private Banking and Mass-marketed Schemes

The creation and growth of the welfare state in the aftermath of World War I and the associated increase in personal and capital taxation prompted the first concerted attempts by wealthy individuals to hide their personal wealth in order to evade tax. The basic strategy for what has become known as 'offshore private banking' has been for wealthy individuals to hold their savings and income-earning assets offshore where they will be hidden from tax authorities as well as safeguarded in regard to other financial liabilities and risks associated with litigation, bankruptcy, divorce and arbitrary confiscation by authoritarian regimes. As will be discussed in greater detail in Chapter 5, it was in the late nineteenth century that the Swiss started to develop a reputation for using bank secrecy to attract international investment, a strategy which is central to their position as one of the world's top offshore financial centres, with an estimated US$2 trillion under management (Hollingshead 2010). While the Swiss did not codify national bank secrecy provisions until the 1934 Swiss Banking Act the practice was well established by the conclusion of World War I (Chaikin 2005). The issue of bank secrecy dominated negotiations at the League of Nations during the 1920s where proposals to develop a tax treaty system, including a robust system of multilateral information exchange, saw vehement opposition by both the International Chamber of Commerce (ICC) and the Swiss government (Rixen 2008, 120; Picciotto 1992).

The Swiss may have pioneered bank secrecy in the late nineteenth and early twentieth centuries but in the context of growing geopolitical instability and rising taxes the strategy was soon emulated by other European states, among them Austria, Monaco, Luxembourg, Liechtenstein and then, by the 1960s, Panama, the Cayman Islands and Bermuda (Palan 2003). By the century's end the use and abuse of 'secrecy jurisdictions' for international tax evasion, money laundering and terrorist financing had become a major issue, leading to the creation of specialist intergovernmental agencies such as the Financial Action Task Force (FATF) and the Joint

International Tax Shelter Information Centre (JITSIC) as well as NGOs such as Global Financial Integrity and the Tax Justice Network. Whereas a wealthy elite had traditionally practised offshore private banking discreetly, a series of more recent high profile cases such as that involving the Swiss bank UBS (Chapter 5) has highlighted the widespread use of secrecy jurisdictions for illicit purposes. This growing awareness of private banking abuse has been a key driver of recent reforms in relation to money laundering and transnational organised crime, allowing investigators access to personal financial information in cases relating to serious criminal activity (Sharman 2011). However, countries such as Switzerland have been determined to retain sufficient secrecy provisions to protect clients from more routine tax and administrative enquiries in an attempt to preserve both their reputations and their lucrative private banking business.

As in other areas of international tax governance, the growing awareness of the exploitation of anomalies and loopholes in the existing regime created additional demand for tax planning services which in turn led to the development of new and innovative products designed to circumvent new and tighter regulations. Since the late 1990s there has been a proliferation of mass-marketed international tax schemes which combined with the growth of e-commerce have fundamentally changed the nature and extent of private banking (Owens 2005). What was once an exclusive and highly personalised service tailored to wealthy clients investing tens of millions of dollars has now become available to middle-income earners establishing accounts with balances as low as $500 (US Senate 2006).

The illicit nature of using offshore accounts in a secrecy jurisdiction means that until recently there has been little reliable data and a good deal of speculation on the prevalence and growth of the practice. A synoptic review of studies published between 2002 and 2005 by Murphy (2006) estimated that high wealth individuals hold an estimated $US9 trillion in offshore accounts, which translates into approximately US$250 billion in lost revenue (see also Gravelle 2009). However, most commentators now believe that such estimates were conservative and overestimated disclosure of offshore accounts by high wealth individuals. Indeed a recent survey by Henry (2012, 5) argues that 'at least $21 to $32 trillion as of 2010 has been invested virtually tax free through the world's still expanding black hole of more than 80 offshore secrecy jurisdictions'. Domestic tax authorities responded to the challenge with a two-part strategy which sought to promote compliance through targeted education campaigns while also increasing enforcement efforts and highlighting successful convictions as a deterrent (Braithwaite 2009). Despite more concerted unilateral efforts to track financial flows to and from secrecy jurisdictions the promoters of offshore products generally have had the measure of regulators. One simple yet effective approach has been through the issuing of credit cards that have allowed investors to access their investments without having to repatriate funds through domestic bank accounts (Palan 2005, 43; Sharman 2010). Despite more concerted efforts to limit the use of secrecy jurisdictions for illegal activities most of this effort focused on money laundering and, after September 11 on terrorist financing. As a consequence, until the financial crisis at least, it has been business as usual for international tax evasion (Sharman 2011).

The status quo concerning private banking was disrupted after 2005 following a number of specific cases and investigations, the two most prominent of which were the United States UBS case and the Liechtenstein LBT tax affair. Both cases saw the disclosure of information on over 25000 bank accounts including those of billionaire Californian property developer Igor Olenicoff who held US$7.2 billion in offshore accounts, thus evading US$200 million in taxes (Mathiason 2008). The realisation that bank secrecy had been seriously compromised has sent shockwaves throughout the private banking industry with firms trying to salvage their battered reputations by cooperating with authorities (Browning 2008). As will be discussed in greater detail in Chapters 5 and 6, the success of the US tax authorities has had two significant consequences. First, tax authorities have capitalised on the situation by launching various amnesties or Voluntary Disclosure Schemes (VDSs) whereby taxpayers can declare undisclosed income and pay outstanding liabilities without being subjected to penalties or criminal charges (Chapter 6). Second, the UBS case in particular has led key core OECD member states such as the US, the UK and Germany to introduce more aggressive unilateral anti-evasion measures (Chapter 5). While the success of VDSs has varied and the effectiveness of recent unilateral measures remains unclear, in combination the OECD claims that compliance initiatives introduced since the height of the crisis have yielded €14 billion in additional revenues from 100000 wealthy individuals (OECD 2011a).

Despite this progress a central question considered in this book is whether recent gains are likely to be consolidated with enduring commitments to end bank secrecy on a more permanent basis. One conclusion that is clear is that bank secrecy is the frontline in the wider battle against international tax evasion; as such it is a central theme in the analysis that follows.

Corporate Structures and Offshore Evasion

International business organisations such as the International Chamber of Commerce (ICC) and the United States Council for International

Business (UNCIB) have argued that international tax evasion is largely perpetrated by wealthy individuals. In contrast they claim that MNCs and other entities actively engaged in international business have a multitude of legitimate reasons for using complex offshore structures in their business models. While it is true that many offshore structures are used for legitimate non-tax reasons and that many more are used for legal tax 'planning' or 'mitigation' purposes, in the absence of greatly improved tax and financial transparency, it is not obvious that there is a clear demarcation between tax evasion undertaken by individuals and the international tax strategies employed by firms. For example, it is relatively easy for an individual to avoid regulations which specifically target individuals rather than firms (such as the EU Savings Directive discussed in Chapter 4) by establishing a corporate structure. Moreover, using shell companies and other exotic entity structures has been at the heart of elaborate worldwide international tax evasion schemes. Given our focus on the relationship between tax transparency and international tax evasion the following section outlines some of the entity structures and legal strategies that have been used to conceal the identity of assets held in offshore jurisdictions.

Shell entities and offshore subsidiaries
The creation of subsidiary companies to book profits in low-tax offshore locations has long been the cornerstone of most international tax planning strategies employed by MNCs but such strategies are increasingly used to facilitate illegal evasion (Tanzi 1995, 75–80). As noted above, as early as the 1960s US authorities passed the CFC laws with the aim of ensuring that passive income earned in a controlled foreign subsidiary (usually defined as a 50 per cent or greater ownership stake) would be taxed as if the company was a resident (Arnold 2000). Owing to the initial success of this anti-avoidance provision, within a matter of years the vast majority of developed economies had followed the US lead and introduced their own CFC laws. However CFC rules and other unilateral anti-avoidance provisions suffer from two weaknesses. At a theoretical level they effectively pierce the sovereignty of offshore jurisdictions by treating legally registered entities as if they were resident in the same country as their parent company. At a practical level a more significant constraint on unilateral anti-avoidance provisions is 'that the resident country needs to know whether a taxpayer keeps funds offshore. Thus, they hinge on effective exchange of information to be effective' (Rixen 2008, 78).

Given such limitations the demand for entity structures that could be used to conceal tax liabilities has increased dramatically in recent years. This trend has been reinforced by improvements in communications and information technology making it possible to manage complex webs of corporate subsidiaries designed to obscure and reallocate income, assets and debt (Desai 2005, 188; Sharman 2010, 7). As noted above, the British Virgin Islands and its population of 22000 is home to 800000 registered companies (Sharman 2010, 6; Palan et al. 2010, 57), while a detailed 2008 US Government Accountability Office study found banking giant Citigroup operating no fewer than 427 subsidiaries in secrecy jurisdictions (GAO 2008, 25). Such data clearly indicate that there are significant tax and other financial and risk management benefits through establishing entities offshore.

Even assuming that a secrecy jurisdiction is willing to disclose tax information, which may increasingly be the case, their ability to provide reliable tax information is undermined by lax corporate governance laws and a limited capacity to verify the bona fide owners of registered companies. One response to this challenge has been the promotion of so-called 'Know Your Customer' regulations whereby banks, tax authorities and other regulators are required to know the physical identity of account holders or the beneficial owners of registered corporations and other entities. While some headway has been made on this front with major initiatives from both the Financial Action Task Force (FATF) and the OECD, this progress has been offset by the creation of innovative new offshore schemes designed to obscure the identity of the beneficial owners of offshore entities.

Trusts and foundations and establishing beneficial ownership
One of the most popular ways of concealing the beneficial owner of offshore assets is through the creation of trusts. Indeed, the inadequate regulation of trusts was a common reason why the Global Forum recently found that 19 jurisdictions (of a total of 59 assessed as of early 2012) had insufficient legal means to establish the beneficial ownership of assets (OECD 2011b). Historically, under equity law a trust was established to allow a nominated trustee to manage assets independently of their legal owner. While there are a number of legitimate uses of trusts they are attractive for tax planning purposes for at least two reasons. First, they can be used to separate the legal management of assets from their true owners. As a trustee is required to pay tax on income produced by a trust, there are clear incentives to establish a trust in a secrecy jurisdiction making it very difficult to establish the identity or ultimate beneficiary of the assets held within the trust. The situation is compounded by the fact that there is often no legal requirement to register trusts making it very difficult for tax authorities or other investigators to establish the true beneficiaries of the structure. Traditionally trusts were designed as a legal instrument for transferring wealth and the settlor of a trust could not be a beneficiary;

however most offshore centres ignore this inconvenient detail by using various nominee arrangements (Palan et al. 2010, 92). The end result is that an offshore trust can ensure that even if bank secrecy in an offshore jurisdiction is compromised, the identity of the account owner will still be concealed. Investigators may be able to determine the identity of the lawyer or accountant who acts as a trustee, but it will be far more difficult to establish the original settlor and beneficiaries (who may be one and the same). Due to the lack of registration requirements noted above it is difficult to establish the precise extent of offshore trust use, although a recent survey by the Society of Trust and Estate Practitioners (cited in Palan et al. 2010, 93) estimated that offshore trusts managed some 350 000 accounts with assets of between US$3 and US$8 trillion. While much of this activity may be legitimate estate planning, without greater transparency and more robust governance it is difficult to avoid the conclusion that offshore trusts are an important instrument for international tax evasion.

Foundations provide another legal structure that can be used in an offshore context to conceal the true identity of owners. While foundations were established to manage income and assets for charities and other designated purposes, the fact that offshore centres require minimal disclosure concerning settlors who 'donate' to foundations and their beneficiaries, combined with their no or low-tax status, provides ample opportunity for abuse (Palan et al. 2010, 93). Arguably the most widely used form of foundation for tax evasion purposes is the Liechtenstein *Anstalt* and while reliable data on their use is scarce they were widely used by the Marcos family in the 1980s to hide their ill-gotten wealth (Picciotto 2011, 241; Sharman 2010, 6), while more recently it has been estimated that as many as 80 000 such foundations may have been created for a mainly offshore clientele (Palan 2010, 94).

Opaque corporations

Trusts and foundations are widely used both for the legitimate management of estates and charitable organisations as well as for obscuring the true ownership of offshore assets. However there are limits to the extent to which an investor can use trusts to actively control and manage a complex business and so a more complex corporate structure may be required. The central role of the corporation in contemporary capitalism is hardly surprising given the numerous advantages that they confer. As noted above, corporations feature a separate legal personality and are treated as discrete entities within international tax law. Moreover, corporations can raise external capital through debt, bonds or issuing equity, while also providing liability protection to investors.

We have already noted that the way in which corporations use subsidiary firms in low-tax jurisdictions to 'book' profitable transactions is central to almost all international tax planning strategies. Rather than outlining and assessing the myriad of tax mitigation strategies used by international business our focus is on the more blatant ways in which specific types of corporate entities found in secrecy jurisdictions are used to evade tax. While legal international tax avoidance and planning remains a significant threat to the integrity and sustainability of national tax systems it can be argued that national governments have some capacity to respond to such threats through unilateral or coordinated anti-avoidance provisions as long as they can establish the beneficial owners and financial activities of offshore firms. For this reason it is necessary to focus on offshore corporate structures that provide financial and tax secrecy.

IBCs
Corporations operating under robust governance provisions with rigorous filing requirements and an obligation to maintain a comprehensive and accurate registry of shareholders provide few opportunities for international tax evasion, especially in the current era of increasing tax information exchange. However, in their quest to attract capital many secrecy jurisdictions have departed from best practice so far as corporate governance is concerned by allowing, and in many cases promoting, corporate entities that conceal their beneficial owners. Such structures allow their owners to exploit many of the benefits of incorporation while allowing them to conceal income and assets. Generically such entities are referred to as International Business Corporations, or IBCs. While there is a good deal of variation between jurisdictions the majority of IBCs share the following characteristics:

- Minimal or no corporate taxation with the host country charging a modest annual registration fee;
- Minimal filing requirements and few obligations to appoint office-bearers;
- Nominee directors often allowable to disguise real management;
- The ability to engage in a full range of business activities; and
- Ability to conceal the real owner of the corporation through issuance of bearer shares.

Of these characteristics the ability to use bearer shares, or shares where no registry of ownership is maintained clearly represents the greatest threat to tax and financial transparency. While allowing the use of bearer shares is becoming less common in the face of mounting international pressure, secrecy jurisdictions are developing innovative ways of complying with requirements to issue registered shares while still conceal-ing the true owners of companies. Strategies include allowing a nominee of a trust to own shares, introducing bank-style secrecy provisions to protect share registries, or simply failing to commit the administrative resources to maintain an up-to-date registry (Desai 2005). The prolifera-tion of such strategies is a central reason why in 2009 the Global Forum implemented an enhanced peer review regime (discussed in later chapters) which assesses both the legislative framework in a given jurisdiction *and* the ability of a jurisdiction to exchange information in practice. The hope is that jurisdictions that fail to maintain adequate share registries or do not hold adequate information on the beneficial owners of corporate entities will be identified in 'Phase 2' peer review reports (Chapter 6).

Exempt corporations and exotic structures

There has been growing resolve amongst OECD countries to tighten anti-avoidance provisions and curtail the blatant use of IBCs for taxa-tion purposes. For example, the number of offshore firms that have been taxed under the CFC provisions of the jurisdiction in which their parent company is registered has increased over the last decade. Such trends are encouraging, but many analysts argue that both the scope and effective-ness of these regimes needs to be enhanced (Pinto 2009). As with all his-torical attempts to improve offshore regulation, secrecy jurisdictions have met these anti-avoidance provisions with innovative responses designed to protect their international tax businesses and remain one step ahead of regulators (Braithwaite and Drahos 2000).

CFC provisions typically target entities that are registered offshore but have little physical presence and do not undertake significant economic activity in their country of registration. Such attacks on so-called 'post-box companies' are intended to force subsidiaries to hold full tax residency in either the jurisdiction of the parent company or to establish a real busi-ness offshore. While the latter option may still facilitate tax competition, it eliminates the situation described above where post-box corporations used for tax purposes can be established for negligible cost and are subject to minimal tax and lighter regulation than domestic firms that conduct real business activities in the secrecy jurisdiction. However the exempt corpora-tion is an audacious structure designed to protect the IBCs' ability to avoid compliance with the domestic tax laws of any state. The defining feature of an exempt corporation is that it is granted residency in a secrecy jurisdic-tion on the basis that it is owned and managed within that jurisdiction. However, contrary to these general requirements, an exempt company can be deemed to be controlled elsewhere and therefore not subject to the tax laws applying to firms resident in the offshore jurisdiction (Palan et al.

2010, 87). Predictably such corporations are effectively stateless, deliberately falling between the claims of competing tax jurisdictions (Sharman 2010). Clearly loopholes which allow companies to register in an offshore jurisdiction and yet not be subject to its tax and corporate governance (and information exchange) provisions threaten to undermine the integrity of the emerging tax transparency regime. While the EU in particular has taken significant steps to eliminating the abuse of exempt corporations in the Channel Islands, where they were pioneered, there are concerns that their use is becoming more common beyond Europe.

CONCLUSION

This chapter has provided an overview of the nature and extent of international tax evasion. On the one hand, the sheer magnitude of the threat that international tax evasion poses, denying governments approximately $250 billion per year – more than 15 times the sum spent on humanitarian aid globally in 2011 – ensures that the issue is gaining prominence on the international political agenda (Palan et al. 2010; GHA 2011). However the chapter has also highlighted the significant challenges that stand in the path of effective tax cooperation and governance.

First and foremost are the financial interests of those actors who benefit from the preservation of the policy status quo. A constant in the politics of international taxation over the last half a century has been an alliance of those taxpayers (either corporate or individual) who seek aggressively to avoid or evade their tax obligations using offshore strategies, financial service providers who create, market and manage schemes to facilitate such offshore strategies, and those jurisdictions which have or provide a regulatory environment that supports such activities. This alliance is informal, often tacit in nature. However, as this book will argue, the structural power of such a coalition is significant and helps explain why small, seemingly powerless secrecy jurisdictions have until recently been able successfully to counter moves to enhance tax transparency.

A second feature of the international tax regime which represents a major obstacle to cooperation is the fact that the international tax regime as described above has been designed to protect the sovereign right of states to make tax law. Generally, national governments have been unwilling to commit to uniform standards for tax and financial data exchange or to allow foreign governments actively to pursue offshore tax investigations that contradict domestic law or in which they have no significant tax interest (Eccleston 2011; Rixen 2008). When the state-centric and sovereignty-preserving nature of the international tax regime is combined with the ability of firms or individuals to separate the physical location of their business from the legal jurisdiction in which their business is carried out then it is little wonder that there has been a boom in the 'virtual offshore world' (Palan 2003).

Ironically, because of the growth in offshore secrecy jurisdictions, the international tax system, which was devised to preserve the fiscal sovereignty of states and their right to tax and spend in accordance with domestic political imperatives, has been seriously compromised. Yet despite a growing awareness of the problem, political solutions remain elusive. This, as will be argued in more detail in the next chapter is because international tax cooperation can be defined as a classic 'collaboration problem' or a situation in which international agreement delivers net benefits to the international community at large, but individual states may gain advantages from defection (Martin and Simmons 1998). Under such circumstances compliance becomes a more significant concern and the ability to enforce an agreement on potential defectors, either through sanctions, reputational costs or some other political or economic means becomes critical.

The remainder of this book assesses the prospects for addressing the central governance challenges associated with the international tax regime and analysing whether changes that have occurred in international tax regulation during and in the immediate aftermath of the financial crisis represent genuine reform and are likely to be sustainable. This task begins in Chapter 2 which establishes the theoretical foundations for the analysis that follows, while Chapter 3 assesses the ways in which the institutional impediments and governance challenges outlined above manifested themselves in the politics of international tax cooperation in the late 1990s and early 2000s.

REFERENCES

Arnold, Brian J. (2000) 'Controlled Foreign Corporation Rules, Harmful Tax Competition, and International Taxation', in *World Tax Conference Report*, Toronto: Canadian Tax Foundation, 1–26.

Arnold, Brian J. and Michael J. McIntyre (2002) *International Tax Primer*, Netherlands: Kluwer Law International.

Braithwaite, John (2001) 'Through the Eyes of the Advisors: A Fresh Look at Tax Compliance of High Wealth Individuals', Centre for Tax System Integrity Working Paper no. 21, Canberra: Australian National University, available at http://ctsi.anu.edu.au/publications/WP/21.pdf (accessed November 2011).

Braithwaite, John and Peter Drahos (2000) *Global Business Regulation*, Cambridge: Cambridge University Press.

Braithwaite, Valerie (2009) *Defiance in Taxation and Governance: Resisting and*

Dismissing Authority in a Democracy, Cheltenham, UK and Northampton, MA, USA: Edward Elgar.

Browning, Lynnley (2008) '2 Indicted in UBS Tax Investigation', *New York Times*, 13 May 2008, available at http://www.nytimes.com/2008/05/13/business/world business/13iht-14tax.12857910.html?_r=1 (accessed July 2012).

Chaikin, David (2005) 'Policy and Fiscal Effects of Swiss Bank Secrecy', *Revenue Law Journal*, **15** (1), 90–110.

Cohen, Benjamin (1977) *Organizing the World's Money: The Political Economy of International Monetary Relations*, New York: Basic Books.

Dale, Richard S., Johnnie E.V. Johnson and Tang Leilei (2005), 'Financial Markets Can Go Mad: Evidence of Irrational Behaviour During the South Sea Bubble', *Economic History Review*, **58** (2), 233–71.

Desai, Mihir A. (2005) 'The Degradation of Reported Corporate Profits', *Journal of Economic Perspectives*, **19** (4), 171–92.

Eccleston, Richard (2011) 'Revolution or Evolution: Sovereignty, the Financial Crisis and the Governance of International Taxation', *Journal of Applied Law and Policy*, **3** (1), 12–24.

GAO (2008) *International Taxation: Large U.S. Corporations and Federal Contractors with Subsidiaries in Jurisdictions Listed as Tax Havens or Financial Privacy Jurisdictions*, Government Accountability Office, December, GAO–09–157.

GHA (2011) *Global Humanitarian Assistance Report 2011*, available at http://www.globalhumanitarianassistance.org/ (accessed December 2011).

Graetz, Michael J. and Michael M. O'Hearh (1997) 'The "Original Intent" of U.S International Taxation', *Duke Law Journal*, **46** (5), 1021–109.

Gravelle, Jane (2009) 'Tax Havens: International Tax Avoidance and Evasion', Congressional Research Service Report for Congress, 9 July, 7-5700.

Henry, James (2012) *The Price of the Offshore Revisited: New Estimates for Missing Private Wealth, Income, Inequality and Lost Taxes*, Tax Justice Network, available at http://www.taxjustice.net/cms/upload/pdf/Price_of_Offshore_Revisited_120722.pdf (accessed July 2012).

Hollingshead, Ann (2010) *Privately Held, Non-Resident Deposits in Secrecy Jurisdictions*, Global Financial Integrity, available at http://www.gfintegrity.org/storage/gfip/documents/reports/gfi_privatelyheld_web.pdf (accessed March 2011).

IMF (2000) 'Offshore Financial Centres: IMF Background Paper', Washington DC, International Monetary Fund, available at http://www.imf.org/external/np/mae/oshore/2000/eng/back.htm (accessed November 2010).

Keohane, Robert and Joseph Nye (1977) *Power and Interdependence*. Boston, MA: Little Brown and Company.

Loader Wilkinson, Tara (2010) 'European Tax Amnesties Lure Cash Back', *Dow Jones Wealth Bulletin*, 8 February, available at http://www.efinancialnews.com/story/2010-02-08/european-tax-amnesties-lure-back-cash (accessed July 2012).

Martin, Lisa and Beth Simmons (1998), 'Theories and Empirical Studies of International Institutions', *International Organization*, **52** (4), 729–57.

Martin, Isaac, Ajay Mehrotra and Monica Prasad (eds) (2009) *The New Fiscal Sociology*, New York and London: Cambridge University Press.

Mathiason, Nick (2008) 'Tax Scandal Leaves Swiss Giant Reeling', *Observer*, 29 June, available at http://www.guardian.co.uk/business/2008/jun/29/ubs.banking (accessed July 2012).

Moya, Elena (2009) 'Hedge Funds in Cayman Islands withdraw from UK Banks', *Guardian,* 15 June available at http://www.guardian.co.uk/business/2009/jun/15/private-equity-tax-avoidance-cayman-islands (accessed July 2012).

Murphy, Richard (2006) 'The Price of Offshore', Tax Justice Network Briefing Paper, available at http://www.richard.murphy.dial.pipex.com/ThePriceofOffshore.pdf (accessed July 2012).

O'Brien, Robert and Marc Williams (2010) *Global Political Economy*, 3rd edn, London: Palgrave Macmillan.

OECD (1998) *Harmful Tax Competition: An Emerging Global Issue*, Paris: OECD.

OECD (2011a) 'Global Forum Delivers Concrete Results to the Cannes G20 Summit', Media Release, 26 October, available at http://www.oecd.org/document/7/0,3746,en_21571361_44315115_48940615_1_1_1_1,00.html (accessed October 2011).

OECD (2011b) *Global Forum on Transparency and Exchange of Information for Tax Purposes: Tax Transparency 2011: Report on Progress*, Paris: OECD.

Owens, Jeffrey (2005) 'Abusive Tax Shelters: Weapons of Tax Destruction', *Tax Notes International*, 5 December.

Palan, Ronen (2003), *The Offshore World: Sovereign Markets, Virtual Places, and Nomad Millionaires,* Ithaca, NY: Cornell University Press.

Palan, Ronen, Richard Murphy and Christian Chavagneux (2010) *Tax Havens: How Globalization Really Works*, Ithaca, NY: Cornell University Press.

Picciotto, Sol (1992) *International Business Taxation: A Study in the Internationalization of Business Regulation*, London: Weidenfeld and Nicolson.

Picciotto, Sol (2011) *Regulating Global Corporate Capitalism*, Cambridge: Cambridge University Press.

Pinto, Dale (2009) 'A Proposal to Reform Income Anti-tax-deferral Regimes', *Australian Journal of Taxation*, **12** (2), 41–75

Radaelli, Claudio M. (1997) *The Politics of Corporate Taxation in the European Union: Knowledge and International Policy Agendas*, London: Routledge.

Radaelli, Claudio M. and Ulrike S. Kraemer (2008) 'Governance Areas in EU Direct Tax Policy', *Journal of Common Market Studies*, **46** (2), 315–36.

Rixen, Thomas (2008) *The Political Economy of International Tax Governance: Transformations of the State*, New York: Palgrave Macmillan.

Sharman, Jason (2006) *Havens in the Storm*, Ithaca, NY: Cornell University Press.

Sharman, Jason (2010) 'Shopping for Anonymous Shell Companies: An Audit Study of Financial Anonymity and Crime', *Journal of Economic Perspectives*, **24** (4), 127–40.

Sharman, Jason (2011) *The Money Laundry: Regulating Criminal Finance in the Global Economy*, Ithaca, NY: Cornell University Press

Sharman, Jason and Percy Mistry (2008) *Considering the Consequences: The Developmental Implications of Initiatives on Taxation, Anti-Money Laundering and Combating the Financing of Terrorism*, London: Commonwealth Secretariat.

Stewart, Jim (2005) 'Fiscal Incentives, Corporate Structure and Financial Aspects of Treasury Management', *Accounting Forum*, **29** (3), 271–88.

Strange, Susan (1988) *States and Markets*, London: Blackwell.

Tanzi, Vito (1987) 'Quantitative Characteristics of the Tax Systems of Developing Countries', in David Newbery and Nicholas Stern (eds), *Tax Systems for Developing Countries*, Oxford: Oxford University Press, pp. 171–96.

Tanzi, Vito (1995) *Taxation in an Integrating World.* Washington DC: Brookings Institution Press.

The Economist (2006) 'Tax Avoidance: Shopping for Low Tax Rates is no Crime', 6 May.

Tax Justice Network (2009) 'Financial Secrecy Project', available at http://www.fin ancialsecrecyindex.com/documents/WhatIsASecrecyJurisdiction.pdf (accessed November 2010).

US Senate (2006) *Tax Haven Abuses: The Enablers, The Tools, and Secrecy*, a Report of the Permanent Subcommittee on Investigations, available at http:// www.levin.senate.gov/imo/media/doc/supporting/2006/PSI.taxhavenabuses.080 106.pdf (accessed July 2012).

Zorome, Ahmed (2007) 'The Concept of Offshore Financial Centers: In search for an Operational Definition', Washington: IMF Working Paper, available at http://www.imf.org/external/pubs/ft/wp/2007/wp0787.pdf (accessed November 2010).

2. The dynamics of global governance

> Once formed, international regimes rarely become static, unchanging structures. On the contrary, they normally set in motion highly dynamic social practices that change continually – sometimes dramatically – in response to both endogenous forces and exogenous pressures. (Young 1999, 133)

The international tax regime that has evolved over the past century poses both governance challenges and opportunities. The sovereignty-preserving nature of international taxation combined with the extent to which it impacts on financial interests provides strong incentives for international regulatory competition in relation to tax matters. At the same time, the magnitude of the financial costs of regulatory arbitrage and the growing threat that international tax evasion poses to national tax systems provide strong incentives to create an international tax regime that will establish a robust foundation for international tax cooperation. In short, the governance of international taxation provides an important case study into the political economy of global economic governance in the twenty-first century.

Recent developments in international tax governance are of broader significance because they provide insights into the critical question of regime change and evolution. As will be outlined in Chapter 3, the international tax regime has evolved over the course of the twentieth century, with the political commitment to providing effective regulation waxing and waning in concert with changing political and economic circumstances. The period since the last years of the twentieth century in particular has seen significant variation in the commitment to cooperation, from the initial enthusiasm for the OECD's HTC initiative in the late 1990s and its effective defeat by the Bush Administration and a coalition of financial interests including key secrecy jurisdictions a few years later, to the current drive to enhance international tax transparency that has gained traction during the financial crisis.

Such events provide a unique opportunity to assess the relative importance of national interests and international organisations in combination with prevailing political, economic and ideational conditions in shaping the governance of international taxation. In these terms this study is animated by, and seeks to contribute to, the existing theoretical knowledge on institutional change and the dynamics of global governance. Given this ambition, the following pages provide a synoptic overview of the literature on cooperation in global economic governance with an emphasis on the factors that prompt states to commit to and comply with an existing regime.

METHODOLOGICAL FOUNDATIONS

The rich literature on global governance may highlight the complex politics of international cooperation, but its methodological diversity also poses problems for research design. Indeed eminent scholars such as Robert Keohane (2005) have lamented that 'social science is not yet at the point where a theory about such a multifaceted phenomenon as cooperation in world politics can be devised and tested'. While Keohane is correct to suggest that formal testing is problematic, it is possible, and indeed desirable, to use the existing literature on global governance to establish a coherent analytical framework to help establish the causal inferences that influence international cooperation in relation to taxation issues. To this extent the literature on international regimes represents a valuable resource that will generate research questions and guide the empirical analysis to 'assist in making events more intelligible through a greater interpretive scheme' (Kay 2006).

In more specific terms, this study employs an 'analytical' or theoretically informed narrative method by employing a combination of inductive and deductive strategies to devise, refine and evaluate theories of international regime change (Rixon 2008, 14–15; Levi et al. 1998; Kay 2006). In the first instance the relevance of existing theories of international cooperation and regime change are assessed in the context of the general developments in international tax regulation over the past decade. The specific objective of this synoptic review is to identify and assess theoretically informed accounts as to why states commit to and comply with existing international regimes. These theoretical claims will then be refined and assessed in light of the empirical account of the changing nature of international cooperation and the changing essence of the international tax regime in recent years. This empirically grounded strategy is preferable to a purely deductive approach given the diversity of economic, political and ideational forces driving change in the global economy in recent years. By casting a wide net the aim is to develop a 'synthetic interpretation of change' that can accommodate and analyse the diverse range of factors shaping international tax regulation (Keohane 2009, 40). Similarly Katzenstein has recently advocated greater 'analytical eclecticism' as an 'intellectual stance that supports efforts to complement, engage, and selectively utilize theoretical constructs embedded in contending research traditions to build complex arguments that bear on substantive problems of interest to both scholars and practitioners' (Sil and Katzenstein 2010, 411). Overall the broad methodological goal is to develop and assess a theoretical framework which is sensitive to the full range of temporal processes that influence international cooperation while remaining sufficiently structured to be subject to falsification (Scharpf 1997; George 1979, 49).

The detailed empirical research presented in the following chapters is therefore designed to evaluate the propositions and research agenda set out in the remainder of this chapter with a view to making an original contribution to our theoretical knowledge of international tax governance. The aim of this strategy is to achieve Young's (1999, 132) methodological ambition of developing accounts of global governance that 'join general knowledge with an in-depth understanding of individual cases'.

SYSTEMIC THEORIES OF REGIME CHANGE

Explaining international cooperation in an inherently anarchical international system goes to the core of international relations and global governance scholarship. Predictably there is a rich literature on the factors that influence international cooperation in world affairs. Arguably, as was discussed briefly in the introduction, the most influential strand of this research is regime theory which, since the late 1970s, has argued that rational states would create 'sets of principles, norms, rules, and decision-making procedures around which actors' expectations converge in a given area of international relations' (Krasner 1983). Predictably the pioneering research on international regimes was framed by the prevailing orthodoxy within international relations scholarship at the time in that both liberal and more sceptical realist traditions could be identified. Rather than providing a comprehensive summary of the evolution of regime theory, our task here is to identify potential explanations of the recent changes in the international tax regime with a specific emphasis on explanations of regime participation and compliance. The account begins by assessing the relevance of realist accounts of regime formation and change before presenting a more detailed examination of the insights that can be drawn from liberal regime theory.

Regimes, as Krasner's seminal definition attests, are created to promote and sustain international cooperation in an inherently anarchical international system. At a theoretical level, the existence of international regimes designed to promote international cooperation would seem to be at odds with realist ontological precepts that world politics is shaped by states' ongoing quest for survival and self-help. However, as a host of realist scholars acknowledge, international regimes have become an increasingly prominent feature of world affairs in recent times. Realists contend that regimes will be created and sustained when they allow powerful states to protect and promote their privileged position in the international system. Three central insights can be drawn from this literature. First, effective leadership is critical to the creation and efficacy of international regimes. Regimes capable of addressing collaboration problems with significant distributional consequences require a serious commitment of resources which will only be forthcoming if powerful states have an enduring interest in the regime's existence. Reflecting this, hegemonic stability theory of the 1970s, argued that the supply of regimes would be closely related to the capacity of a hegemonic power to promote and enforce international agreements (Gilpin 1981; Krasner 1983). However, with declining US power since the 1970s and a growing reluctance to provide international leadership, there has been a good deal of research from both liberal and realist scholars alike on the possibility and form of non-hegemonic leadership (Keohane 1984, 50). On this question realists have been influenced by both empirical research on international cooperation and by theoretical work on group dynamics and cooperation and now acknowledge the critical role of 'privileged groups' and a 'concert of great powers' in providing regime leadership (Olson 1965; Schelling 1978). The analysis that follows will assess the extent and changing nature of group leadership among key states in the international tax regime.

The second important insight from realist accounts of international regimes relates to an often critical assessment of their efficacy. Specifically the realist approach helps explain the often partial and ineffective nature of regime implementation. Put simply, in a state-based international order national governments may consent to international agreements for reasons of political expediency with little intention of implementing these commitments if they run contrary to national interests. This is especially true in the case of highly contested governance arenas in which agreements involve significant costs or require substantial domestic political reform. This dynamic helps explain why implementation is widely regarded as the Achilles heel of global governance and why there has been a proliferation of 'sham regimes' in recent years (Young 1999; Drenzer 2007, 81–5; Joachim et al. 2008). In light of this literature, it is necessary to explore the dynamic relationship between regime participation and effectiveness in relation to the international tax transparency regime over the past decade. For example, did states commit to the OECD's original HTC initiative because they regarded it as being ineffective? And will the greater focus on implementation and compliance since the financial crisis have an impact on participation?

Finally, both realists and liberals have long acknowledged that changing state interests will impact on regime formation, participation and compliance (Keohane and Nye 1977). Traditionally the focus of realist scholarship has been on the effect of structural economic and geopolitical changes within the international system on state interests, with Krasner (1983) invoking a geological metaphor in which the tectonic plates on which international politics has its foundations periodically shift with dramatic consequences for the world order (Cohen 2008, 103). While the analysis that follows will be cognisant of the impact of structural changes on the agendas and interests of great powers, a more recent and relevant trend in realist theory has been to open the 'black box' of the state by giving more detailed consideration to the role of domestic politics (albeit influenced by structural developments) in shaping state interests (Drezner 2007; Moravcsik 1997). An ambition of this book is to build on the work of neo-realists such as Drezner by making a contribution to a more comprehensive understanding of the complex interactions between international events, domestic politics and international organisations in the international tax arena. However, before returning to this theme later in the chapter, it is first necessary to outline the key contributions of liberal regime theory.

Liberal Insights

Regime theory, with its emphasis on how to understand and promote international cooperation, is rightly regarded as a liberal research agenda. Presciently, scholars such as Keohane and Nye (1977) argued that with increased economic integration and overlapping sovereignty, or *complex interdependence*, there would be increased demand for and interest in international cooperation. Beyond this fundamental functionalist insight, perhaps the most significant and distinctive contribution made by scholars is that international regimes influence the ways in which states and other significant actors in world affairs assess the benefits or otherwise of engaging in international cooperation. In contrast to realists, first generation liberal scholars, such as Keohane and Nye, argued that negotiations and agreements within regimes had the potential to promote and sustain co-operation through reducing uncertainty and reassuring participants.

The central claim is that while actors participate in international regimes to further their interests, conceptions of such interests are inherently bounded by uncertainty and incomplete information (Simon 1982; Keohane 1984, ch. 4). Given the uncertainty surrounding the creation of international agreements strategic interactions within an international regime can influence preferences through promoting shared understandings of governance problems and the best regulatory solutions to them. Critically, given the interdependence associated with international governance problems, regimes provide insights into the likely conduct of rival states and the prospects of third-party compliance – considerations that are essential to sustainable cooperation. The core claim is that while international regimes do not override self-interest, they do affect calculations of self-interest (Keohane 2005, xi). This approach is still within the rationalist framework, yet in contrast to many of the game-theory inspired models associated with 'Open Economy Politics' (OEP) that followed, the notion that states and other participants in international regimes have fixed egoistical interests is questioned. Accepting that the structure and dynamics of international regimes influence the calculation of self-interest and the prospects of international cooperation gives rise to the more important question of how regime dynamics shape patterns of economic diplomacy. It is in relation to this critical question that rationalist and constructivist scholars offer distinctive theories of endogenous regime dynamics.

Liberal institutionalists identify three endogenous processes – social learning, establishing focal points and shaping expectations – that can enhance international cooperation and influence regime change. It has long been recognised that regimes that promote and sustain interaction among regime participants can foster information exchange and social learning (Haas 1983). The former process refers to the ways in which the sharing of policy knowledge, evidence and ideas reduces uncertainty in relation to complex governance strategies and international agreements, while the latter acknowledges that with time fundamental understandings of the nature of governance problems and the ways in which they should be tackled can change (Young 1999, 62; Ostrom 1990). Arguably the OECD's greatest contribution to global governance, both in the tax arena and beyond, has been to host so-called 'generative regimes' in which policy experts from member states can discuss policy problems and work towards developing agreed solutions (Woodward 2009). These regimes have been instrumental in setting standards and shaping the international agenda in numerous policy arenas. Significantly there is evidence that such internal negotiation and bargaining has facilitated regime change and adaptation (Checkel 2005). While internal negotiations and learning within 'epistemic communities' or 'transgovernmental networks' can provide the foundations for building and adapting international agreements, many critics argue that in order to achieve robust cooperation this type of technically oriented regime needs to be linked to and engage with key decision-makers. For example, Haas's research on epistemic communities suggests that in order to be effective, agendas developed by generative regimes need to be able to make persuasive claims and enjoy the support of influential brokers with access to key decision-makers (1990). In a similar vein, Coats and Colander (1989) argue that the existence of personal and organisational networks linking policy experts and decision-makers is central to the dissemination of ideas. Given such claims a central element of the research agenda that follows is assessing the extent to which social learning occurred in the international tax regime as well as the nature and consequences of inter-organisational relationships between the OECD, member states and key decision-making forums such as the G20.

The second way in which international regimes can reduce uncertainty surrounding complex global governance issues is through identifying and promoting key focal points. An important insight from the game theory literature which resonates with real world economic diplomacy is the existence of multiple equilibria, or the reality that there are a number of possible solutions to a particular international governance problem. Given this complexity and the associated limits on information concerning the likely costs and benefits of alternative agreements, international regimes can help identify and promote one viable solution among many. Historically, as will be discussed in Chapter 3, the OECD has performed an important role in identifying regulatory 'focal points', which once accepted by a critical mass of member states, can become a de facto international standard. Such a regime may be subject to increasing returns and once a tipping point is reached states that hitherto were not parties to an agreement will have significant incentives to adopt the emerging international standard. As we saw in the previous chapter, this dynamic is true of the DTA regime, which courtesy of the OECD model treaty, provides certainty and reduces transaction costs while still allowing for incremental change.

When governance problems resemble coordination problems in that all actors have an incentive to comply, then establishing a focal point may be enough to sustain an international agreement. However, in the case of collaboration problems (such as the Prisoner's Dilemma), or a governance regime where agreement will deliver net benefits to the international community at large, but individual states may benefit from defection, then the issue of compliance becomes a more significant concern (Martin and Simmons 1998). Under these circumstances the ability to enforce the agreement on potential defectors, either through sanctions, reputational costs or some other political or economic means becomes critical. Here the liberal institutionalist literature invokes the concept of the 'shadow of the future' or the idea that if an international agreement becomes established, and there is a credible threat of retaliation against non-compliant states, then there are much stronger incentives to comply with the regime

(Axelrod and Keohane 1993; Dal Bo 2005). As with the more benign case of coordination problems described above, there is potential for a regime, once established, to influence state expectations and behaviour and promote compliance with international agreements. Indeed the most sophisticated 'folk theorem' modelling of international cooperation highlights how over the course of time, with multiple and repeated games, the expectations of actors change such that malign collaboration problems can be transformed into more benign coordination problems (Abbott and Snidal 2002). This demonstrates the dynamic nature of cooperation. As Keohane (2005, x) argues, harmony is 'an intensely political process of mutual adjustment in a situation of actual and potential discord'.

BEYOND SYSTEMIC THEORIES OF CHANGE

Systemic explanations of international cooperation provide useful insights into the centrality of interests, leadership and power dynamics in international cooperation but also overlook critical factors that may influence regime participation and compliance. These omissions have given rise to a revisionist literature on the dynamics of global governance which tackles the important questions of institutional evolution and adaption from a range of increasingly sophisticated perspectives (Djelic and Sahlin-Andersson 2006; Hasenclever et al. 2000). The unifying agenda informing revisionist theories of international regimes is an interrogation of the rationalist assumption that state interests are either fixed or, at the very least, structurally determined. In contrast, the literature outlined below variously contends that endogenous socialisation within regimes, changing inter-organisational relationships and networks and developments at the level of domestic politics can all influence a state's willingness to participate in and comply with an international agreement.

Sociological Approaches

The defining assumption of liberal regime theory is that rational actors hold externally defined interests with the extent and nature of cooperation shaped by prevailing institutional incentives. The claim that internal regime dynamics not only reduce uncertainty, but can have a broader and independent influence on the construction of interests can be traced back to key contributions in Goldstein and Keohane's edited volume *Ideas and Foreign Policy* (1993), which argued that regimes are inherently social institutions wherein institutionalised and recurring interaction among participants is likely to have an independent impact on the preferences and behaviour of regime participants (Keohane 2009). However more recent research in the sociological tradition goes a good deal further than the claims of 'weak cognitivists', and their study of how ideas mediate the process through which interests are translated into preferences (Hasenclever et al. 1997, 2000), with fully fledged constructivists highlighting the constitutive (as opposed to causal) role of ideas and the social construction of knowledge in shaping interests in world affairs (Abdelal et al. 2010). This 'deep' constructivist research agenda, with its distinctive ontological and epistemological foundations, cannot easily be integrated into a unified theory of international regime change but, at an empirical level, this literature does provide important insights into the potential role of ideational factors in shaping changing patterns of international cooperation (Hasenclever et al. 2000).

Perhaps the most relevant sociological process for explaining changing patterns of regime compliance is the literature on institutional socialisation and its central claim that through a process of sustained institutional interaction, actors gradually adapt their behaviour, which, over time, can lead to interest convergence and cooperation (Bearce and Bondanella 2007). In specific terms, institutional socialisation suggests that international organisations, such as the OECD, and the forums and regimes they facilitate, make an independent and positive contribution to international cooperation and global governance. In contrast to rationalist accounts described above, sociological theories of institutional socialisation argue that sustained international engagement and deliberation potentially lead to a more fundamental reassessment of beliefs and interests (Finnemore 1996; Johnston 2001). This literature highlights different processes that lead to varying depths of socialisation. On this last point Checkel (2005) makes a useful distinction between *Type 1*, or 'shallow' socialisation, which is consistent with liberal accounts in which rational actors accept institutionally appropriate rules and behaviours yet through participation in the regime may adapt strategies in order to achieve outcomes (Haas 1990), and deeper 'constitutive' *Type 2* socialisation, which occurs when, over time, actors assume new interests and even the identity of the organisation in which they participate. For our purposes it is important to note that evidence of this process takes the form of states or state actors 'internalising' new values to the extent that new interests and behaviour become accepted norms. Beyond establishing evidence of shifting values among state actors, it is also necessary to establish clear causal mechanisms and pathways from international institutions to member governments. In the absence of such evidence it is possible that international cooperation could be the product of exogenous developments or changing domestic interests and priorities generated independently from international socialisation processes.

Beyond the impact of prevailing norms and ideas within international regimes this study will also evaluate the changes in the broader ideational climate and how the financial crisis in particular impacted on the policy and regulatory priorities of states and the legitimacy of international agreements. Indeed the role of ideas has a long history in political economy analysis, from Marxist concerns with hegemony, legitimation and false consciousness, to Keynes's observation that interests were not rational but 'fickle things' which are constituted by ideas (Blyth 2002, 42). At this structural level ideational frameworks are significant because they can influence the prospects of international cooperation in at least two important ways. Firstly policy paradigms that provide 'descriptions and theoretical analyses that specify cause and effect relationships' (Campbell 1998, 384) have a significant impact on the policy agenda. Emerging paradigms, or what Stone (1989) refers to as 'causal stories', create a cognitive model of the world which can both discredit the status quo and be used by political leaders and policy entrepreneurs to formulate policy solutions to prevailing political and economic problems. The literature on economic crises is particularly relevant to the study at hand because during moments of flux, such as the height of the financial crisis in late 2008, not only do the material circumstances confronting actors change but the very policy paradigms used to interpret the political world may also be displaced. Hall (1989, 1993) argues that this process is shaped by the supply of ideas and the extent to which powerful political actors mobilise behind a new paradigm. Blyth (2002) takes the causal role of ideas further and suggests that in moments of political upheaval, or 'Knightian uncertainty', ideas are foundational in shaping interests and providing blueprints for new institutional orders. In short, crises are clearly catalysts for fundamental political change both at the level of domestic politics and in international economic diplomacy (Eccleston 2007, ch. 1).

Beneath the role of policy paradigms ideas also mediate debates concerning the policy agenda and the broader legitimacy of rival policy options. Such processes occur at a number of levels. First, dominant ideas play a significant role both in defining policy problems and in the generation of viable policy solutions. In this sense ideas play an important agenda-setting function. Second, embedded norms influence what the broader public regard as being politically acceptable. Such norms are what Campbell (2004, 96) defines as 'public sentiments', or the normative background assumptions that constrain decision-making and institutional change by limiting the range of programmes that decision-making elites are likely to perceive as acceptable and legitimate both to their constituents and themselves (Campbell 1998, 384; Weir and Skocpol 1985, 119).

This increasingly prominent sociological literature suggests three levels at which changing ideational conditions associated with the financial crisis may have shaped the regime dynamics and patterns of international cooperation:

1. Within regimes sustained interaction may lead to the construction and dissemination of new norms and logics of appropriate action – the institutional socialisation hypothesis.
2. Financial crisis may have provided an ideational moment of flux in which the regulatory status quo was undermined and strategically located policy entrepreneurs could formulate and promote a new regulatory order.
3. Finally, at the level of public sentiment, the financial crisis may have undermined the electoral legitimacy of the existing regulatory order, enhancing the reformist resolve of national governments at the international level.

Reflecting these developments in constructivist theory, the empirical analysis that follows will examine the extent to which interactions within the international tax regime promoted an expert consensus, providing a focal point for regulatory initiatives, or whether the regime fostered more fundamental 'deep socialisation', driving shifts in prevailing norms held by key regime participants. Finally the study will explore the extent to which the financial crisis influenced both the regulatory reform agendas of state actors independent of key international organisations within the international tax regime and the political support these agendas enjoyed by the mass public.

Reflecting the established dichotomy in the literature this chapter so far has distinguished between endogenous and exogenous processes and their impact on patterns of international cooperation. While this is a useful organising principle, few would argue that there is a clear demarcation between internal and external regime dynamics. Indeed, as the empirical analysis in the following chapters will demonstrate, internal dynamics and ideational trends work in concert with broader structural forces which operate above the level of the state in the global political economy. Above all else this process is mediated by changing relationships between organisations as well as domestic political imperatives. Given these dynamics it is necessary to broaden the analysis beyond the established parameters of the academic debate and give consideration to how inter-organisational networks and relationships, as well as domestic political imperatives, shape patterns of international cooperation.

Networks and Inter-organisational Dynamics

The most significant institutional consequence of the financial crisis to date has been the transformation of existing international financial institutions (most notably the G20), such that they have taken on new agendas and functions (Streeck and Thelen 2005; Thelen 2002). In part, this affirms the argument that institutional adaptation is preferable to the creation of new organisational structures because it is less time consuming and requires a relatively modest investment of diplomatic capital – commodities in short supply at the height of the financial crisis (Eilstrup-Sangiovanni 2009, 205). In specific terms, we witnessed the conversion of the G20 from a ministerial-level forum, whose role had hitherto focused on agenda-setting and 'widening existing mindsets and promoting policy paradigms', to a leaders' forum charged with responsibility for coordinating and implementing the global response to the financial crisis (Porter 2010; Hillman 2010). However, given the G20's (and indeed all of the Gs) lack of a secretariat (Beeson and Bell 2009; Garrett 2010), developing and implementing detailed policy prescriptions in a timely manner required intense cooperation with established intergovernmental organisations such as the IMF and the OECD. Indeed the deepening of G20-led vertical inter-organisational networks in global economic governance and its impact on patterns of international cooperation is arguably the most significant aspect of the initial global response to the financial crisis (Eccleston et al. 2010). Given such developments it is necessary to assess the impact of these inter-organisational networks and negotiations on patterns of international tax cooperation.

Five years prior to the financial crisis Anne-Marie Slaughter predicted that network governance 'would become a key feature of the world order in the twenty first century' (Slaughter 2004, 1). This insight was based on the observation that traditional, treaty-based intergovernmental organisations simply do not have the breadth of expertise, flexibility or speed of decision-making to solve many of the contemporary problems in global governance, notably those that arise as crises (Reinicke et al. 2000; Slaughter 2004; Ruggie 2002; Helleiner and Pagliari 2010; Eilstrup-Sangiovanni 2005). In contrast, networks, with their largely informal modes of exchange and coordination, promise flexibility in terms of their objectives, membership and, by virtue of their members' access to formal organisations, use of a range of regulatory instruments that can be employed in the pursuit of international cooperation. Importantly it has been argued that a networked world order can complement existing state actors and intergovernmental organisations and regimes (Kahler 2009). Networks, it is argued, are ultimately about enhancing relationships between organisations and individuals based on mutual needs (Reinicke et al. 2000; Eilstrup-Sangiovanni 2005). At a functional level networks can facilitate mutually beneficial resource exchange, promoting the efficacy of global governance. This has certainly been evident during the financial crisis with, for example, the G20 exploiting the OECD's expertise in relation to international taxation issues to improve international tax transparency (Wouters et al. 2010; Porter 2010).

Significantly the rise of the G20 Leaders' Forum during the financial crisis represents a distinctive form of vertical network in global governance in which the G20 assumes a new 'superordinate' relationship with the wide range of horizontal networks and international organisations. As noted above, at the height of the crisis the G20's role was transformed to that of an important node in what had previously been a loosely coordinated web of international economic actors (Wouters et al. 2010). Critically the G20 acted as an executive forum establishing a clear set of priorities and granting subordinate actors, organisations and networks a mandate to pursue their various agendas. Yet, far from being simply hierarchical, these network relations were characterised by mutual dependence. The evidence presented in this book suggests that the G20 afforded organisations such as the OECD increased legitimacy and authority, institutional prestige and resources, if only in relation to specific areas of work. On the other hand, partner organisations reciprocated with expertise and developed reform agendas and pre-existing diplomatic and interpersonal networks that have the potential to enhance decision-making and implementation. Given such claims and evidence, it is necessary to evaluate the impact of the G20's rise and the deepening of associated inter-organisational networks and patterns on the international tax regime. If the leadership of the G20 was a decisive factor in garnering international support for international tax transparency then we must also consider how dependent the regime is on ongoing G20 leadership and support. We return to this theme in the final chapter.

The Domestic Politics of International Cooperation

International relations scholarship has traditionally focused on the political relationships between states, with realist approaches in particular paying scant attention to domestic political considerations (Bull 1972; Katzenstein 1978, 4–5). Yet, at an empirical level, the renewed enthusiasm for the OECD's tax information exchange regime which has been evident since the mid-2000s has, in part, been the consequence of changing domestic considerations within key states such as the United States (Chapter 5). Similarly the preparedness of secrecy jurisdictions to comply with the regime is, in part, dependent on domestic considerations. Given such evidence there is a clear need to move beyond systemic theories of international relations, with their exogenous (and relatively static) conceptions of state interests, and towards a more comprehensive account which assesses the combined influences of domestic and international factors in an explanation of international regime change. Fortunately a good many pioneering scholars have embarked on the difficult journey of trying to integrate theories of domestic politics into a comprehensive account of world affairs. This section will be devoted to a brief summary of the most relevant approaches to the study at hand before concluding with a summary of the research agenda for the remainder of the book.

Few, if any, contemporary international relations scholars would argue that domestic factors have no bearing on state interests. As Kingsbury et al. (2005) have argued, we can only understand regime change if we 'understand that that interstate and domestic politics are not separate realms but intertwined entities'. The real barrier to a more integrated theory of world affairs is largely methodological with most scholars opting to exclude detailed consideration of the domestic in the interests of parsimony. For example, Robert Keohane, whose *After Hegemony* (1984) includes many references to the ways in which domestic political and economic factors influence the motivation and ability of states to provide international leadership, acknowledges that the under-theorisation of the domestic is largely because 'I did not know how to incorporate a sophisticated theory of domestic politics into my analysis in a cogent and parsimonious way' (2005, xiii). While theoretical parsimony may be desirable, in this case the significance of domestic political developments justifies casting the causal net more widely, even if the subsequent analysis is more complex and subject to a range of interpretations. This is precisely why the study employs an ideographic method, albeit one in which the empirical analysis is animated by the extant literature and theorising.

Serious scholarship on the relationship between domestic politics and international relations can be traced to the late 1970s with Peter Katzenstein's *Between Power and Plenty* (1978) and Peter Gourevitch's paper in *International Organization*, 'The Second Image Reversed' (1978). Significantly for the study at hand, Katzenstein highlighted how variations in foreign policy both between states and across time could be explained by variations in domestic institutional structures as well as the changing nature of governing coalitions. Gourevitch's contribution to the debate complemented Katzenstein's by demonstrating the ways in which international imperatives shape patterns of domestic politics, especially in smaller, open economies. Taken together these accounts represent the first serious attempt to describe and theorise the complex and interdependent relationship between domestic politics and foreign economic policy.

Despite having been on the international political economy research agenda for over thirty years, attempts to develop an integrated and robust theory linking international behaviour (and in our case cooperation) to domestic political considerations have been elusive. For example, Putnam's (1988) model of the 'two-level game' sought to explain how states attempt to reconcile domestic and international imperatives to maximise political advantage. While the approach has a certain elegance, its plausibility is compromised by the assumption that the domestic and international are separate political spheres mediated by the state. At this level Putnam's approach, and indeed much of the 'American School' literature which followed, fails to do justice to Katzenstein and Gourevitch's central claim that the domestic and international realms are interdependent (Cohen 2008, 128–9).

Attempts to develop a general theory linking domestic politics to an account of international behaviour may have been disappointing, but more recent research has yielded significant, albeit incremental progress. One notable contribution which focuses specifically on the issues of regime formation and effectiveness is Daniel Drezner's work (2007) on international cooperation. Writing from a neo-realist perspective Drezner argues that effective global governance is critically dependent on converging great-power interests. Yet his analysis builds on earlier contributions from Moravcsik (1997) in arguing that (in relation to economic issues in particular) state interests are largely shaped by domestic considerations (Drezner 2007, 6). The model assumes that a state's economic interests and power are largely a product of its domestic political economy. In situations where international regulatory commitments may deliver net national benefits, yet have a detrimental impact on sectoral economic interests (as is often the case), then Drezner accepts that domestic politics matters. More specifically that entrenched, immobile industries can often use their structural power, or 'voice' using Hirschman's (1970) terminology, to shape state preferences at an international level. This framework for linking the interests and structural power of key economic actors at a domestic level represents a significant contribution to the literature although it could be argued that more emphasis could be granted to the importance of governing coalitions and changing administrations (as suggested by Katzenstein 1978), or to the potentially significant role of ideas in framing national policy responses to demands for international regulation.

Another approach which yields important insights into the relationship between domestic politics, state interests and patterns of global governance is the emerging 'Everyday Political Economy' literature which seeks to highlight the way in which changing patterns of social relations have a 'bottom up' effect on domestic political agendas and imperatives which in turn influence state interests at the international level (Elias 2010; Hobson and Seabrooke 2007). This emerging literature is significant in that it reminds us of Polyani's ([1944] 2001) often forgotten insight that economic relations are ultimately embedded in patterns of social relations. The implication is that if diplomatic strategies and subsequent international agreements do not enjoy popular support then they are vulnerable to a grassroots movement for change. Clearly examples of this process have been evident since the onset of the financial crisis in 2007 with the Occupy Wall Street movement being the most prominent example. More optimistically the reverse may be true in that changing interests at a domestic level may bolster the prospects for achieving international cooperation.

Finally, significant contributions to our understanding of the impact of domestic politics on patterns of international cooperation have also come from the more empirically grounded, inductive research on regimes which concludes that new governments, new patterns of interest group politics and institutional innovations all have the potential to influence a state's commitment to an international agreement (Underdal 1998; Young 1999; Singer 2004). This research advocates an idiographic method in which empirical research should aim to establish the complex ways through which domestic imperatives shape international postures and the extent to which international developments feed back into the domestic sphere. The collective goal of such scholarship is to identify the extent (perhaps limited) to which common processes and patterns of influence occur across different policy arenas and historical periods and by so doing, to attempt to develop more general knowledge from detailed case studies (Young 1999, 155).

RESEARCH AGENDA

Having outlined the semi-inductive method which informs this study and provided a strategic survey on the literature on international regime change, the final task for this chapter is to describe the specific research agenda which will be pursued over the remainder of the book. The empirical analysis that follows traces the historical development of the international tax regime from its early twentieth-century origins (Chapter 3) through to the recent period of rapid change in the immediate aftermath of the financial crisis (Chapters 4, 5 and 6). Yet this account goes beyond a traditional narrative in that the analysis is designed to provide insights into the competing explanations of international regime change described

Table 2.1   Levels of analysis in international regime dynamics

Level of analysis	Relevant variables
Structural/international	Geopolitical interests; state leadership, economic conditions and interests; policy paradigms
Organisational politics	Institutional socialisation; institutional entrepreneurship; inter-organisational networks
Domestic politics	Changing governing coalitions; changing domestic financial imperatives; changing domestic political economy imperatives

in this chapter. In this sense the study aims to provide an empirically grounded explanation of regime change which is both animated by and contributes to existing theoretical debates on international regime change.

One strategy employed in institutional analysis to create a coherent synthesis from otherwise complex causal processes is the creation of clear levels of analysis (Thelen and Steinmo 1992; Thelen 1999). In the case at hand it is useful to distinguish between processes at the international/ structural level, processes within and between international organisations and, finally, processes at the domestic political level. As a first approximation the various processes that can affect international regime change described in this chapter can be allocated as set out in Table 2.1.

By necessity the schema in Table 2.1 should be regarded as a framework for identifying and assessing discrete causal processes that have the potential to influence patterns of international cooperation. In reality changing patterns of international cooperation will be a consequence of complex combinations of these processes and dynamics, which have not been captured by this framework. Moreover, as Keohane and Nye (1977) suggested in the late 1970s, it is possible, indeed likely, that patterns of regime change are shaped by the complex interaction of international, organisational and domestic factors. More recently, similar claims have been made by institutional theorists who emphasise the need to study not only the relationships between institutions and their broader context but also the role of situated agents and the central role of agent choice in driving regime change (Bell 2011).

For example, a change in governing coalition or a change of administration within a great power may result in a new determination to provide leadership at the international level. Most significantly, the financial crisis and its aftermath have clearly had an effect across all three levels of analysis in that it has influenced geopolitical interests and prevailing paradigms concerning international financial regulation. At the organisational level the crisis led to the promotion of the G20 as the key international forum for formulating a response to the crisis, as well as providing unprecedented opportunities for organisations with existing regulatory expertise to promote ready formed policy agendas. At the domestic level the financial crisis has influenced all of the processes described in the framework, from influencing government coalitions to placing advanced democracies under unprecedented financial pressure. The aim of the empirical analysis presented in the chapters that follow is to systematically explore these complex relationships and their consequences. In pursuing this agenda it is hoped that we can glean theoretical insights from this important case study of regime change.

REFERENCES

Abbott, Kenneth and Duncan Snidal (2002) 'Filling in the Folk Theorem: The Role of Gradualism and Legalization in International Cooperation to Combat Corruption', Paper presented at the American Political Science Association Meetings, Boston, 30 August, available at http://www.international.ucla.edu/cms/files/Duncan_Snidal.pdf (accessed July 2012).

Abdelal, Rawi, Mark Blyth and Craig Parsons (eds) (2010) *Constructing the International Economy*, Ithaca and London: Cornell University Press.

Axelrod, Robert and Robert Keohane (1993) 'Achieving Cooperation under Anarchy: Strategies and Institutions', in David Baldwin (ed.), *Neorealism and Neoliberalism: The Contemporary Debate*, New York: Columbia University Press, pp. 85–115.

Bearce, David and Stacy Bondanella (2007) 'Intergovernmental Organizations, Socialization, and Member-State Interest Convergence', *International Organization*, **61** (4), 703–33.

Beeson, Mark and Stephen Bell (2009) 'The G20 and International Economic Governance: Hegemony, Collectivism or Both?' *Global Governance*, **15** (1), 67–86.

Bell, Stephen (2011) 'Do We Really Need Constructivist Institutionalism to Explain Institutional Change?' *British Journal of Political Science*, **41** (4), 883–906.

Blyth, Mark (2002) *Great Transformations: Economic Ideas and Institutional Change in the Twentieth Century*, Cambridge: Cambridge University Press.

Bull, Hedley (1972) 'International Relations as an Academic Pursuit', *Australian Outlook*, **26** (3), 251–65.

Campbell, John (1998) 'Institutional Analysis and the Role of Ideas in Political Economy', *Theory and Society*, **27** (3), 277–409.

Campbell, John (2004) *Institutional Change and Globalization,* Princeton, NJ: Princeton University Press.

Checkel, Jeffrey T. (2005) 'International Institutions and Socialization in Europe: Introduction and Framework', *International Organization*, **59** (4), 801–26.

Coats, Alfred William and David C. Collander (1989) 'An Introduction to the Spread of Economic Ideas', in Alfred William Coats and David C. Colander (eds), *The Spread of Economic Ideas*, New York: Cambridge University Press, pp. 1–19.

Cohen, Benjamin J. (2008) *International Political Economy: An Intellectual History*, Princeton, NJ and Oxford: Princeton University Press.

Dal Bo, Pedro (2005) 'Cooperation under the Shadow of the Future: Experimental Evidence from Infinitely Repeated Games', *American Economic Review*, **95** (5), 1591–604.

Djelic, Marie-Laure and Kerstin Sahlin-Andersson (2006) *Transnational Governance*, Cambridge: Cambridge University Press.

Drezner, Daniel (2007) *All Politics is Global: Explaining International Regulatory Regimes*, Princeton, NJ: Princeton University Press.

Eccleston, Richard (2007) *Taxing Reforms: The Politics of the Consumption Tax in Japan, the United States, Canada and Australia*, Cheltenham, UK and Northampton, MA, USA: Edward Elgar.

Eccleston, Richard, Peter Carroll and Aynsley Kellow (2010) 'Handmaiden to the G20? The OECD's Evolving Role in Global Governance', Paper presented at the Australian Political Science Association Conference, University of Melbourne, Melbourne, 27 September.

Eilstrup-Sangiovanni, Mette (2005) 'Transnational Networks and New Security Threats', *Cambridge Review of International Affairs*, **18** (1), 7–13.

Eilstrup-Sangiovanni, Mette (2009) 'Varieties of Cooperation: Government Networks in International Security', in Mette Kahler (ed.) *Networked Politics: Agency, Power and Governance*, Ithaca: Cornell University Press, pp. 194–227.

Elias, Juanita (2010) 'Locating the "Everyday" in International Political Economy Which Lies on the Other Side of Silence', *International Studies Review*, **12** (4), 603–9.

Finnemore, Martha (1996) *National Interests in International Society*, Ithaca: Cornell University Press.

Garrett, Geoffrey (2010) 'G2 in G20: China, the United States and the World after the Global Financial Crisis', *Global Policy*, **1** (1), 29–39.

George, Alexander L. (1979) 'The Causal Nexus between Cognitive Beliefs and Decision-Making Behavior: The Operational Code Belief System', in Lawrence S. Falkowski (ed.), *Psychological Models in International Politics*, Boulder, CO: Westview, pp. 95–124.

Gilpin, Robert (1981) *War and Change in International Politics*, Cambridge: Cambridge University Press.

Goldstein, Judith and Robert Keohane (eds) (1993) *Ideas and Foreign Policy: Beliefs, Institutions and Political Change*, Ithaca: Cornell University Press.

Gourevitch, Peter (1978) 'The Second Image Reversed', *International Organization*, **32** (4), 881–912.

Haas, Ernst B. (1983) 'Words Can Hurt You, or Who Said What to Whom About Regimes', in Stephen D. Krasner (ed.), *International Regimes*, Ithaca: Cornell University Press, pp. 23–59.

Haas, Ernst B. (1990) *When Knowledge is Power: Three Models of Change in International Organizations*, Berkeley, CA: University of California Press.

Hall, Peter (1989) *The Political Power of Economic Ideas: Keynesianism Across Nations*, Princeton, NJ: Princeton University Press.

Hall, Peter (1993) 'Policy Paradigms, Social Learning and the State: The Case of Economic Policymaking in Britain', *Comparative Politics*, **25** (3), 275–96.

Hasenclever, Andreas, Peter Mayer and Volker Rittberger (1997) *Theories of International Regimes*, Cambridge: Cambridge University Press.

Hasenclever, Andreas, Peter Mayer and Volker Rittberger (2000) 'Integrating Theories of International Regimes', *Review of International Studies*, **26** (1), 3–33.

Helleiner, Eric and Stefano Pagliari (2010), 'The End of Self Regulation? Hedge Funds and Derivatives in Global Financial Governance', in Eric Helleiner, Stefano Pagliari and Hubert Zimmermann (eds), *Global Finance in Crisis: The Politics of International Regulatory Change*, Oxford: Routledge, pp. 74–90.

Hillman, Jennifer (2010) 'Saving Multilateralism: Renovating the House of Global Economic Governance for the 21st Century', Brussels Forum Paper Series, The German Marshall Fund of the United States, Washington DC.

Hirschman, Albert. O. (1970), *Exit, Voice and Loyalty*, Cambridge, MA: Harvard University Press.

Hobson, John M. and Leonard Seabrooke (eds) (2007) *Everyday Politics of the World Economy*, Cambridge: Cambridge University Press.

Joachim, Jutta, Bob Reinalda and Bertjan Verbeek (eds) (2008) *International Organizations and Implementation: Enforcers, Managers, Authorities?* Abingdon and New York: Routledge.

Johnston, Alastair Iain (2001) 'Treating International Institutions as Social Environments', *International Studies Quarterly*, **45** (4), 487–515.

Kahler, Miles (2009) 'Networked Politics: Agency, Power and Governance', in Miles Kahler (ed.), *Networked Politics: Agency, Power and Governance*, Ithaca: Cornell University Press, pp. 1–22.

Katzenstein, Peter (1978) *Between Power and Plenty: Foreign Economic Policies of Advanced Industrial States*, Madison: University of Wisconsin Press.

Kay, Adrian (2006) *The Dynamics of Public Policy: Theory and Evidence,* Cheltenham, UK and Northampton, MA, USA: Edward Elgar.

Keohane, Robert (1984) *After Hegemony: Cooperation and Discord in the World Political Economy*, Princeton, NJ: Princeton University Press.

Keohane, Robert (2005) *After Hegemony: Cooperation and Discord in the World Political Economy*, Princeton, NJ: Princeton University Press.

Keohane, Robert (2009) 'The Old International Political Economy and the New', *Review of International Political Economy*, **16** (1), 34–46.

Keohane, Robert and Joseph Nye (1977) *Power and Interdependence*, Boston, MA: Little Brown and Company.

Kingsbury, Benedict, Nico Krisch and Richard B. Stewart (2005) 'The Emergence of Global Administrative Law', New York University Public Law and Legal Theory Working Papers, Paper 17, available at http://lsr.nellco.org/nyu_plltwp/17 (accessed July 2012).

Krasner, Stephen D. (ed.) (1983) *International Regimes*, Ithaca: Cornell University Press.

Levi, Margaret, Robert Bates, Avner Greif, Jean-Laurent Rosenthal and Barry Weingast (1998) *Analytic Narratives*, Princeton, NJ: Princeton University Press.

Martin, Lisa and Beth Simmons (1998) 'Theories and Empirical Studies of International Institutions', *International Organization*, **52** (4), 729–57.

Moravcsik, Andrew (1997) 'Taking Preferences Seriously: A Liberal Theory of International Politics', *International Organization*, **51** (4), 513–53.

Olson, Mancur (1965) *The Logic of Collective Action*, Cambridge, MA: Harvard University Press.

Ostrom, Elinor (1990) *Governing the Commons: The Evolution of Institutions for Collective Action*, Cambridge: Cambridge University Press.

Polyani, Karl ([1944] 2001) *The Great Transformation: The Political and Economic Origin of Our Time*, Boston: Beacon Press.

Porter, Tony (2010) 'Why International Institutions Matter in the Global Credit Crisis', *Global Governance*, **15** (1), 3–8.

Putnam, Robert D. (1988) 'Diplomacy and Domestic Politics: The Logic of Two-Level Games', *International Organization*, **42** (3), 427–60.

Reinicke, Wolfgang and Francis Deng, with Jan Martin Witte, Thorsten Benner, Beth Whittaker and John Gershman (2000) *Critical Choices: The United Nations, Networks, and the Future of Global Governance*, Ottawa, ON: GPP.

Rixen, Thomas (2008) *The Political Economy of International Tax Governance: Transformations of the State*, New York: Palgrave Macmillan.

Ruggie, John (2002) 'The Theory and Practice of Learning Networks: Corporate Social Responsibility and the Global Compact', *Journal of Corporate Citizenship*, **5** (2), 292–6.

Scharpf, Fritz W. (1997) *Games Real Actors Play: Actor-Centered Institutionalism in Policy Research*, Boulder, CO: Westview.

Schelling, Thomas C. (1978) *Micromotives and Macrobehavior*, New York: W.W. Norton & Company.

Sil, Rudra and Peter Katzenstein (2010) 'Analytical Eclecticism in the Study of World Politics: Reconfiguring Problems and Mechanisms across Research Traditions', *Perspectives on Politics*, **8** (1), 411–31.

Simon, Herbert (1982) *Models of Bounded Rationality*, Cambridge: Cambridge University Press.

Singer, David A. (2004) 'Capital Rules: The Domestic Politics of International Regulatory Harmonization', *International Organization*, **58** (3), 531–65.

Slaughter, Anne-Marie (2004) *A New World Order*, Princeton, NJ: Princeton University Press.

Stone, Deborah (1989), 'Causal Stories and the Formation of Policy Agendas', *Political Science Quarterly*, **104** (1), 281–300.

Streeck, Wolfgang and Kathleen Thelen (2005) 'Introduction: Institutional Change in Advanced Political Economies', in Wolfgang Streeck and Kathleen Thelen (eds), *Beyond Continuity: Institutional Change in Advanced Political Economies*, Oxford: Oxford University Press, pp. 1–39.

Thelen, Kathleen (1999) 'Historical Institutionalism in Comparative Perspective', *Annual Review of Political Science*, **2**, 369–404.

Thelen, Kathleen (2002) 'How Institutions Evolve: Insights from Comparative-Historical Analysis', in James Mahoney and Dietrich Rueschemeyer (eds), *Comparative Historical Analysis in the Social Sciences*, New York: Cambridge University Press, pp. 208–40.

Thelen, Kathleen and Sven Steinmo (1992) 'Historical Institutionalism in Comparative Perspective', in K. Thelen, S.H. Steinmo and F. Longstreth (eds), *Structuring Politics: Historical Institutionalism in Comparative Analysis*, Cambridge: Cambridge University Press, pp. 369–404.

Underdal, Arild (1998) 'Explaining Compliance and Defection: Three Models', *European Journal of International Relations*, **4** (1), 5–30.

Weir, Margaret and Theda Skocpol (1985) 'State Structures and the Possibility for "Keynesian" Responses to the Great Depression in Sweden, Britain and the United States', in Peter B. Evans, Dietrich Rueschemeyer and Theda Skocpol (eds) *Bringing the State Back In,* New York: Cambridge University Press, pp. 107–68.

Woodward, Richard (2009) *The Organisation for Economic Cooperation and Development*, Oxford: Routledge.

Wouters, Jan, Steven Sterkx and Tim Corthaut (2010) 'The International Financial Crisis, Global Financial Governance and the European Union', Working Paper No. 52 – September, Leuven Centre for Global Governance Studies, Leuven, Belgium.

Young, Oran R. (1999). *Governance in World Affairs*, Ithaca: Cornell University Press.

.

3. Politics without conviction: the OECD's failed Harmful Tax Competition initiative

The international tax regime has been almost a century in the making. Whereas the various international agreements and conventions brokered by the OECD up to the 1980s focused largely on alleviating the risk of double taxation, the last two decades have seen more emphasis on reducing the incidence of international tax evasion and avoidance. Despite these efforts to improve anti-evasion measures, until very recently initiatives aimed at enhancing international tax transparency have enjoyed a mixed record at best. This chapter provides an overview of attempts to improve international tax transparency and information exchange since the late 1980s as well as offering an explanation as to why the OECD's concerted effort to end what it defined as 'Harmful Tax Competition' in the late 1990s and early 2000s was almost universally regarded as a failure.

This historical analysis of the debates concerning the origins of the tax transparency and information exchange agenda as well as the barriers to reform represents an important foundation for the study of the changing nature of the tax transparency regime presented in subsequent chapters. As the extant literature on institutional and policy dynamics explains, a grounded, longitudinal research strategy is necessary for two significant reasons. First, conceptually there may be broad acceptance that change occurs when an entity assumes different characteristics over time (Kay 2006, 7), but all too often insufficient consideration is given to what constitutes an existing policy or regulatory framework during the pre-reform period of stability and the factors that have prevented policy change. As Campbell (2004) has argued, it is often necessary to understand the impediments to political change and the forces that sustain such resistance in order to fully understand the process of regime change.

Second, such accounts stress that regimes consists of complex layers of institutions and while change may occur at some levels there may well be continuity at others (Campbell 2004; Hay 2002; Pierson 2004; Kay 2006). For example, while there is a good deal of evidence that the financial crisis represents a critical juncture – one that precipitated significant change in the international tax regime, as Chapter 4 will argue – the specific policy response arising from the crisis was shaped by established institutions and using existing policy instruments. As a consequence contemporary institutional scholars categorise such processes as 'punctuated evolution', and because regimes comprise a number of interrelated and overlapping or 'nested' institutions, dramatic change at one level of the system may be offset by stability in other key institutions (Pierson 2004, 136). This process of layering suggests that the dynamics of regime change can only be understood by focusing both on critical junctures, such as the immediate aftermath of the financial crisis, and on the broader context in which policy changes occur (Campbell 1998, 2004; Thelen 1999, 383).

The next section of the chapter describes the growing extent of offshore tax evasion during the 1980s and 1990s and how an increasing awareness of the problem among policymakers put the issue of tax transparency and harmful tax competition more generally on the international political agenda. The majority of the chapter is devoted to providing an overview of the policy response to this challenge, with an emphasis on the OECD's Harmful Tax Competition (HTC) initiative launched in 1998. This account is then supplemented with a synopsis of the published academic analysis of the HTC project and the various explanations for its failure. Taken together the chapter describes and evaluates the measures that were taken during the late 1990s and early 2000s and why they largely failed to improve the exchange of tax information in practice. In so doing, the chapter allows us to establish both how and why the regime has changed since 2007.

GLOBALISATION AND THE EMERGING OFFSHORE THREAT

Debates about the causes, extent and implications of economic globalisation have been the subject of innumerable policy debates, academic articles and popular analyses in recent years. Despite the contested nature of these issues, few would dispute the empirical fact that patterns of cross-border capital flows and investment increased dramatically in the later 1980s and into the 1990s (Helleiner 2005). The causes of economic globalisation are complex, but most explanations highlight the gradual demise of Bretton Woods capital controls in the decade after the US devaluation of 1971 and subsequent financial innovations and associated liberalisation in major market centres such as Wall Street and the City of London. By 1986 those EU economies that had resisted liberalisation were forced to follow the American and British lead courtesy of the Single European Act (Tanzi

1995; Braithwaite and Drahos 2000). As a result of these developments the volumes of foreign exchange transactions and cross-border capital flows have increased significantly. For example, the Bank of International Settlement (BIS) estimates that the daily turnover on foreign markets rose from $US60 billion per day in 1983 to $3.2 trillion per day in 2007 (BIS 2007). This 50-fold increase in international capital flows, when combined with the fact that the value of world trade in goods and services merely doubled over the period, highlights the extraordinary internationalisation of finance over the past quarter of a century.

By the late 1980s there were growing concerns that economic globalisation was undermining effective financial regulation, with Susan's Strange's *Casino Capitalism* acting as a clarion call to academics and regulators alike (1986). In the international tax arena, policymakers and analysts were also becoming increasingly concerned about the impact of increased capital mobility on the integrity of national tax systems. Small numbers of wealthy individuals may have physically moved their savings to traditional secrecy jurisdictions such as Switzerland since the early twentieth century (Chapter 1), but the ease of moving assets for tax purposes as a result of financial liberalisation, combined with what Palan (2002) has described as the 'commercialisation of sovereignty', dramatically increased the scale and potential risk of international tax evasion. As the then director of the IMF's Fiscal Affairs Department argued in 1995, without greatly improved administrative cooperation the increasingly mobile nature of capital posed a fundamental threat to the international tax regime because 'In an increasingly integrated world the application of the residence principle and the attempt to tax income on a global basis will only be possible if there is full and efficient exchange of information between tax authorities' (Tanzi 1995, 82). Beyond blatant international tax evasion, the risk of avoidance and aggressive international tax planning was also growing as a result of the increasing use of tax concessions to attract offshore investment and income. As a confidential OECD briefing paper prepared in the mid-1990s noted:

> The deregulation of exchange and capital controls and the liberalization of financial markets during the last two decades have considerably increased the mobility of capital. In the wake of these events, a number of preferential tax regimes have been, or are about to be, established by OECD Member and non-Member countries to attract, in particular, financial and other service activities. (OECD 1997, 6)

We possess reasonably accurate data on international capital flows (such as those cited above), courtesy of international institutions such as the BIS and the International Monetary Fund (IMF); reliable information on the extent of international tax evasion and the extent to which it has increased is, however, more difficult to obtain. Because tax evasion by its very nature involves concealing financial information from tax authorities, any measure of the extent of the phenomenon necessarily involves a degree of guesswork (Palan et al. 2010, 46–7). The available data on investments held in offshore jurisdictions and the precise extent of international tax evasion may be a little sketchy, but the broad trends are clear and were becoming a cause for concern among policymakers in advanced and relatively high-tax countries by the early 1990s. According to data collected by the OECD in the mid-1990s for an unpublished background paper for the HTC project, market sources suggested a significant increase in investor interest in offshore evasion possibilities through the use of offshore investment funds. As of 1995 it was estimated that there was in excess of $1 trillion in tax-free environments (OECD 1997, 5; Figure 3.1). Even at this early stage it was clear that secrecy jurisdictions were playing an increasingly important yet poorly understood role in the emerging global financial system. When a watershed report published by the IMF in 1994 claimed that as much as half of cross-border lending was routed through secrecy jurisdictions international tax avoidance and evasion became a major issue (Cassard 1994).

THE INTERNATIONAL RESPONSE TO THE OFFSHORE THREAT

Despite the fact that strong economic growth continued to underpin corporate and capital revenues, by the mid-1990s concern about the growing threat of international tax competition and evasion was such that the issue reached the international political agenda (Webb 2004, 795). In the European Union both France and Germany held long running concerns about the detrimental impact of international tax evasion and the growing risk of international tax competition, with German authorities estimating revenue losses of as much as $12 billion per annum relating to undeclared savings held in Switzerland, Austria and Liechtenstein (Sharman 2006, 29; *The Economist* 1997). The OECD's first published report on the extent of international tax competition and evasion was produced in 1991 and not only highlighted the threats such competition posed to corporate taxation but argued that tax-related distortions threatened the efficient allocation of capital in the global economy (OECD 1991). These growing concerns transformed the issue from a technical policy debate to an international political concern when the then European Competition Commissioner

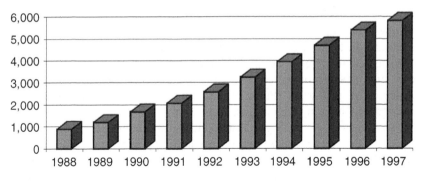

Source: OECD 1997.

Figure 3.1   Growth in offshore investment funds, 1988–97

(Italian Prime Minister since November 2011), Mario Monti, urged action via a European Council of Finance Ministers paper published in March 1996 (Eden and Kudrle 2005, 118; Sharman 2006, 29). On the other side of the Atlantic American authorities were also warming to the idea of a coordinated international strategy on international tax issues after earlier unilateral attempts to improve tax transparency among Caribbean financial centres yielded only mixed results (Hudson 1998; Picciotto 1992, 169; Kudrle 2003). This emerging consensus among the major powers took the form of concrete action at the G7 leaders' summit in Lyon in 1996. Specifically the summit communiqué instructed the OECD to investigate harmful tax competition and report back to the G7 in 1998:

> Finally, globalisation is creating new challenges in the field of tax policy. Tax schemes aimed at attracting financial and other geographically mobile activities can create harmful tax competition between States, carrying risks of distorting trade and investment and could lead to the erosion of national tax bases. We strongly urge the OECD to vigorously pursue its work in this field, aimed at establishing a multilateral approach under which countries could operate individually and collectively to limit the extent of these practices. We will follow closely the progress on work by the OECD, which is due to produce a report by 1998. (G7 1996)

As a result of this call to action the OECD Council established a series of 'Special Sessions on Tax Competition' which met for the first time on 8–9 October 1996, initiating what would be an 18-month process in which the OECD would undertake technical research, establish study groups and engage in consultation both between and beyond the organization's membership in order to establish a multilateral approach to addressing 'Harmful Tax Competition'.

The OECD's Harmful Tax Competition Initiative

The G7's 1996 mandate and the OECD's subsequent work culminated in the publication of the OECD's seminal report *Harmful Tax Competition: An Emerging Global Issue* (OECD 1998). Rather than presenting a detailed account of the politics of the OECD's HTC initiative between 1998 and 2006 (for excellent summaries see Webb 2004; Eden and Kudrle 2005; Sharman 2006; Rixen 2008; Palan et al. 2010, 210–221; Palan 2002 and 2003; Woodward 2006), our primary focus here is on identifying the forces that undermined its success. As was noted above, it is often necessary to understand the impediments to political change and the forces that sustain such resistance in order to fully understand institutional and regime change.

The OECD HTC initiative was ambitious from the outset in that it had a dual mandate. First the OECD sought to identify tax havens, and the definition that was negotiated for the purpose of the 1998 report had four elements:

(i)   No or nominal taxes;
(ii)   Lack of effective exchange of information;
(iii) Lack of transparency;
(iv)   No substantial economic activity required. (OECD 1998, 23)

More controversially, and reflecting concerns about tax competition, the project also sought to identify Preferential Tax Regimes (PTRs), which generally met transparency standards and were OECD member states, but sought to attract international investment by offering generous tax concessions, or tax rates which were either very low or were not available to domestic firms and investors (OECD 1998). As outlined in the previous chapter, calls to reduce international tax competition through harmonisation have always raised a host of theoretical and normative concerns and this was certainly the case in relation to the HTC initiative. A major risk with trying to implement multilateral measures against PTRs was a lack of broad-based support for tax harmonisation across the OECD's membership. While France had long held concerns that countries such as Ireland, who at the time offered a 10 per cent corporate tax rate on foreign firms who relocated (which was later replaced with a general 12.5 per cent corporate rate), were precipitating a destructive 'race to the bottom' so far as capital taxation was concerned, the United States and British governments had long opposed the agenda, arguing that it threatened the sovereign right of national governments to set budget priorities according to domestic political imperatives (Weschler 2001).

Perhaps more importantly the PTR agenda posed numerous ideological challenges for the OECD given that promoting economic competition was at the core of the neo-liberal policy prescriptions it had been promoting since the 1980s (Mahon and McBride 2008). Not only was a good deal of energy (and the majority of the 1998 HTC report) devoted to the vexed issue of when tax competition was desirable and when it was harmful, but, as we shall see below, secrecy jurisdictions were able to use this inconsistency successfully to undermine the legitimacy of the OECD's campaign. As Sharman has highlighted (2006, 119; Scott 1990), small states can successful undermine hegemonic powers by using dominant ideas against those who promote them. Indeed an OECD official acknowledged in a more reflective moment that it might have been a mistake to use the language of 'harmful tax competition' because 'As an economist, how can I ever say anything bad about competition' (quoted in Webb 2004, 800). Given these vexed issues, and after much deliberation, the 1998 report generally endorsed broad-based tax competition and instead focused on 'ring fencing', or tax concessions which were only available to foreigners (OECD 1998, 14–16). The debate about tax harmonisation may have been conceptually separate to the broader push to improve tax transparency, but at a political level the two issues were often conflated, which further undermined the OECD campaign.

Responses to the 1998 report
Despite being a central focus of the 1998 report, commitment to promoting tax harmonisation soon waned, both within the OECD and among member states. While the HTC progress report published in 2000 (OECD 2000; Webb 2004, 806) identified 47 policies across both OECD member and non-member states which 'potentially' constituted harmful practices, a reluctance to make definitive assessments concerning whether specific taxes met the standard was underpinned by an equally vague commitment to conduct peer review assessments by 2003, by which time the OECD had been forced to abandon the harmful competition agenda. From this point onwards the focus was on the increasingly controversial and contested debate concerning secrecy jurisdictions and tax transparency.

At least initially the campaign to identify and potentially coordinate collective measures against tax havens (as defined above) enjoyed broad-based support among OECD member states and soon after the publication of the 1998 report 41 jurisdictions had been identified and faced the prospect of sanctions or 'defensive measures' unless they changed their ways. Clearly this represented a major threat to the booming offshore financial services industry and few were surprised when secrecy jurisdictions themselves embarked on a campaign to limit and perhaps defeat the OECD initiative. A common theme across many of the excellent studies of the ensuing 'battle' between the OECD and secrecy jurisdictions between 1998 and 2001 was the success with which secrecy jurisdictions, many of which are small and relatively powerless compared with OECD member states, successfully used rhetoric and widely accepted norms to undermine the legitimacy of their larger rivals (in particular see Webb 2004; Sharman 2006).

Despite the OECD rhetoric claiming that the regime aimed to restore 'a level playing field' in relation to international tax matters, the HTC was dogged by claims that the regime was inconsistent and privileged the interests of wealthy OECD member states. Specifically identified tax havens argued that the OECD regime offended principles of procedural justice because they were not adequately consulted and the timelines to implement reforms were too short, especially given the lack of transitional support from OECD member states. The tax havens (as defined by the OECD) also pointed out that the OECD campaign contradicted the advice from the World Bank and IMF to exploit their low-tax status to develop their financial services industries (Sharman and Mistry 2008). At the level of interest group politics, the OECD failed to mobilise civil society groups who were in favour of tax justice; combined with the traditional lack of a business constituency for improving international tax compliance and the complaints from the OECD's own Business Industry Advisory Council (BIAC), it was clear that the agenda was politically vulnerable (Eccleston 2009). In contrast the financial services sector mobilised behind the secrecy jurisdictions and forced a number of major concessions including the removal of provisions that only firms who could demonstrate substantial business activity in offshore jurisdictions could claim tax residency (Persaud 2001; Webb 2004, 807–10). This significant development ensured that the HTC initiative would pose little threat to the aggressive, legal, international tax planning strategies pursued by so many of the world's MNCs. Instead the OECD would have to settle for creating information exchange provisions designed to prevent wealthy individuals concealing income and savings offshore.

The most damaging criticism of the initiative was the accusation of OECD hypocrisy in demanding compliance from non-member states identified as tax havens while ignoring prominent member states with equally secretive regimes, among them Switzerland and Luxembourg (Woodward 2006, 690; Webb 2004, 807; Carroll and Kellow 2011, 140). As OECD member states, Switzerland and Luxembourg (and to a lesser

extent Belgium and Austria) were always going to be in an invidious position in relation to any proposal to promote tax transparency, given that
their lucrative banking sectors have been built on a foundation of client
secrecy (see Chapter 2 above; Palan et al. 2010, 115–16). Likely dissent was
a particular problem given the OECD's commitment to decision-making
by consensus which meant that either Switzerland or Luxembourg had
the power to veto the entire project. Indeed this very issue came to the
fore in March 1998 when the OCED's Committee on Fiscal Affairs had to
approve the final HTC report.

Both Switzerland and Luxembourg strongly disagreed with the definition of a tax haven proposed in the report and had no intention of dismantling their secrecy laws. But rather than veto the report they agreed to
abstain from the vote. Under the OECD's 'mutual agreement' provisions
this meant that neither country would be bound by the final decision
(Carroll and Kellow 2011, 140). While this was a deft procedural move it
greatly undermined the moral authority of the HTC project because the
OECD was left trying to impose a standard, and potentially sanctions, on
non-members, while some of its own members were exempt. This double
standard was fully exploited by the secrecy jurisdictions themselves who
portrayed the project as 'a coercive and hypocritical exercise in big-power
bullying by states and organizations that sought to re-write rules of economic competition in their own favour' (Sharman 2006, 9). When the
Commonwealth Secretariat and other groups promoting the collective
interests of the small secrecy jurisdictions argued that this was a form of
discrimination which was contrary to both neo-liberal orthodoxy and
the OECD's stated aim of establishing a 'level playing field', the exemp-
tion of Switzerland and Luxembourg became untenable. In November
2001 the OECD gave a reluctant commitment that it would not impose
'defensive measures' against non-member states until all OECD members
met the standard. In effect this meant that any enforcement measures
were dependent on Switzerland and Luxembourg's compliance which,
according to Woodward (2004, 119), rendered the entire regime 'virtually meaningless'. This chapter of the HTC debate is especially relevant
to more recent developments because it highlights just how the legitimacy
and effectiveness of any multilateral attempt to improve tax transparency
is critically dependent on Swiss support. For this reason the second half of
Chapter 5 is devoted to analysing the domestic politics of the tax transparency debate in Switzerland in the aftermath of the financial crisis.

HTC as incremental reform

Despite the largely successful campaign against the HTC initiative,
an enduring contribution of the 1998 HTC report and subsequent

negotiations was that it narrowed the regulatory agenda to a focus on enhancing information exchange. The ensuing technical work successfully established and won international support for the OECD's 2002 *Model Agreement on Exchange of Information on Tax Matters*, which in turn served as the basis for changes made in 2005 to Article 26 (on information exchange) of the OECD Model Tax Convention which removed bank secrecy provisions and requirements that requested countries hold a domestic tax interest in the information being sought (OECD 2011). The fact that the standard is based on exchange of information on request, as opposed to automatic data transfer, has been the subject of much criticism (Neslund 2009; Meinzer 2012; detailed in Chapter 6), but it has nonetheless provided a conceptual and legal framework for subsequent negotiations conducted during the financial crisis. As Rixen has argued (2008, 188), the technical and contested nature of the international taxation regime results in considerable inertia and a situation in which it is preferable to persevere with 'the existing institutional setup even though its shortcomings are widely recognised'.

The strong path dependency associated with the international tax regime has technical, legal and normative elements. At a technical and legal level it is important to recall that the international tax regime is a web of bilateral agreements between states which are loosely coordinated by agreed standards such as the OECD Model Convention. While a rules-based multilateral tax system based on international law with associated enforcement mechanisms, such as the World Trade Organization, may be more effective (Pinto and Sawyer 2009; Sawyer 2009), creating such a system would necessitate dismantling the more than 2000 DTAs in existence as well as the domestic tax provisions they reflect. Not only would such reform impinge upon the fiscal sovereignty of states, but such radical change would also be extremely disruptive for international business. These high levels of regulatory inertia have led commentators such as Doernberg (2000, as quoted in Rixen 2008, 189) pessimistically to conclude that 'One might describe the current international tax system as the second worst imaginable – the worst system being whatever would replace the current system.'

A second reason for pursuing an incremental approach that focuses on improving the effectiveness of the existing regime through enhanced administrative cooperation and information exchange is that unlike calls to promote tax harmonisation, this agenda was consistent with neo-liberal norms (Blyth 2003). Given that improving tax transparency could be justified on the grounds that it would address information asymmetries and improve global economic efficiency, neither the secrecy jurisdictions themselves, nor the commercial interests involved in international finance could make credible claims against the reforms. As Michael Webb (2004, 809) concluded, 'In normative terms, the havens' arguments were simply not persuasive when measured against the criteria of liberal economic ideology.'

Taken together these constraints help explain why small and relatively powerless states were able to successfully undermine the OECD's attempt to increase international tax harmonisation and end the practice of using secrecy jurisdictions for tax planning purposes regardless of whether the entity concerned was engaged in real economic activity within the jurisdiction. Despite these developments modest progress was achieved in terms of developing an international standard for the exchange of information for tax purposes with a view to improving the effectiveness of existing enforcement and anti-evasion measures. Equally significant was that the OECD took some preliminary yet important steps towards developing a process for engaging and facilitating participation with non-member states. The creation of the Global Tax Forum in 2002 may not have yielded short-term results but, as we shall see in Chapter 4, the forum did go on to serve as the basis for the revised Global Forum on Transparency and Information Exchange for Taxation Purposes (created in 2009) which greatly enhanced the ability of non-OECD jurisdictions to participate in the administration of the international tax regime. However, despite this progress, the implementation of the OECD's tax transparency agenda was undermined in the short term by waning political support for reform in the United States as a coalition of corporate interests and the secrecy jurisdictions took their fight to the then recently elected and largely sympathetic administration of George W. Bush.

United States Capitulation

International relations scholars have long argued that effective global governance is critically dependent on the leadership of states with 'great power' or 'hegemonic' status (Kindleberger 1973; Krasner 1976). In the latter part of the twentieth century this mantle has clearly fallen on the United States and, despite some decline in recent years, the US remains both the world's largest economy and continues to host the most world's most significant capital markets. Given this position of power in the international economic system there is a consensus that financial regulation is critically dependent on US support because, as the extensive literature on 'club standards' suggests, any regulations that are not enforced on American listed entities or in United States markets can easily be circumvented (Drezner 2007, 75–8; Martin 1993). This is particularly true in relation to international taxation because at an organisational level, the OECD is critically dependent on American funding; the fact that the United States provides 25 per cent of the OECD's 'Part One' budget makes it difficult for the organisation to pursue an agenda that is contrary to US interests (Carroll and Kellow 2011, 15; Woodward 2009, ch. 2).

Given the controversial nature of the HTC project and the central role of the US in both the international tax regime and in financing and supporting OECD activities, there was always a distinct possibility that George W. Bush's victory in the November 2000 US Presidential Election would influence the politics of international tax cooperation. We have already noted that US governments have been the driving force behind the majority of multilateral tax initiatives in recent decades (Eden and Kudrle 2005). The corollary is that the absence of support from Washington would seriously undermine attempts by others to regulate international taxation. Given that the Bush Presidency coincided with the escalating debate about the OECD project, the incoming administration provided secrecy jurisdictions and their clients with an unprecedented opportunity effectively to veto the OECD's HTC agenda. Not only was the Bush Administration an enthusiastic advocate of supply-side tax cuts (Suskind 2004, Hacker and Pierson 2005), it was also openly hostile to the type of multilateral regime being proposed by the OECD. This ideational climate was reinforced by the fact that 2001 saw the Bush Administration and its 'neo-con' supporters at the zenith of their political influence. Given this more hostile domestic political environment in the United States, analysts were unsurprised when interests opposed to the OECD agenda launched an aggressive campaign focusing on the new administration and Congress. Theoretically these developments support claims outlined in Chapter 2 that changing governing coalitions at a domestic level can have a profound impact on foreign economic policy (Katzenstein 1978).

A central development in the campaign within the United States (as will be discussed in more detail in Chapter 5) was the formation of the Centre for Freedom and Prosperity (CFP) which was founded in October 2000 in part to highlight the impact of the OECD initiative on tax sovereignty and competition (Ring 2009, 186–90; Easson 2004). Over the winter of 2000–01 the CFP executed a very successful campaign which mobilised both conservative representatives and members of the Democratic black caucus who were concerned that the OECD agenda would threaten development in poor Caribbean states, which it was argued could lead to an increase in illegal drug trafficking and money laundering in the region (Ring 2009, 188). Given the success of this campaign and the turning political tide in the US, few were surprised when the newly appointed Treasury Secretary Paul O'Neil announced in May 2001 that:

The United States does not support efforts to dictate to any country what its own tax rates or systems should be, and will not participate in any initiative to harmonise world tax systems. (O'Neil as quoted in Denny 2001)

Beyond this statement that the Bush Administration would not support any attempts to promote harmonisation or other impediments to a state's fiscal sovereignty (although the OECD had already largely conceded this), there were also rumours that the Bush Administration was opposed to any regime designed to enhance information exchange and threatened to cut its funding to the OECD if it failed to heed its advice (Sharman 2006, 61; Palan et al. 2010, 217; Carroll and Kellow 2011, 140). However, the terrorist attacks of September 2001 and the clear imperative to detect terrorist financing bolstered the ailing transparency agenda and ensured that there would be notional support for the OECD's tax transparency agenda alongside parallel initiatives promoted by, among others, the Financial Action Task Force (FATF), the Financial Stability Forum (FSF) and the Basel Committee (Eden and Kudrle 2005, 121; Sharman 2011).

Politics without Conviction

By 2002 the OECD's HTC initiative may not have been formally abandoned but it was, in the eyes of most commentators, 'watered down beyond recognition' (Palan et al. 2010, 217). What remained was a commitment to enhance tax transparency which, if effectively implemented had the potential to limit the most blatant forms of international tax evasion. However the OECD standard required only that secrecy jurisdictions had to give an undertaking to exchange tax information on request in relation to criminal and civil matters in order to be removed from its tax haven blacklist. Given that compliance could be achieved simply by expressing an intention to enter into limited tax information exchange agreements, few were surprised when by September 2004 only five of the original 35 jurisdictions identified in the 2000 progress report were still identified by the OECD as harmful tax havens (Eden and Kudrle 2005, 122; OECD 2000; OECD 2004). While this clearly represented incremental reform, as will be explained in more detail in Chapter 6, critics claim that bilateral tax information exchange agreements (or TIEAs), the main legal instrument in the post-2002 OECD regime, were too difficult to negotiate and that the burden of proof required to lodge a request for tax information was too high (Palan et al. 2010, 216; Tax Justice Network 2009).

Perhaps the most damning criticism of the effectiveness of the TIEAs is the fact that only a handful of requests for information had been lodged under the new regime (Palan et al. 2010, 34). While jurisdictions involved in the Global Forum process may have been nominally compliant with the modest information exchange standard it was promoting, there is little evidence that the regime was *effective* in terms of having a material impact on the extent of international tax evasion (Joachim et al. 2008). Certainly the evidence from this period suggested that the OECD's HTC initiative was the victim of a 'vertical disintegration' of global governance in that an international agreement had failed to have a material impact as a result of a lack of political commitment to implementation at the level of nation states (Underdal 1998). At this point it is sufficient to note that in 2006 the majority of academic analysts and business commentators agreed that the OECD's Harmful Tax Competition initiative had largely failed to achieve its primary objective of undermining the role of secrecy jurisdictions in international tax evasion (Sharman 2006; Woodward 2006, 693; Picciotto 2011; Webb 2004; Eden and Kudrle 2005; Sullivan 2007). As Palan et al. (2010) argue, this was a period of 'politics without conviction'.

BARRIERS TO INTERNATIONAL TAX COOPERATION

The evolution of the international tax regime in the years leading up to the financial crisis highlights the ways in which the complex interactions between high politics, changing economic conditions and interests, prevailing norms, interest group and domestic politics all shape the broad parameters of international tax cooperation and how these interactions were mediated by the institutional structure of the governance regime. Above all else, this complexity demands what Kantian scholars describe as an *ideographic* research method, one that is sensitive to the historically specific ways in which complex processes drive political change. Yet this does not mean that it is desirable to present a purely descriptive account of the multitude of variables that have shaped the politics of international taxation in recent years, but rather that the discussion that follows needs to take the form of an analytical narrative that is particularly attentive to likely causes of stability or change within the regime based on established empirical and theoretical analysis. To this end it is important to summarise the variables which limited or constrained the prospects of achieving international tax cooperation in the decade leading up to the financial crisis.

The first conclusion that can be drawn from the extant literature on international tax cooperation is that the support of powerful states is a pre-condition both to effecting change and to ensuring compliance with the regime. As Rixen has argued, the need for the support of a 'concert of great powers' to achieve effective international tax cooperation is largely a consequence of the structure of the international tax governance problem (Rixen 2008, 182–5). More specifically, international taxation can be described as an asymmetrical Prisoner's Dilemma because despite potential system-wide welfare benefits from cooperation, there are clear financial incentives for individual jurisdictions to defect from the regime because offering tax concessions or secrecy can be used to attract mobile capital. Moreover, the regime is asymmetrical because the greater the number of states engaging in effective cooperation the greater (in theory at least) the potential benefits from defection. Under these circumstances, and in contrast to more benign coordination problems, solidarity among major players is essential if cooperation and enforcement are to be effective. These themes will be explored in greater detail in the following chapter, but the main practical conclusion that we can draw from this analysis is that effective international tax cooperation must be underpinned by the support of all major financial powers, including the United States, in order to have any prospect of success. In these terms the Bush Administration's thinly veiled hostility to the HTC agenda effectively scuttled any prospect of the OECD's 1998 HTC report achieving its objectives. The lesson that can be drawn from this is that future reform efforts must focus on an agenda, such as enhanced information exchange, that enjoys broad support on both sides of the Atlantic.

Solidarity among the major powers may be a pre-condition for effective international tax governance but this raises a question that has all too often been neglected by 'rationalist' accounts of international tax cooperation: How and why does a state's political commitment to international agreements change over time? Reflecting the growing acceptance that domestic and international politics are deeply interconnected, rather than being separate realms (Chapter 2), it is necessary to engage in empirically grounded research on the factors that influence a state's commitment or otherwise to an international regime (Underdal 1998; Young 1999; Singer 2004). Chapter 5 is devoted to evaluating the domestic politics of international tax cooperation in the United States and Switzerland given their critical role in the international tax regime.

The lack of American support for the OECD's HTC initiative after 2001 may have been the decisive factor in the failure to achieve international cooperation beyond a commitment to information exchange on request, but as all of the published accounts of the period suggest, political support for the agenda was in serious decline prior to George W. Bush's election victory in 2001. This finding suggests that a determination among powerful states to end offshore tax abuse may not, on its own, be enough to ensure success unless proposed reforms are regarded as being legitimate and are administered in a consistent manner according to a democratic process. Scholarly analysis of the HTC initiative highlights the fact that small and relatively powerless states can successfully resist regulatory initiatives being promoted by great powers if such proposals run contrary to established norms and political practices (Webb 2004; Sharman 2006). In terms of norms, opponents of the HTC highlighted the fact that the OECD's initial attempts to limit tax competition and to link tax residency to economic activity contravened central tenets of neo-liberal economic theory (which had been hitherto been promoted by the OECD and other international financial institutions) as well as established principles of state sovereignty. As Sharman concluded (2006, 145–6), this is a clear example of what James Scott (1990) describes as 'symbolic ju-jitsu' in which structurally weak actors can prevail over the powerful in political conflicts by using the rhetoric and norms promoted by the elite against them: 'The dominant group is . . . least able to take liberties with those symbols in which they are most heavily invested' (Scott quoted in Sharman 2006, 145). In short, hypocrisy of this nature leaves the powerful politically vulnerable.

The second dimension of this vulnerability concerns the lack of demo-cratic participation and due process in the original HTC initiative. The nature and desirability of democratic participation in global governance remains deeply contested. Despite debates about the extent to which non-state actors and citizens should be able to participate in interna-tional decision-making, there is a broad consensus that, as a minimum, states should be afforded a degree of participation in forums which seek to regulate their activities (Clark 2007). Beyond the need for democratic participation, the legitimacy of international regimes is critically depend-ent on non-discrimination, that is, all states should be equally bound by international agreements. Again, as was described above, the HTC failed both of these tests, which seriously compromised the political viability of the regime. At the level of participation, the early stages of the project, including the preparation of the 1998 HTC report, were prepared without sufficient consultation with non-OECD member states despite the poten-tially profound impact the initiative would have on them. While this lack of engagement was partially addressed through the creation of the original Forum on Harmful Tax Practices, the reality was that non-OECD member states felt they had little input into the HTC agenda or subse-quent deliberations. The final and most damaging criticism of the HTC agenda was the abstention of Switzerland and Luxembourg in April 1998 under the OECD's mutual agreement provisions. As we have noted above, this blatant hypocrisy rendered the HTC virtually meaningless unless all OECD member states agreed to be bound by the regime (Woodward 2006).

The majority of academic accounts of the various attempts to limit offshore tax abuse highlight the OECD's inability to couch its reform agenda in a way that was consistent with accepted norms and how this undermined the legitimacy and political viability of the agenda. While the available evidence supports such claims, it is also important to acknowledge the success that groups opposed to offshore regulation had in terms of mobilising a coalition of small states and financial interests against the reforms and the effectiveness of lobbying in the realm of overt politics. Beyond the ideational factors noted above, the success of campaigns conducted by the Centre for Freedom and Prosperity and the Commonwealth Secretariat must also, in part, be explained by the structural power of the financial actors whose interests they promoted together with the absence of a countervailing coalition of public interest groups prepared to campaign for tax justice. Reflecting these dynamics, the analysis of post-2007 international tax politics will be sensitive to the patterns of interest group politics including the rise of public interest groups such as the Tax Justice Network and Uncut, as well as broader public sentiments concerning the use of offshore financial services. In combination the rise of public interest groups concerned about international tax matters and greater awareness of international tax issues among the voting public have the potential to counter the inevitable political response from financial interests opposed to proposals designed to improve international tax transparency.

CONCLUSION

The historical analysis presented in this chapter suggests that the prospects for reforming international tax governance depend on successfully meeting four broad conditions – the support of great powers, a robust compliance regime, prevailing norms and the demands of domestic political circumstances – each of which have a range of dimensions. In terms of securing and maintaining the support of a concert of great powers it is essential that any reform agenda enjoy support on both sides of the Atlantic. For this reason it would be prudent to focus, in the first instance at least, on enhancing tax transparency rather than on a more ambitious agenda concerned with enhancing international tax harmonisation or moving to a system of formula apportionment. Beyond the level of international support, clearly the sustainability and effectiveness of any reforms to the international tax regime will be influenced by institutional innovations that enhance and consolidate support for the new regime, effectively increasing the costs associated with failing to implement any international commitments. For this reason the chapters that follow will carefully assess the role of the G20 Leaders' Forum in order to establish its role in shaping the post-crisis reform agenda and garnering and maintaining support for international tax cooperation.

In terms of the political implications of prevailing norms and ideas, the lesson from the pre-crisis experience documented in this chapter is that proposed reforms must be consistent with dominant norms and especially those being espoused and promoted by key actors in the international financial system. To this extent the analysis below will assess the resilience of neo-liberal ideas in the aftermath of the financial crisis and the extent to which reform proposals are consistent with dominant ideas. The second set of norms that will inevitably influence the legitimacy of any attempt to enhance international tax cooperation concern the process used to reach any international agreement and the extent to which any such agreement is applied in a consistent manner. To this end smaller financial centres and non-OECD member states must be allowed to participate fully in setting and administering any new international standards, which must subsequently be applied in a consistent manner. Reflecting this goal, Chapter 6 will be devoted to assessing the legitimacy and effectiveness of the revised Global Forum on Transparency and Information Exchange for Tax purposes (established in 2009) which is charged with the responsibility for implementing the changes to the international tax regime agreed at the height of the financial crisis.

Prevailing norms and the power and preferences of great powers may be the central concerns of international relations scholars, but the evidence presented above suggests that there is also a need to assess the complex ways in which international developments impact on the domestic politics of international tax cooperation. A central consideration here is the role of interest group politics and the extent to which pro-financial centre interests can influence domestic law makers and the degree to which the issue of international taxation gains prominence on the domestic political agenda. Given that this study is designed to be sensitive to past patterns of politics and the factors that have historically undermined international tax cooperation the analysis presented in the ensuring chapters is designed to assess how the financial crisis and its aftermath precipitated change in the international tax regime.

REFERENCES

BIS (2007) Bank of International Settlements, *Quarterly Review*, September 2007, available at http://www.BIS.org (accessed June 2011).
Blyth, Mark (2003) 'The Political Power of Financial Ideas: Transparency, Risk

and Distribution', in Jonathan Kirshner (ed.), *Monetary Orders*, Ithaca: Cornell University Press.

Braithwaite, John and Peter Drahos (2000) *Global Business Regulation*, Cambridge: Cambridge University Press.

Campbell, John (1998), 'Institutional Analysis and the Role of Ideas in Political Economy', *Theory and Society*, **27** (3), 377–409.

Campbell, John (2004), *Institutional Change and Globalization*, Princeton, NJ: Princeton University Press.

Carroll, Peter and Aynsley Kellow (2011) *The OECD*, Cheltenham, UK and Northampton, MA, USA: Edward Elgar.

Cassard, Mark (1994) 'The Role of Offshore Centers in International Financial Intermediation', IMF Working Paper No 107, Washington DC

Clark, Ian (2007) *International Legitimacy and World Society*, Oxford: Oxford University Press.

Denny, Charlotte (2001) 'OECD to Defy Bush over Tax Havens', *Guardian*, 12 May, available at http://www.guardian.co.uk/business/2001/may/12/7 (accessed July 2012).

Drezner, Daniel (2007) *All Politics is Global: Explaining International Regulatory Regimes*, Princeton, NJ: Princeton University Press.

Easson, Alex (2004) 'Harmful Tax Competition: An Evaluation of the OECD Initiative', *Tax Notes International*, **34** (10), 1037–77.

Eccleston, Richard (2009) 'Business and International Tax Regulation: Business Associability, Strategy and Influence at the OECD', Paper presented to Research Committee 38 (Business and Politics) IPSA World Congress, Santiago, July.

The Economist (1997) 'European Tax Disharmony', 3 April.

Eden, Lorraine and Robert T. Kudrle (2005) 'Tax Havens: Renegade States in the International Tax Regime?' *Law & Policy*, 27 (1), January 2005, 100–127.

G7 (1996) 'Lyon Summit – Economic Communiqué', available at http://www.g8.u toronto.ca/summit/1996lyon/communique.html (accessed May 2010).

Hacker, Jacob and Paul Pierson (2005) *Off Center: The Republican Revolution and the Erosion of American Democracy*, New Haven, CT: Yale University Press.

Hay, Colin (2002), *Political Analysis: A Critical Introduction*, Basingstoke: Palgrave Macmillan.

Helleiner, Eric (2005) 'The Monetary and Financial System', in John Ravenhill (ed.), *Global Political Economy*, Oxford: Oxford University Press.

Hudson, Alan (1998) 'Reshaping the Regulatory Landscape: Border Skirmishes around the Bahamas and Cayman Offshore Financial Centres', *Review of International Political Economy*, **5** (3), 534–64.

Joachim, Jutta, Bob Reinalda and Bertjan Verbeek (eds) (2008) *International Organizations and Implementation, Enforcers, Managers, Authorities?* Oxford: Routledge.

Katzenstein, Peter (1978) *Between Power and Plenty: Foreign Economic Policies of Advanced Industrial States*, Madison: University of Wisconsin Press.

Kay, Adrian (2006) *The Dynamics of Public Policy: Theory and Evidence*, Cheltenham, UK and Northampton, MA, USA: Edward Elgar.

Kindleberger, Charles (1973) *The World Depression, 1929–1939*, Berkeley: University of California Press.

Krasner, Stephen (1976) 'State Power and the Structure of International Trade', *World Politics*, **28** (3), 317–47.

Kudrle, Robert (2003) 'Are There Two Sides to the Tax Issue?' Paper presented to the International Studies Association Conference, Portland.

Mahon, Rianne and Stephen McBride (eds) (2008) *The OECD in Transnational Governance*, Vancouver: UBC Press.

Martin, Lisa (1993) *Coercive Cooperation: Explaining Multilateral Economic Sanctions*, Princeton, NJ: Princeton University Press.

Meinzer, Markus (2012) 'The Creeping Futility of the Global Forum's Peer Reviews', Tax Justice Network Tax Justice Briefing (March), available at http://www.taxjustice.net/cms/upload/GlobalForum2012–TJN–Briefing.pdf (accessed March 2012).

Neslund, Kristofer (2009) 'Why Tax Information Exchange Agreements are "Toothless"' (16 July), available at http://www.cpa2biz.com/Content/media/PRODUCER_CONTENT/Newsletters/Articles_2009/Tax/Toothless.jsp (accessed 1 June 2011).

OECD (1991) *Taxing Profits in a Global Economy: Domestic and International Issues*, Paris: OECD.

OECD (1997) 'Economic Impact of Low-Tax Jurisdictions', Working Party No. 2 on Tax Policy Analysis and Tax Statistics, OECD Archive file DAFFE/CFA/WP2(97)25

OECD (1998) *Harmful Tax Competition: An Emerging Global Issue*, Paris: OECD.

OECD (2000) *Improving Access to Bank Information for Tax Purposes*, Paris: OECD.

OECD (2002) *Model Agreement on Information Exchange on Tax Matters*, Paris: OECD.

OECD (2004) *OECD Global Forum Progress Report*, Paris: OECD

OECD (2011) 'Article 26 of the OECD Model Tax Convention on Income and Capital', available at http://www.oecd.org/document/53/0,3746,en_2649_33747_33614197_1_1_1_1,00.html (accessed July 2012).

Palan, Ronen (2002) 'Tax Havens and the Commercialization of State Sovereignty', *International Organization*, **56**, 152–78.

Palan, Ronen (2003) *The Offshore World: Sovereign Markets, Virtual Places and Nomad Millionaires*, Ithaca: Cornell University Press.

Palan, Ronen, Richard Murphy and Christian Chavagneux (2010) *Tax Havens: How Globalization Really Works*, Ithaca: Cornell University Press.

Persaud, Avinash (2001) 'The Knowledge Gap', *Foreign Affairs*, **80** (2), 107–17.

Picciotto, Sol (2011) *Regulating Global Corporate Capitalism*, Cambridge: Cambridge University Press.

Picciotto, Sol (1992) *International Business Taxation*, London: Quorum.

Pierson, Paul (2004) *Politics in Time: History, Institutions and Social Analysis*, Princeton and Oxford: Princeton University Press.

Pinto, Dale and Adrian Sawyer (2009) 'Towards Sustaining the Future of Taxation: Is a World Tax Organization Necessary and Feasible in Today's Globalized World?' *Australian Tax Forum*, **24** (2), 179–205.

Ring, Diane (2009) 'What's at Stake in the Sovereignty Debate? International Tax and the Nation-State', *Virginia Journal of International Law*, **49** (1), 154–233.

Rixen, Thomas (2008) *The Political Economy of International Tax Governance: Transformations of the State*, New York: Palgrave Macmillan.

Sawyer, Adrian (2009) *Developing a World Tax Organisation: The Way Forward*, Bath: Fiscal Publications.

Scott, James (1990) *Domination and the Art of Resistance: Hidden Transcripts*, New Haven, CT: Yale University Press.

Sharman, Jason (2011) *The Money Laundry*, Ithaca: Cornell University Press.

Sharman, Jason (2006) *Havens in a Storm: The Global Struggle for Tax Regulation*, Ithaca: Cornell University Press.

Sharman, Jason and Percy Mistry (2008) *Considering the Consequences: The Development Implications of Initiatives on Taxation, Anti-Money Laundering and Combating the Financing of Terrorism*, London: Commonwealth.

Singer, D. (2004) 'Capital Rules: The Domestic Politics of International Regulatory Harmonization', *International Organization*, **58**, 531–65.

Strange, Susan ([1986] 1997) *Casino Capitalism*, Manchester: Manchester University Press.

Sullivan, Martin (2007) 'Lessons from the Last War on Tax Havens', *Tax Notes*, **116**, 327–37.

Suskind, Ron (2004) *The Price of Loyalty: George W. Bush, the White House and the Education of Paul O'Neill*, New York: Simon and Schuster.

Tanzi, Vito (1995) *Taxation in an Integrating World*, Washington DC: Brookings Institution Press.

Tax Justice Network (2009) 'Tax Information Exchange Agreements – Briefing Paper', April 2009, available at http://www.taxjustice.net/cms/upload/pdf/TJN_0903_Exchange_of_Info_Briefing_draft.pdf (accessed 28 February 2010).

Thelen, Kathleen (1999), 'Historical Institutionalism and Comparative Politics', *Annual Review of Political Science*, **2**, 369–404.

Underdal, Arild (1998) *The Politics of International Environmental Management*, New York: Kluwer.

Webb, Michael (2004) 'Defining the Boundaries of Legitimate State Practice: Norms, Transnational Actors and the OECD's project on Harmful Tax Competition', *Review of International Political Economy*, **11**, 37–58.

Weschler, William (2001) 'Follow the Money', *Foreign Affairs*, **90** (4), 40–57.

Woodward, Richard (2006) 'Offshore Strategies in Global Political Economy: Small Islands and the Case of the EU and OECD Harmful Tax Competition Initiatives', *Cambridge Journal of International Affairs*, **19**, 685–99.

Woodward, Richard (2009) *The Organization for Economic Cooperation and Development*, London: Routledge.

Young, Oran (1999) *Governance in World Affairs*, Ithaca: Cornell University Press.

4. The financial crisis and the politics of international tax cooperation

By the mid-2000s the campaign to promote international tax transparency was floundering, characterised by analysts as being the victim of a 'politics without conviction' (Palan et al. 2010). Yet contrary to expectations, there has since been significant and unexpected progress insofar as tax information exchange agreements are concerned. Whereas before 2006 a mere 11 OECD TIEAs had been signed, renewed enthusiasm for tax transparency has been such that some 440 had been agreed by late 2011 (see Figure 4.2 below). Beyond this progress on bilateral information exchange agreements there have been significant parallel developments, including the agreement of all OECD member states (including Switzerland) to the revised Article 26 of the OECD Model Tax Convention with provisions requiring parties to exchange tax information under 'foreseeably relevant' circumstances irrespective of bank secrecy provisions. This chapter analyses the rejuvenation of the international tax transparency regime with particular reference to the impact of structural and organisational variables on patterns of international cooperation, while Chapter 5 will be devoted to assessing the influence of domestic politics on the regime.

At first blush casual observers may be tempted to conclude that renewed interest in international tax issues in recent years is a logical and inevitable consequence of the financial crisis that could readily be explained by structuralist accounts of regime change described in Chapter 2. While the financial crisis has provided an important context for recent changes in the international tax regime, it is equally apparent that causation is complex and multi-dimensional. Indeed the tax regulation movement was gaining momentum prior to the financial crisis and the progress that has been achieved since 2009 was far from inevitable. At the level of institutional innovations arguably the April 2009 G20 leaders' meeting in London represents something of a watershed in terms of the consolidation of the OECD regime, because world leaders moved beyond general platitudes to making firm commitments to the OECD's established agenda on tax transparency and information exchange. But the G20's endorsement of the OECD's tax transparency agenda was itself a consequence of lobbying and diplomacy, which suggests that there is a good deal of agency in the international responses to the financial crisis, with key actors, international organisations and broader public sentiments all contributing to recent developments. The task of this chapter is both to describe the recent progress that has been made in terms of improving tax transparency and information exchange and to apply the literature outlined in Chapter 2 to establish how a combination of structural pressures connected with the financial crisis and associated organisational developments have shaped the international tax regime. Chapter 5 builds on this analysis by evaluating the complementary role of domestic political developments in shaping these changes.

THE FINANCIAL CRISIS AND THE RISE OF THE G20

The financial crisis that has afflicted world markets since 2007 arguably represents the most significant shock to the global economy since the Great Depression. At the height of the crisis in late 2008 the global financial system froze, sending world production, trade and asset prices into sharp decline. By early 2009 the IMF had dubbed the crisis 'The Great Recession'. While the international banking system was stabilised over the course of 2009 and 2010, an ongoing sovereign debt crisis in the eurozone has compromised the global recovery and significant risks and legacy issues remain.

Historically, moments of political and economic crisis have given rise to significant institutional and political change (Gourevitch 1986; Helleiner 2009). Such accounts stress the importance of 'critical junctures' as the rare but transformative moments when existing political orders are deposed and new interests, ideas and institutions prevail (Hall 1993; Collier and Collier 1991; Pierson 2000; Blyth 2002; Kay 2006). This literature suggests that the financial crisis had the potential to precipitate radical change in the governance of the global economy – although surprisingly the financial crisis seems to have done little to undermine the credibility of and political support for the pre-financial crisis liberal order (Helleiner and Pagliari 2010; Gill 2010; Crouch 2011). Within the specific context of the international taxation arena, the literature on the transformative nature of economic crises suggests that the economic dislocation associated with the financial crisis and the way in which it has highlighted deficiencies in existing regulatory structures and frameworks may be able to explain the transformation in the international tax regime described within this volume. Finally, at the level of political leadership and strategy, there is evidence that crises often prompt a strong response from governments keen to demonstrate that they are taking responsibility for the economic malaise and are capable of devising and implementing mitigating policies (Sinclair 2010a).

The main discussion in this chapter begins with a brief assessment of the structural economic impact that the financial crisis had on the global economy and on the financial interests of member states and of the ideational consequences of the crisis. The objective here is not to provide another detailed account of the wider economic impact of the financial crisis, but rather to evaluate the impact of the crisis on the interests and strategies of key actors in the international tax regime.

At an instrumental level the financial crisis had an immediate impact on the policy priorities of national governments as policymakers sought to pursue dual strategies for stabilising domestic banks – first through the provision of short-term loans and then later through the employment of varying combinations of state guarantees and equity contributions. Using public funds to recapitalise banks was successful to the extent that it mostly prevented large-scale bank failures; however the approach did not manage to restore sufficient confidence in financial markets to sustain bank lending. The ensuing credit squeeze and the subsequent decline in lending and private investment ensured that the financial crisis soon spread to the real economy. By the end of 2008 governments of all industrial economies were engaged in unprecedented attempts to support economic growth through a combination of low interest rates and unprecedented fiscal stimulus as well as through experimental monetary strategies such as quantitative easing.

Beyond the immediate task of attempting to support domestic economic activity, the transnational scope and severity of the financial crisis soon forced world leaders to engage in informal and then more institutionalised forms of economic cooperation. The most significant innovation in terms of international economic cooperation was the creation of the G20 Leaders' Forum, a development that is described in greater detail below. Despite precipitating these radical policy responses and new forms of international cooperation, somewhat surprisingly the impact of the financial crisis on the prevailing ideas and paradigms concerning the operation and governance of the global economy remains remarkably modest (Sinclair 2010a; Tarullo 2008; Gill 2010).

Whereas a crisis of the severity of that which engulfed the international financial system in 2008 might have been expected to call into question the intellectual foundations on which neo-liberal globalisation is built, leading to a conscious reassessment and redefinition of the governance of the global economy (Hall 1993; Kay 2006), such a paradigm shift has not occurred. Instead the intellectual consensus has not been on replacing neo-liberal globalisation but on enhancing its governance through improved regulation and greater transparency in the hope of limiting the pervasive externalities and market failures that triggered the crisis (Stiglitz 2010). The resilience of the neo-liberal order may be explained by the absence of a coherent or credible alternative, or perhaps because neo-liberalism has become so deeply institutionalised in what Stephen Gill refers to as the 'new constitutionalism of disciplinary neo-liberalism' (Gill 2008, 2010; Lesage and Vermeiren 2011). Whatever the explanation for neo-liberalism's durability, the consequence has been an absence of broad-based support for more radical proposals to re-regulate global finance, such as through the introduction of a Tobin tax. However the determination to reform the neo-liberal financial order through enhanced prudential supervision, risk management and transparency has given rise to various regulatory reforms which have had a direct impact on the international tax regime.

In addition to creating a climate for international financial reform, the financial crisis represents the greatest challenge to the public finances of advanced industrial economies since the Second World War. A combination of deteriorating revenues and expensive fiscal stimulus packages and financial bailouts has resulted in almost unprecedented budget deficits and spiralling public debt. In the United States the federal deficit peaked at 12.8 per cent of GDP in 2009 while general government gross debt is expected to reach 111 per cent of GDP by 2014 (IMF 2011, 71). Similarly, in the United Kingdom an equally bleak deficit of £175 billion (10.3 per cent of GDP) was recorded in the 2009–10 financial year while other EU states such as Greece, Portugal and by late 2011 Italy and Spain face fully fledged sovereign debt crises (Schifferes 2009; Reinhart and Rogoff 2009) (see also Figure 4.1). The fiscal and associated political challenges arising from the financial crisis are all the more serious given that recently introduced austerity measures will have to continue into the 2020s to put the public finances of the worst affected countries back on to a sustainable footing. In an attempt to move towards such sustainability, governments have been forced to impose new taxes, and devote increased resources to tax enforcement and compliance. In this context initiatives designed to limit revenue losses through international tax evasion represent a politically palatable way of increasing revenue.

Finally, the financial crisis has ignited broader political interest in what had hitherto been highly technical regulatory issues dominated by international organisations and business interests. As Helleiner et al. (2010) argue, financial crises provide unique conditions that highlight the costs of regulatory failure to both taxpayers and society at large, mobilising public opinion behind agendas for regulatory reform. For example, Chapter 5 describes how Barack Obama's sponsorship of the Stop Tax Haven Abuse

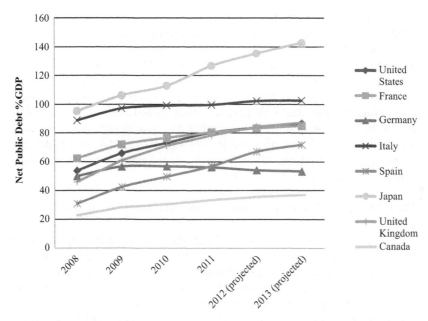

Source: IMF, *Fiscal Monitor* (2011, 70).

Figure 4.1   Net public debt in select industrial economies 2008–13

Act in February 2007 became a political asset as the financial crisis intensified during the 2008 Presidential campaign. More generally, there has
been a significant increase in NGO activism through groups such as the
Tax Justice Network, Uncut and Christian Aid (author interview). Not
only has international tax regulation become politicised in the aftermath
of the crisis, but with the legitimacy of corporate actors who promote
international tax planning at historical lows, initiatives aimed at curtail-
ing international tax evasion enjoyed relatively strong domestic political
support. Political resolve to enhance international tax transparency has
also been reinforced by complementary initiatives aimed at ending bank
secrecy. While tax haven abuse was not the cause of the financial crisis,
the use of secrecy jurisdictions by many of the investment banks, insurers
and hedge funds at the centre of the crisis served to heighten uncertainty
and concerns about solvency and counterparty risk (Palan et al. 2010). As
a consequence of this diagnosis, financial regulators, such as the newly
established Financial Stability Board (FSB), have assumed a fresh determination to shed light on derivatives markets, hedge funds and other
'off-balance sheet' positions held by banks and other financial actors.

For example, after more than two decades of self-regulation the financial crisis prompted national regulators to demand greater financial transparency with regard to hedge funds and derivatives markets by 'developing mechanisms for cooperation and information sharing between relevant authorities in order to ensure oversight is maintained' (G20 2009 as quoted in Helleiner and Pagliari 2010, 77). By happy coincidence this determination to increase financial transparency promises to have positive 'spillover effects' in terms of enhancing the quality and availability of tax-relevant information regarding funds held in OFCs (Pierson 2004) and highlights the significance of interactions between nested regimes in terms of driving regulatory change (Crouch 2005).

The G20–OECD Relationship and the Rejuvenation of the Global Forum

As mentioned previously the rise and the consolidation of the G20 Leaders' Forum is the most obvious institutional consequence of the financial crisis with significant implications for the global tax regime. The inaugural G20 leaders' summit held in Washington in November 2008 was designed to give the evolving response to the financial crisis a broad and emphatic mandate. Hence, while the detailed content of the financial reform agenda and precise nature of emergency economic settings were established through existing organisations and networks, the G20 acted as a de facto executive forum providing coordination and much needed political authority to ensure a decisive response (Porter 2010; Wouters et al. 2010; Garrett 2010).

Rather than precipitating a new international financial architecture the financial crisis resulted in the conversion of existing financial institutions, such as the G20, enabling them to take on new agendas, functions, and in some cases, deepening relationships with other actors within that architecture (Streeck and Thelen 2005; Thelen 2002; Pierson 2004). This strategy is consistent with a more general claim amongst institutional theorists that adapting existing institutions to meet emerging challenges is less time consuming and is more efficient than creating new institutions from the ground up (Eilstrup-Sangiovanni 2009). In specific terms we witnessed the conversion of the G20 from a ministerial-level forum, whose role had hitherto focused on agenda-setting and 'widening existing mindsets and promoting policy paradigms', to a leaders' forum charged with responsibility for coordinating and implementing the global response to the financial crisis (Porter 2010; Hillman 2010). Whilst the first hastily convened G20 leaders' summit held in Washington in November 2008 had unrivalled political power to set the global economic agenda, given the G20's (and indeed all of the Gs) lack of a secretariat (Beeson and Bell 2009; Garrett

2010), developing and implementing detailed policy prescriptions required either the creation of a new international bureaucracy, which was simply not feasible given the time constraints, or the support of established intergovernmental organisations such as the IMF, the FSF (now FSB) and the OECD. It was the latter option that was selected, necessarily entailing a rapid increase in the frequency, intensity and nature of the already existing relationships between the FSF/FSB, the G20 and bodies such as the IMF and the OECD.

By the second G20 leaders' meeting, held in London in April 2009, the two working groups established in Washington had developed detailed proposals to regulate hedge funds and derivatives markets, and to reform the process of calculating and managing financial risk and to improve the regulation of ratings agencies. Perhaps the most important decision made at the April 2009 meeting was to charge the IMF and a new and expanded Financial Stability Forum, to be called the Financial Stability Board (FSB), with responsibility for providing comprehensive oversight of the trends and risks in international finance broadly defined (G20 2009a; Woods 2010).

At the height of the crisis this technical regulatory agenda was perhaps secondary to the political imperative shared by world leaders concerning the need to be seen to be responding decisively to the crisis and to be engaged in a tangible 'referential' response to what was emerging as the most significant global recession since the 1930s (Edelman 1977). This situation also provided a significant opportunity for the more entrepreneurially minded leaders of intergovernmental organizations (IGOs), such as the OECD, to advance related issues on their agendas. As we have noted, secrecy jurisdictions may not have directly caused the financial crisis (Palan et al. 2010), but the veil of secrecy they provided for banking and investment transactions had long been a hindrance to effective domestic and international financial regulation. Moreover, the international tax evasion that secrecy jurisdictions facilitated further undermined the finances of states struggling under rapidly escalating levels of public debt. In these circumstances a proposal for improving international tax transparency was arguably an idea whose time had come (Kingdon 1984). It was under these circumstances that the OECD, with the support of key states on both sides of the Atlantic, was able to enter into a symbiotic relationship with the enhanced G20 Leaders' Forum to promote its international tax agenda (Lesage 2010).

Against this backdrop, combined with its prior work on the issue and long-standing relationship with the G20 Finance Ministers' Forum, the OECD was able successfully to promote its international taxation agenda. The inaugural November 2008 G20 leaders' meeting identified the OECD's framework for enhancing tax information exchange as being a 'medium term priority'. Significantly, and in part because developing and reaching agreement on detailed proposals on financial reform were more elusive (author interview September 2009), the G20 enhanced its commitment to the OECD's tax transparency agenda at the second leaders' meeting in London in April 2009 committing the G20:

> To take action against non-cooperative jurisdictions, including tax havens. We stand ready to deploy sanctions to protect our public finances and financial systems. The era of banking secrecy is over. We note that the OECD has today published a list of countries assessed by the Global Forum against the international standard for exchange of tax information. (G20 2009b)

This declaration and a commitment to identify non-cooperative jurisdictions and potentially to impose sanctions, such as increased withholding taxes, against them, was in some regards similar to the declarations made in the late 1990s, but given the context of the financial crisis and the increasingly central role of the G20 the declaration represented a watershed in terms of the international commitment to tax transparency. Yet this assessment and listing exercise was not without controversy, in part because of the possible ramifications. Perhaps the clearest case where divergent state interests influenced the G20's deliberations was in relation to the Chinese territories of Hong Kong and Macau which have long been used as regional secrecy jurisdictions. Reports suggest that the Chinese government took umbrage at the OECD's initial negative assessment of Hong Kong and Macau as non-cooperative jurisdictions and threatened to withdraw support for both the tax transparency initiative and the entire London summit unless they were removed from the list. Given the threat this posed to China's multi-billion dollar support to the IMF, British Prime Minister Brown and US President Obama brokered a compromise whereby China was placed on the OECD 'white list' of compliant jurisdictions and it was noted that the territories of Hong Kong and Macau had committed to the international standard (Lesage 2010; Hall et al. 2009; Watt et al. 2009). This successful compromise maintained the G20's support for the tax transparency initiative but, as always, highlights the dependence of the regime on the support of major powers.

By the third leaders' summit in Pittsburgh in September 2009, and after extensive lobbying from the OECD Secretary General (author interview September 2009), the G20 had agreed to support the creation and funding of a newly expanded Global Forum on Tax Transparency and Information Exchange, organised through the OECD, which would be charged with systematically evaluating the implementation of and compliance with the new global standard. According to the Pittsburgh communiqué:

We are committed to maintain the momentum in dealing with tax havens, money laundering, proceeds of corruption, terrorist financing, and prudential standards. We welcome the expansion of the Global Forum on Transparency and Exchange of Information, including the participation of developing countries, and welcome the agreement to deliver an effective program of peer review. The main focus of the Forum's work will be to improve tax transparency and exchange of information so that countries can fully enforce their tax laws to protect their tax base. We stand ready to use countermeasures against tax havens from March 2010. (G20 2009c)

While these pronouncements were a reiteration of the OECD's established tax agenda they were significant because they represented an unprecedented high-level political commitment to the regime as well as an undertaking to finance a new forum, allowing it to conduct a more robust 'field based' peer review process (author interview September 2009). In the OECD's own words:

The support of the G20 has been instrumental in bringing the work of the Global Forum to the fore of today's public policy agenda. The emphasis they have placed on ensuring that jurisdictions, as members of the global financial community, implement the standards, has had a direct impact on the pace of implementation. (OECD 2010, 16)

The evidence suggests that the evolving inter-organisational relationship between the G20 and the OECD following the onset of the financial crisis had a significant impact on the international tax regime. The G20's political and financial support for the tax information exchange agenda represented a major fillip for the OECD. However this relationship was one of interdependence because while subordinate at the level of power relations, the OECD has almost unrivalled expertise and policy capacity in the international tax arena as well as an established reform agenda in relation to international tax transparency (Eccleston et al. 2010). This was an extremely valuable political resource in late 2008 given the political pressure on the G20 to develop a timely response to the crisis. In the short term the OECD was able to exploit this resource advantage, winning endorsement for its tax information exchange standard as well as securing additional financial resources to assist with its implementation. However, it is necessary to reiterate that this mutually beneficial exchange of resources was not inevitable. It is important to acknowledge the value of entrepreneurial leadership and bargaining strategies in the formation of inter-organisational networks. At a diplomatic level the OECD Secretary General Gurria, aided by Jeffrey Owens, the Director of the OECD's Centre for Tax Policy and Administration, was proactive and successful in terms of promoting the OECD's international tax agenda at successive

G7 and then G20 leaders' meetings. In the words of one senior OECD official 'our real impact has been in terms of setting a reform agenda – at the height of the crisis we were able to offer world leaders a considered and coherent course of action' (author interview September 2009). In other words, the OECD's established expertise, combined with the entrepreneurial skills of Gurria and Owens, proved attractive to the G20 in the context of the financial crisis.

The power-dependency relationship described above also suggests that the international agreements for the OECD's tax transparency framework forged at the height of the financial crisis can be understood in terms of the OECD's (and organisations in other regulatory arenas) ability to supply policy solutions in the face of overwhelming demands by the international community. This conceptualisation of the causes of international cooperation resonates with John Kingdon's influential analysis of the agenda-setting process in domestic politics (1984) which distinguished between the supply of policy ideas, or what he defined as the 'policy stream' and the broader political demands and pressures confronting governments. For Kingdon, change occurs when the supply of policy solutions meets prevailing political demands, creating a momentary 'policy window' where policy and political agendas meet. This framework is particularly relevant to the case at hand because it emphasises that both domestic political circumstances and imperatives as well as elite opinion and organisational politics influence patterns of international cooperation. Also significant is Kingdon's emphasis on the importance of agency in that policy entrepreneurs play a critical role in linking their agendas to existing policy problems. Central in this is the ability to frame policy solutions in innovative ways and the ability to build political coalitions and enhance the legitimacy of policy change (Kingdon 1984, 188–91; Pierson 2004, 137). The most successful policy entrepreneurs and architects of institutional reform, such as OECD Secretary General Gurria, tend to be powerful brokers situated at the intersection of important policy networks (Pierson 2004; Polsky 2000).

This analysis suggests that the rejuvenation of the international tax transparency regime can be explained in terms of the OECD's ability to exploit the acute demand for a coherent regulatory response to the financial crisis. In contrast to realist theories and the claim that organisations are instruments of state interests, this 'brokerage' role implies that organisations such as the OECD can act autonomously and make an important contribution to global governance through promoting mutually beneficial relationships with and between key states and international institutions. While this process clearly differs from that described in the literature on institutional socialisation and its emphasis on interaction and deliberation within (rather than between) forums (Bearce and Bondanella 2007; Checkel 2005), the networking role of international organisations described above largely complements institutional socialisation. Whereas the institutional socialisation highlights internal learning and accommodation within an organisational forum, networking and brokerage describes a process whereby ideas are mobilised beyond an epistemic community or specialist transgovernmental networks in response to broader structural developments and challenges in the international system.

Like the *Type 1* institutional socialisation described in Chapter 2, this process relies on a combination of ideational resources and the more instrumental foundations of state interests. Ideas matter, because as the wider literature on agenda-setting makes clear, culture, norms and discourse play a role both in defining policy problems and the appropriateness of specific reform agendas (Kuran 1995; Stone 1997; Finnemore and Sikkink 2001). Yet, as has been argued both above and in the literature on the political economy of taxation more generally, prevailing economic conditions – including economic crises and significant budget deficits – also play an important role in creating the political demand for tax reform (Hallerberg and Basinger 1998). In summary, the rise of the emerging international tax transparency regime up the global regulatory reform agenda in the aftermath of the financial crisis can only be understood in terms of the relatively unique economic, ideational and political conditions which prevailed in 2008–09. However, reaching an international agreement on the need to address a specific economic governance problem is only the first, albeit important, step towards achieving a sustainable and effective solution. We now turn our attention to the specific institutional and regulatory innovations that have been implemented in the tax transparency arena since the height of the financial crisis, before analysing the domestic viability of the regime in Chapter 5 and its effectiveness in Chapter 6.

ENHANCING INTERNATIONAL TAX TRANSPARENCY

While many analysts continue to argue that the recent achievements of the OECD are relatively modest (Picciotto 2011; Avi-Yonah 2009, 793; Spencer 2010; Meinzer 2012), by historical standards these developments represent a promising first step towards curbing the use of secrecy jurisdictions to conceal income and investments from 'onshore' tax authorities. However, before moving on to a preliminary assessment of the efficacy and outlook for the emerging international tax regime in Chapter 6, it is first necessary to document the manner in which the structural and institutional developments described above have shaped the international tax regime since 2009. The remainder of this chapter will be devoted to this task, first describing the creation and activities of the rejuvenated Global Forum for Transparency and Exchange of information for Tax Purposes, and then sketching some of the more significant unilateral measures implemented by key OECD member states designed to enhance tax transparency.

The Revised Global Forum

The G20's April 2009 request of the OECD to 'develop an effective peer-review mechanism to assess compliance' assumed a tangible form at the Global Forum's Mexico City meeting of 1–2 September 2009 (G20 2009b). Reflecting the growing political commitment to international tax transparency, this meeting agreed to a number of important substantive and procedural changes to the regime. In terms of the forum processes the most significant changes included the introduction of a more robust, two-stage peer review process designed to establish the extent to which forum members (of whom there were 101 in late 2011) complied with the emerging tax information exchange regime. In contrast to the original Global Forum, established in 2000, which assessed compliance with the OECD standard based on whether the jurisdiction under review had established an appropriate legal and regulatory framework to support information exchange, the revised peer review process also involved assessing the extent to which tax information is exchanged in practice. This 'Phase 2', field-based assessment regime was a response to critics who argued that prior to 2009 no consideration was given as to whether the jurisdiction under review had the capacity or willingness to exchange information in practice. When combined with the fact that forum members only had to sign a modest 12 TIEAs to be assessed as having 'substantially implemented' the old standard, it could credibly be argued that the regime was largely symbolic and did little to enhance international tax transparency (Webb 2004; Palan et al. 2010, 218). In addition to subjecting member states to this enhanced two-phase peer review process, the forum committed to conducting a post-assessment follow-up process to ensure that countries continue to honour their commitments and keep the international community informed of any policy changes which may influence their ability to exchange tax information (OECD 2011b). The differences between the Global Forum's pre-2009 annual assessment regime and the enhanced peer review process can be summarised as shown in Table 4.1.

Beyond these changes to the peer review process the Global Forum has

Table 4.1   *Comparison of pre-crisis annual reviews and post-crisis Global Forum process*

	'Old' annual assessments	Enhanced peer reviews
Basis	Information provided by each jurisdiction is reviewed by the secretariat but not subject to in-depth analysis. All jurisdictions have an opportunity to comment prior to publication.	Information is verified by an assessment team consisting of at least two legal experts assigned by member jurisdictions, and one member of the Global Forum secretariat. The report produced by the assessment team is then presented to the 30-member Peer Review Group for consideration and approval before being presented to the whole Global Forum for adoption.
Scope	Information that is 'relevant to transparency and effective exchange of information for tax purposes'.	Reviews are based on the Terms of Reference agreed by the Global Forum, which breaks down the international standards into 10 essential elements necessary to achieve effective exchange of information.
Outcome	Purely factual description of the jurisdictions' legal and regulatory framework for transparency and exchange of information.	Phase 1 reports contain determinations as to whether elements essential to the effective exchange of information are in place or whether improvements are needed. Phase 2 reports will contain ratings as to the extent to which the jurisdiction complies with the international standard
Follow-up	The annual assessments are updated by asking jurisdictions to indicate any changes that have occurred in the previous year.	Following publication of a report, jurisdictions can be asked to report back to the Peer Review Group with an oral update after 6 months and a written report after 1 year detailing changes made in response to the recommendations made by the Global Forum. It is contemplated that a procedure will be established to review determinations made in light of changes made.

Source: Adapted from OECD (2010, 20).

also elaborated and refined the criteria against which a country under review should be assessed. The ten central elements of transparency and exchange of information are provided below, but at this stage it is necessary to focus on the two most important elements of the framework. First, we have noted that the Global Forum's previous position of recognising a country as having 'substantially implemented' the international standard on having signed a threshold of 12 TIEAs was widely criticised on the grounds that a secrecy jurisdiction could meet the standard without compromising its offshore business by entering into agreements with obscure states of little economic significance rather than the financial centres on which they rely for investment (Murphy 2010). In contrast, the revised criteria represent an incremental shift away from the arbitrary 12-agreement threshold towards a requirement that members' 'network of information exchange agreements should cover all relevant partners'. This is suggestive of a more nuanced review regime which attempts to establish the quality and relevance of exchange agreements rather than just an arbitrary quantum. While it is still too early to make a definitive assessment of how this new standard will be assessed in practice, it does promise an incremental improvement over the pre-2009 regime.

A second dimension to the more nuanced assessment regime established after the Mexico City meeting is a gradual move away from the blunt distinction between states who were regarded as being compliant, having 'substantially implemented' the OECD standard, and those jurisdictions that were regarded as being non-cooperative. Given that the revised Global Forum is to assess compliance across 10 criteria (see Box 4.1) with particular reference to all relevant partners, then a more nuanced ranking system is required. As part of the 'Phase 2' review process the Global Forum will establish a rating system with jurisdictions under review being assessed as: (i) compliant; (ii) largely compliant; (iii) partially compliant; or (iv) non-compliant (OECD 2010, 14). This assessment procedure promises to provide a more detailed and accurate ranking of a jurisdiction's legislative and practical commitment to exchanging tax information, but as of early 2011 detailed ranking data relating to the first set of states subject to Phase 2 peer reviews had not been published owing to the absence 'Of a subset of jurisdictions representing a geographic and economic cross section of the Global Forum . . . to ensure that the applications of the rating system is consistent across jurisdictions' (OECD 2011b, 25).

The most controversial aspect of the Global Forum's revised standards and procedures for assessing tax information exchange has been the ongoing commitment to the exchange of information on request under circumstances that are 'foreseeably relevant' to the enforcement and

BOX 4.1 SUMMARY OF THE ASSESSMENT CRITERIA USED IN THE REVISED GLOBAL FORUM PROCESS

THE ESSENTIAL ELEMENTS OF TRANSPARENCY AND EXCHANGE OF INFORMATION FOR TAX PURPOSES

A   AVAILABILITY OF INFORMATION

A.1.   Jurisdictions should ensure that ownership and identity information for all relevant entities and arrangements is available to their competent authorities.

A.2.   Jurisdictions should ensure that reliable accounting records are kept for all relevant entities and arrangements.

A.3.   Banking information should be available for all account-holders.

B   ACCESS TO INFORMATION

B.I.   Competent authorities should have the power to obtain and provide information that is the subject of a request under an EOI agreement from any person within their territorial jurisdiction who is in possession or control of such information.

B.2.   The rights and safeguards that apply to persons in the requested jurisdiction should be compatible with effective exchange of information.

C   EXCHANGING INFORMATION

C.1.   EOI mechanisms should provide for effective exchange of information.

C.2.   The jurisdictions' network of information exchange mechanisms should cover all relevant partners.

C.3.   The jurisdictions' mechanisms for exchange of information should have adequate provisions to ensure the confidentiality of information received.

C.4.   The exchange of information mechanisms should respect the rights and safeguards of taxpayers and third parties.

C.5.   The jurisdiction should provide information under its network of agreements in a timely manner.

Source: OECD (2010, 35).

administration of the domestic tax laws of the requesting country. This limitation on information exchange was incorporated in the 2002 OECD *Model Agreement on Exchange of Information in Tax Matters* ostensibly to protect the integrity of tax data and prevent requesting countries engaging in 'fishing expeditions' and has been identified as a major deficiency in the OECD regime ever since. Critics argue that in practice information exchange on request is ineffective because requesting countries require detailed information regarding the taxpayer/s on which they are seeking data including their tax and financial interests (Spencer 2010; Meinzer 2012). This may be possible in a relatively small number of cases where tax authorities have detailed knowledge of offshore schemes acquired via whistle blowers or through amnesties and voluntary disclosure schemes (such as occurred in the UBS and LCT cases described in the following chapter). More often tax authorities will only have limited knowledge concerning the nature and full extent of offshore tax evasion, as a senior tax official from an OECD member state explains:

> Information exchange by request is very useful when you have a taxpayer who you're pretty certain is involved in evasion through a specific jurisdiction. Then you can ask for information and you'd be able to get it – I'm confident about that, but that's a small part of the problem because generally you don't know the people who have evaded in the first place and that's why we need automatic exchange of information. Otherwise they have to be in your sights before you can use information exchange on request and a lot of these people are not. They go to great efforts to not to be. (Author interview March 2010)

Chapter 1 described how offshore tax evasion is critically dependent on the concealment of income and investments from the tax authorities in which a taxpayer is resident. Under these circumstances even a well administered regime providing information exchange on request will only reveal the tip of the iceberg so far as international evasion is concerned. To paraphrase former US Secretary of Defense Donald Rumsfeld (2002): information exchange on request will help counter 'the known unknowns' but will do little to reveal 'the unknown unknowns', which arguably represent the greatest problem. Reflecting such concerns, many analysts, some states and indeed the European Union have argued for a system of automatic information exchange of tax and banking information between tax authorities. In theory the systematic and routine transfer of tax information used in conjunction with data matching technology has the potential to transform offshore tax enforcement. This was tacitly accepted by the OECD in the 1980s under the auspices of the OECD-Council of Europe Multilateral Convention on Administrative Assistance in Tax Matters as well as the OECD's report on *Improving Access to Bank*

Information for Tax Purposes (2000) and is a central feature of the EU Savings Directive introduced in 2005 (Spencer 2005).

Given there is recognition that automatic exchange of tax information is both possible and arguably desirable, the OECD's long-held preference for promoting information exchange on request under foreseeably relevant circumstances has been subject to a range of interpretations. Activists regard the promotion of exchange on request as a 'wasted opportunity' and regard the OECD's continued promotion of a 'flawed standard' as evidence of the organisation's inability to devise and implement a transparency regime that would seriously undermine offshore tax evasion and the powerful financial interests that support this industry (Christensen and Shaxson 2010; Meinzer 2012). An alternative and more optimistic interpretation, which has been reflected in recent developments, is that the OECD's promotion of information exchange on request represents an incremental step towards a more comprehensive system based on automatic information exchange. Certainly this is an argument advanced by the OECD secretariat both privately and in published reports (author interview September 2009). More specifically, neither the 2002 *Model Agreement on Exchange of Information on Tax Matters* (OECD 2002) or Article 26 of the *Model Tax Agreement* prohibit automatic information exchange. For example, Article 5, paragraph 39 of the 2002 model agreement states that while TIEAs do not cover automatic or spontaneous exchange of information 'Contracting parties may wish to expand their co-operation in matters of information exchange for tax purposes by covering automatic and spontaneous exchanges and simultaneous tax examinations.' Indeed, consistent with this view that countries may want to go beyond the baseline standard of exchange of information on request, the OECD has developed a number of procedures, protocols and resources to facilitate automatic or 'routine' tax information exchange including the 1997 *Revised Standard Magnetic Format for Automatic Information Exchange* and a revised 111-page module on 'Automatic Information Exchange' as part of the updated 2006 *Manual on the Implementation of Exchange and Information Provisions for Tax Purposes.* The most recent development on this front has been the OECD's July 2012 acknowledgment that automatic information exchange represents the emerging international standard because it 'can help detect cases of non-compliance even where tax administrations have had no previous indications of non-compliance' (OECD 2012, 19). While the implications of this development are unclear this report represents significant progress towards establishing automatic information exchange as the new international standard.

This dual strategy of allowing and developing resources to support automatic information exchange while insisting that exchange on request is the international standard can best be understood as being a pragmatic response in the face of deep seated political resistance to automatic information exchange. As was noted in Chapter 3, states have been extremely reluctant to cede sovereignty in relation to tax matters and routinely sharing tax and financial data with jurisdictions other than close allies and trading partners has generally been regarded as a bridge too far. More significantly, the offshore financial industry and the financial centres that depend on its trade have been unrelenting in their opposition to automatic information exchange because of a combination of the compliance burden that may result and because of the likely impact such a regime would have on demand for offshore services, including those in OECD member states.

Arguments against automatic information exchange were mobilised during the original HTC debate in the early 2000s with the Bush Administration in particular echoing concerns expressed by the conservative Heritage Foundation that 'international bureaucracies have no moral authority to interfere with national tax laws' (Mitchell 2000) and that the OECD project 'was too broad . . . and was not in line with the Administration's tax and economic priorities' (as quoted in Palan et al. 2010, 217). As we have seen in Chapter 3, given this hostile political environment the OECD was forced to retreat by promoting a more benign standard for information exchange on request including provisions to limit 'fishing expeditions' and allowing requests for information only once 'all other means available in its territory' have been exhausted (OECD 2011a). While keeping the option of automatic information exchange open, it was argued that the 2002 agreement to information exchange on request did represent 'a major step forward for the jurisdictions concerned'. Indeed within the OECD the original 2002 standard has been enhanced to the extent that paragraphs 4 and 5 of Article 26 of the Model Convention were amended in 2005 to make it clear that requests for information cannot be denied on the grounds that the requested jurisdiction has no tax interest in the request or because the request is contrary to bank secrecy provisions. However, despite this progress and the OECD's July 2012 watershed report on the topic, automatic exchange remains a threshold issue. The secrecy jurisdictions themselves acknowledge that while 'Many offshore centers feel empowered to deny cooperation to the OECD in relation to its tax information exchange on request program' this complacency is dangerous because many 'hard line' European countries are successfully promoting automatic exchange that 'would be much more onerous' 'with personal financial confidentiality being eliminated' (Hay 2005 as quoted in Spencer 2010, 51).

One factor that may have prompted the OECD to revisit its hitherto cautious and pragmatic approach to automatic information exchange is rivalry with other international organisations in the tax arena (Sharman 2006, 138–41). While few would dispute the OECD's pre-eminent role in international tax regulation, the EU, the United Nations and the IMF have all proposed variations on the OECD's standards. Of particular interest insofar as automatic information exchange is concerned is the fact that the EU and the UN's Commission of Experts on the Reform of the International Monetary and Financial System (the Stiglitz Commission) have both advocated, and in the case of the EU Savings Directive, have implemented frameworks for the automatic exchange of tax information (Stiglitz 2010, 114–16). In combination with recommendations to enhance the funding and status of the UN Tax Committee and growing political support for automatic information exchange from NGO groups, developing countries and key European states, the OECD may well be forced to incorporate this standard into its model agreements or risk becoming a victim of a 'forum shopping' process whereby states that wish to engage in automatic information exchange do so outside established OECD processes and frameworks.

We will revisit the legitimate concerns about the efficacy of the current OECD standard for tax information exchange on request in Chapter 6, but at this point it is important to acknowledge three key points. First, countries can no longer use bank secrecy and domestic tax interest provisions to deny tax information to treaty partners. Second, the extent to which Global Forum members are willing to exchange tax information in practice is now subjected to higher levels of evaluation courtesy of the Global Forum's enhanced peer review process. Finally, the level of engagement with the Global Forum process and the rate at which states both within the OECD and beyond have entered into tax information exchange agreements since the height of the financial crisis has been quite staggering and arguably represents a 'tipping point' for the regime. As of April 2011 over 650 TIEAs had been entered into under the auspices of the Global Forum regime, a 15-fold increase over the 44 that had been signed prior to the November 2008 Washington summit (see Figure 4.2).

DEVELOPMENTS BEYOND THE REVISED GLOBAL FORUM

The Global Forum may be the most important arena for international tax cooperation but its work has been both complemented and influenced by other international organisations, such as the UN International Tax Committee, the EU and the IMF, and also by increased unilateral enforcement activities within key industrial economies. In this sense

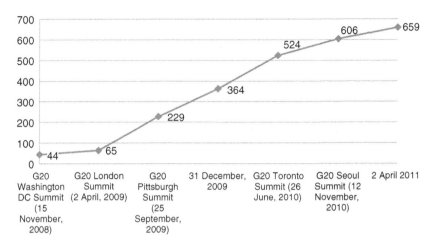

Source: OECD (2011a, 18).

Figure 4.2   TIEAs and DTAs signed between G20 summits

it is appropriate to regard the regulatory framework for international taxation as a 'nested regime' or a 'regime complex' in which more formal organisational structures, such as the Global Forum, are loosely linked to developments in other arenas, including the unilateral activities of major states (Keohane and Victor 2010). The remainder of the chapter is devoted to a brief summary of the largely complementary initiatives undertaken by these organisations as well as some of the more prominent unilateral actions on the part of key states such as the United States, the United Kingdom, France and Germany in the aftermath of the financial crisis. This survey of the broader political context of international tax regulation is necessary because, as was argued in Chapter 2, taxpayer behaviour and patterns of international tax compliance are ultimately shaped by a combination of international, regional and domestic policies.

UN Committee of Experts on International Cooperation in Tax Matters

The UN's involvement in international tax matters pre-dates the creation of the OECD in 1961 and can be traced back to the League of Nation's role in the drafting of the first double tax agreements in the inter-war years (Picciotto 1992). However by the 1950s the role and influence of the UN Fiscal Committee had begun to wane and it was eventually downgraded to the status of an ad hoc committee with limited membership and resources (Sharman 2006, 139). Over the ensuing years the committee's major contribution has been to draft an alternative model double tax agreement which was largely based on the dominant OECD standard but which allocated greater taxing powers to developing countries in receipt of foreign investment (reflecting the 'source' principle) rather than the OECD alternative (Chapter 1). However the UN's marginal role in international taxation began to change amid the HTC debate in the early 2000s as the OECD's reputation and legitimacy were challenged (Sharman 2006, 139–40). The resentment felt by secrecy jurisdictions regarding their regulation by an organisation of which they were not members, combined with a growing concern by the EU and G7 that the OECD's post-2002 information exchange regime would be ineffective, precipitated a move to reinvigorate the ad hoc UN International Tax Committee.

By November 2004 this campaign was successful to the extent that the UN committee was upgraded to the status of full committee (the Committee of Experts on International Cooperation in Tax Matters) with a modest secretariat under the direction of the UN Economic and Social Council (UN 2011, 4). In the aftermath of the financial crisis there have been further moves to expand the UN's role in international tax cooperation to improve the representation of developing countries. In specific terms a proposal to establish a standing intergovernmental commission on international tax cooperation is being considered by the Economic and Social Council (UN 2011). While it seems unlikely that the UN and its member states will commit the resources required to rival the OECD's work in the international tax arena, the UN Committee of Experts has served an important role in providing an alternative forum to the OECD. As was noted above, the UN has played a role in ensuring that issues such as automatic information exchange have remained on the international agenda, and perhaps more importantly, institutional rivalry between the OECD and the UN has forced the OECD to accommodate many of the concerns raised by its critics. The most striking example here has been the OECD's determination to increase participation of non-member states in its international tax programme (as of November 2011 the Global Forum had a membership of 101 following claims in early 2002 that the UN, with its universal membership, was the only organization that could legitimately set international tax standards).

The European Union

The governance of international taxation is complicated by the fundamentally divergent views and interests of national governments. Prominent among these have been simmering transatlantic tensions on tax matters between continental European welfare states on the one hand and the United States (and the UK) on the other. Given such cleavages, the EU is not only a major actor in relation to tax policy within the European Union but it also exerts significant influence at the global level through a combination of its formal membership of key organisations such as the OECD, as a powerful regional voting block and as an actor in its own right (Woodward 2009). It is not possible to provide a comprehensive account of the EU's post-financial crisis international tax initiatives, including the EU Code of Conduct on Business Taxation, progress towards implementation of the EU Savings Tax Directive and Common Consolidated Corporate Tax base as well as the use of the European Court of Justice to impose sanctions against jurisdictions who have been unwilling to implement the EU Anti-Money Laundering Directive (Rixen and Schwarz 2012; Stiglitz 2010, 114). However the Commission has also been active in supporting the Global Forum in numerous ways. The most significant development has been the EU's ECOFIN committee's decision to ensure all member states implement the OECD's standard for information exchange on request. This included a commitment preventing jurisdictions from withholding requested information on the basis that it was held by a bank or financial institution. Of greater significance is that the Commission has initiated a process for establishing automatic information exchange 'aimed at eventually ensuring unconditional exchange of information for eight categories of income and capital' (EU 2010; Murphy 2010). As was argued above, such proposals not only reinforce the progress that has been made via the Global Forum process, but put subtle pressure on the OECD to move towards adopting automatic information exchange as the new global standard.

The IMF and the World Bank Group

The IMF in conjunction with the Financial Stability Forum increased its monitoring of secrecy jurisdictions in the late 1990s. This collaboration resulted in the publication in 2000 of a list of countries which the IMF regarded as secrecy jurisdictions. Having established a list of secrecy jurisdictions the IMF intensified its monitoring and evaluation programme, including a series of 'staff assessments' of the regulation and transparency of secrecy jurisdictions (IMF 2008; Palan et al. 2010, 219–20). Since the onset of the financial crisis the G20 has been largely successful in establishing a clearer institutional division of labour between international financial institutions. As a consequence the IMF has largely concentrated its research efforts on issues of improving the transparency of complex financial instruments, leaving tax information exchange to the Global Forum (IMF 2009). Notwithstanding this new role, the IMF has continued to provide technical assistance to secrecy jurisdictions to help improve tax administration and compliance and has published provocative working papers reporting the size of the international tax evasion problem (Murphy 2010; Lane and Milesi-Ferretti 2010).

Reflecting the World Bank Group's (WBG) central role in development assistance, it too has broadened its traditional role of providing technical assistance aimed at improving domestic tax administration in developing countries to include support in negotiating and implementing tax information exchange agreements. On the enforcement front, the WBG has indicated that development assistance may be linked to recipient countries' compliance with Global Forum standards, providing an added incentive to comply with the standard (WBG 2011).

Unilateral Measures

Enhanced tax transparency and information exchange can be regarded as an indirect method of limiting international tax evasion because rather than prohibiting secrecy jurisdictions from engaging in certain tax practices and policies, the regime enhances the ability of tax authorities in relatively high-tax jurisdictions to implement unilateral anti-avoidance measures (Rixen 2008, 143). To this end it is important to consider progress that has been made in relation to information exchange alongside the unilateral anti-avoidance measures that have been introduced by key states in the international regime. While we assess the efficacy of these initiatives in more detail in Chapter 6, at this stage it is important to note that the financial crisis prompted increased unilateral measures to counter international tax evasion as well as multilateral responses, such as the Global Forum.

In the United States for example, since 2001 there has been a broad and multi-dimensional push to improve offshore compliance which has been quite independent of the OECD (Chapter 5). These efforts have intensified since 2008 through the aggressive prosecution of both individual and corporate cases of international tax evasion, including the long-running UBS case (Mathiason 2009), which has been complemented by voluntary disclosure schemes and more comprehensive legislative measures such as the US Foreign Accounts Tax Compliance Act (FATCA). Similarly, in the United Kingdom the Labour government of Gordon Brown stepped up its commitment to rein in international tax evasion over the course of 2008 and 2009 through leading the G20 initiatives described above and through unilateral strategies that included the instigation of a review into the financial arrangements and regulation of the UK's Crown Dependencies and various voluntary disclosure schemes (Watt 2009; Foot 2009).

As a consequence of acute fiscal pressures and high profile protests by civil society groups concerned about tax justice issues, the Conservative-Liberal Democrat government of David Cameron also seems committed to the issue of offshore tax enforcement, seeking to tax Swiss accounts held by UK residents (Chapter 6) as well as establishing a Treasury Select Committee to investigate corporate tax avoidance (Hawkes and Wearden 2011). However these initiatives have been undermined by the 'Hartnett Scandal' at Her Majesty's Revenue and Customs Service (HMRC) in 2011. On the other side of the English Channel both Germany and France have increased their offshore enforcement efforts.

Germany's political commitment to improving tax transparency assumed a new importance in February 2008 as a result of the 'Liechtenstein-LGT affair' in which German authorities purchased information relating to billions in undeclared savings held by German citizens in Liechtenstein's LGT Bank (Simonian 2009). The scandal resulted in a number of prosecutions as well as a commitment to ending tax evasion in Liechtenstein through unilateral measures and a determination to include the alpine principality in the EU Savings Directive. In an interesting development the French government, frustrated by the reluctance of various Caribbean financial centres to enter into and honour TIEAs unveiled a list of 18 non-cooperative jurisdictions which would be subjected to a 50 per cent withholding tax on interest and dividend payments (the standard rate is 15 per cent) until they complied with French demands (International Tax Review 2010). Indeed the French approach of imposing withholding penalties on non-compliant jurisdictions has also been adopted by Australia, Italy and, as is discussed in the following chapter, the United States, adding to the pressure on secrecy jurisdictions to improve tax transparency.

CONCLUSION: OUTLOOK, SUSTAINABILITY AND IMPACT

The OECD and the Global Forum's work, together with that of other international organisations described above, has arguably created the institutional foundations for improving tax transparency, but it is also important to recognise that there has been a good deal of complementary activity on the part of individual states which has been motivated by a desire to promote offshore compliance with domestic tax laws. Indeed while the OECD has been reluctant to impose sanctions for non-compliance this has not stopped countries such as France and organisations such as the FSB using OECD evaluations in their own separate enforcement activities.

Taken together this suggests that the financial crisis and its immediate aftermath represents something of a tipping point in the international tax regime. Yet any such conclusion by necessity must be qualified by two important sets of considerations. First, our analysis suggests that the ongoing viability of the regime is critically dependent on the continuing support of the key states in the regime, including the United States, the United Kingdom, France and Germany. As we saw during the early 2000s, without the committed political and financial support of these countries the Global Forum runs the risk of becoming a token symbolic gesture. The challenge is that as the immediacy of the financial crisis passes domestic political support for these measures in countries such as the United States will wane while the willingness of secrecy jurisdictions to comply may also abate. Given the importance of domestic politics in explaining the extent and sustainability of international tax cooperation the following chapter is devoted to a more in-depth analysis of the politics of international taxation in the critical cases of the United States and Switzerland.

The second set of considerations – which will be central to determining the success or otherwise of recent progress in relation to enhancing tax transparency – relate to the impact of the evolving regulatory regime on the behaviour of taxpayers, the international financial services industry and on the regulatory behaviour of secrecy jurisdictions themselves. While more time and detailed research is required to make a definitive assessment of the efficacy of the emerging international tax regime, Chapter 6 will describe the parameters of this task and make a preliminary assessment in terms of the progress that has been made to date.

REFERENCES

Avi-Yonah, Reuven (2009) 'The OECD Harmful Tax Competition Report: A Retrospective After a Decade', *Brooklyn Journal of International Law*, **34** (3), 783–95.

Bearce, David and Stacy Bondanella (2007) 'Intergovernmental Organizations. Socialization and Member-State Interest Convergence', *International Organization*, **61** (4), 703–33.

Beeson, Mark and Stephen Bell (2009) 'The G20 and International Economic Governance: Hegemony, Collectivism or Both?' *Global Governance*, **15** (1), 67–86.

Blyth, Mark (2002) *Great Transformations: Economic Ideas and Institutional Change in the Twentieth Century*, Cambridge: Cambridge University Press.

Checkel, Jeffrey T. (2005) 'International Institutions and Socialization in Europe: Introduction and Framework', *International Organization*, **59** (4), 801–26.

Christensen, John and Nicholas Shaxson (2010) 'Time to Black-List the White Wash', *Financial Times*, 18 November.

Collier, Ruth and David Collier (1991) *Shaping the Political Arena*, Princeton, NJ: Princeton University Press.

Crouch, Colin (2005) *Capitalist Diversity and Change: Recombinant Governance and Institutional Entrepreneurs*, Oxford: Oxford University Press.

Crouch, Colin (2011) *The Strange Non-Death of Neo-Liberalism*, Cambridge: Polity Press.

Eccleston, Richard, Peter Carroll and Aynsley Kellow (2010) 'Handmaiden to the G20? The OECD's Evolving Role in Global Governance', Working Paper, available at http://apsa2010.com.au/full-papers/pdf/APSA2010_0228.pdf (accessed March 2011).

Edelman, Murray (1977) *Political Language: Words that Succeed and Policies that Fail*, New York: The Institute for the Study of Poverty.

Eilstrup-Sangiovanni, Mette (2009) 'Varieties of Cooperation: Government Networks in International Security', in Miles Kahler (ed.), *Networked Politics: Agency, Power and Governance*, Ithaca: Cornell University Press, pp. 194–227.

EU (2010) 'Combating Tax Fraud: Agreement on Strengthened Mutual Assistance and the Exchange of Information', Council of the European Union 15094/10, Brussels, 7 December, available at http://europa.eu/rapid/pressReleasesAction. do?reference=PRES/10/279&format=DOC&aged=1&language=EN&guiLang uage=en (accessed July 2012).

Finnemore, Martha and Kathryn Sikkink (2001) 'Taking Stock: The Constructivist Research Program in International Relations and Comparative Politics', *Annual Review of Political Science*, 4, 391–416.

Foot, Michael (2009) *Final Report of the Independent Review of British Offshore Financial Centres*, London, HM Treasury, available at http://webarchive.natio nalarchives.gov.uk/+/http://www.hm-treasury.gov.uk/d/foot_review_main.pdf (accessed July 2012).

Garrett, Geoffrey (2010) 'G2 in G20: China, the United States and the World after the Global Financial Crisis', *Global Policy*, 1 (1), 29–39.

Gill, Stephen (2008) *Power and Resistance in World Order*, 2nd edn, London: Palgrave Macmillan.

Gill, Stephen (2010) 'The Global Organic Crisis', *Monthly Review*, February.

Gourevitch, Peter (1986) *Politics in Hard Times*, Ithaca: Cornell University Press.

G20 (2009a), *Declaration of Strengthening the Financial System*, London, G20, available at http://www.g20.utoronto.ca/2009/2009ifi.html (accessed July 2012).

G20 (2009b), *London Communiqué*, London, G20, available at http://www.eu-un. europa.eu/articles/fr/article_8622_fr.htm (accessed July 2012).

G20 (2009c), *Pittsburgh Communiqué*, Pittsburgh, G20, available at www.ft.com/c ms/s/0/5378959c-aa1d-11de-a3ce-00144feabdc0.html (accessed July 2012).

Hall, Ben, George Parker and Vanessa Houlder (2009) 'Stage Set for Tax Havens Battle', *Financial Times*, 1 April, available at http://www.ft.com/cms/s/0/843987 5c-1f00-11de-a748-00144feabdc0.html#axzz214kAZcfM (accessed July 2012).

Hall, Peter (1993) 'Policy Paradigms, Social Learning and the State: The Case of Economic Policymaking in Britain', *Comparative Politics*, **25** (3), 275–96.

Hallerberg, Mark, and Scott Basinger (1998) 'Internationalization and Changes in Tax Policy in OECD Countries: The Importance of Domestic Veto Players', *Comparative Political Studies*, 31 (3), 321–53.

Hawkes, Alex and Graeme Weardon (2011) 'MP's to Investigate Corporate Tax

Avoidance', *Guardian,* 28 March, available at http://www.guardian.co.uk/busin ess/2011/mar/28/mps-investigate-corporate-tax-avoidance (accessed July 2012).

Hay, Richard (2005) 'Beyond a Level Playing Field: Free(r) Trade in Financial Services', Paper presented at the STEP Symposium, 19–20 September, London.

Helleiner, Eric (2009) 'Special Forum: Crisis and the Future of Global Financial Governance', *Global Governance,* **15** (1), 21–8.

Helleiner, Eric and Stefano Pagliari (2010), 'The End of Self Regulation? Hedge Funds and Derivatives in Global Financial Governance', in Eric Helleiner, Stefano Pagliari and Hubert Zimmermann (eds), *Global Finance in Crisis: The Politics of International Regulatory Change,* Oxford: Routledge, 74–90.

Helleiner, Eric, Stefano Pagliari and Hubert Zimmermann (eds) (2010), *Global Finance in Crisis: The Politics of International Regulatory Change,* Oxford: Routledge.

Hillman, Jennifer (2010) 'Saving Multilateralism: Renovating the House of Global Economic Governance for the 21st Century', Brussels Forum Paper Series, The German Marshall Fund of the United States, Washington DC.

IMF (2008) 'Offshore Financial Centers (OFCs): IMF Staff Assessments', International Monetary Fund, Washington DC, available at http://www.imf.org/ external/np/ofca/ofca.asp (accessed July 2012).

IMF (2009) 'Lessons From the Crisis: IMF Urges Rethink Of How To Manage Global Systemic Risk', *Policy: IMF Survey Magazine,* 6 March, Washington DC: International Monetary Fund available at http://www.imf.org/external/pubs/ ft/survey/so/2009/pol030609a.htm (accessed July 2012).

IMF (2011) *Fiscal Monitor, September 2011,* available at http://www.imf.org/exter nal/pubs/ft/fm/2011/02/fmindex.htm (accessed October 2011).

International Tax Review (2010) 'A Time for Tax Transparency and Clarity', *International Tax Review,* **21** (3), 13–15.

Kay, Adrian (2006) *The Dynamics of Public Policy: Theory and Evidence,* Cheltenham, UK and Northampton, MA, USA: Edward Elgar.

Keohane, Robert and David Victor, (2010) 'The Regime Complex for Climate Change', Harvard Project on International Climate Agreements: Discussion Paper 10-33.

Kingdon, John (1984) *Agendas, Alternatives and Public Policy,* Boston, MA: Little Brown.

Kuran, Timur (1995) *Private Truths, Public Lies: The Social Consequences of Preference Falsification,* Cambridge, MA: Harvard University Press.

Lane, Phillip. R and Gian Milesi-Ferretti (2010) 'Cross-Border Investment in Small International Financial Centres', IMF Working Paper 10/38, International Monetary Fund, Washington DC..

Lesage, Dries (2010) 'The G20 and Tax Havens: Maintaining the Momentum', Paper presented at the conference 'Governing the Global Economy: The Role of the G20', Munk School of Global Affairs, University of Toronto, 18 June.

Lesage, Dries and Mattias Vermeiren (2011) 'Neo-Liberalism at a Time of Crisis: The Case of Taxation', *European Review,* **19** (1), 43–56.

Mathiason, Nick (2009) 'New Threat for UK's Offshore Havens: Tax', *Guardian,* 28 October, available at http://www.guardian.co.uk/business/2009/oct/28/tax-more-tax-havens-told (accessed July 2012).

Meinzer, Markus (2012) 'The Creeping Futility of the Global Forum's Peer Reviews', Tax Justice Network Tax Justice Briefing – March 2012, available at http://www.taxjustice.net/cms/upload/GlobalForum2012-TJN-Briefing.pdf (accessed March 2012).

Mitchell, Daniel (2000) 'An OECD Proposal to Eliminate Tax Competition Would Mean Higher Taxes and Less Privacy,' Heritage Foundation Backgrounder #1395, available at http://www.heritage.org/Research/Reports/2000/09/OECD -Proposal-To-Eliminate-Tax-Competition (accessed July 2012).

Murphy, Richard (2010) 'Of Course There are Trillions Offshore – and Now the IMF Recognises the Fact', Tax Research UK, 15 March, available at http://www. taxresearch.org.uk/Blog/category/imf/ (accessed July 2012).

OECD (1997) *Revised Standard Magnetic Format for Automatic Information Exchange*, Paris: OECD, available at http://www.oecd.org/dataoecd/7/63/40499 533.pdf (accessed July 2012).

OECD (2000) *Improving Access to Bank Information for Tax Purposes*, Paris: OECD, available at http://www.oecd.org/dataoecd/3/7/2497487.pdf (accessed July 2012).

OECD (2002) *Model Agreement on Exchange of Information on Tax Matters*, Paris: OECD, available at http://www.oecd.org/dataoecd/15/43/2082215.pdf (accessed July 2012).

OECD (2006) *Manual on the Implementation of Exchange and Information Provisions for Tax Purposes*, Paris: OECD, available at http://www.oecd.org/ dataoecd/16/23/36647823.pdf (accessed July 2012).

OECD (2010) *Tax Co-Operation 2009: Towards a Level Playing Field: 2009 Assessment by the Global Forum on Transparency and Exchange of Information*, Paris: OECD, available at http://www.oecd.org/dataoecd/25/24/44429779.pdf (accessed July 2012).

OECD (2011a) *The Global Forum on Transparency and Exchange of Information for Tax Purposes: Information Brief* (2011) Paris: OECD, available at http://www. oecd.org/dataoecd/32/45/43757434.pdf (accessed July 2012).

OECD (2011b) *Implementing the Tax Transparency Standards: A Handbook for Assessors and Jurisdictions – Second Edition*, Global Forum on Transparency and Exchange of Information, Paris: Organisation of Economic Development and Cooperation.

OECD (2012) *Automatic Exchange of Information. What it is, How it Works, Benefits, What Remains to be Done*, available at http://www.oecd.org/ctp/exchan geofinformation/AEOI_FINAL_with%20cover_WEB.pdf (accessed July 2012).

Palan, Ronen, Richard Murphy and Christian Chavagneux (2010) *Tax Havens: How Globalization Really Works*, Ithaca: Cornell University Press.

Picciotto, Sol (2011) *Regulating Global Corporate Capitalism*, Cambridge: Cambridge University Press.

Picciotto, Sol (1992) *International Business Taxation: A Study in the Internationalization of Business Regulation*, London: Weidenfeld and Nicolson.

Pierson, Paul (2000) 'Increasing Returns, Path Dependence, and the Study of Politics', *American Political Science Review*, **94** (2), 251–67.

Pierson, Paul (2004) *Politics in Time: History, Institutions and Social Analysis*, Princeton, NJ: Princeton University Press.

Polsky, Andrew J. (2000) 'When Business Speaks: Political Entrepreneurship, Discourse, and Mobilization in American Partisan Regimes', *Journal of Theoretical Politics*, **12** (4), 451–72.

Porter, Tony (2010) 'Why International Institutions Matter in the Global Credit Crisis', *Global Governance*, **15** (1), 3–8.

Reinhart, Carmen M. and Kenneth S. Rogoff (2009) 'The Aftermath of Financial Crises', *American Economic Review*, **99** (2), 466–72.

Rixen, Thomas (2008) *The Political Economy of International Tax Governance: Transformations of the State*, New York: Palgrave Macmillan

Rixen, Thomas and Peter Schwarz (2012) 'The Effectiveness of the EU Savings Directive – Evidence from Four Countries', *Journal of Common Market Studies*, **50** (1), 151–68.

Rumsfeld, Donald (2002) 'DoD News Briefing, February 12 2002', available at http://www.defense.gov/transcripts/transcript.aspx?transcriptid=2636 (accessed January 2011).

Schifferes, Steve (2009) 'UK Economy 'Faces Decade of Pain', BBC News, 23 April, available at http://news.bbc.co.uk/2/hi/business/8015063.stm (accessed July 2012).

Sharman, Jason C. (2006) *Havens in a Storm: the Struggle for Global Tax Regulation*, Ithaca: Cornell University Press.

Simonian, Haig (2009) 'Liechtenstein in Talks with Germany on Transparency', *Financial Times*, 12 August.

Sinclair, Timothy (2010a) 'Global Financial Crises', in Mark Beeson and Nick Bisley (eds), *Issues in 21st Century World Politics*, Basingstoke: Palgrave, 214–24.

Sinclair, Timothy (2010b) 'Round Up the Usual Suspects: Blame and the Sub-Prime Crisis', *New Political Economy*, **15** (1), 91–107.

Spencer, David (2005) 'The Cost of Capital Flight', *Accountancy, Business and the Public Interest*, **4** (2), 151–60, available at http://visar.csustan.edu/aaba/Spencer 2005.pdf (accessed July 2012).

Spencer, David (2010) 'International Tax Cooperation: Centrifugal vs. Centripetal Forces: Part 1', *Journal of International Taxation*, **21** (4), 38–51.

Stiglitz, Joseph E. (2010) *The Stiglitz Report: Reforming the International Monetary and Financial Systems in the Wake of the Global Crisis*, New York: The New Press.

Stone, Deborah (1997) *Policy Paradox: The Art of Political Decision Making*, New York: W.W. Norton and Company.

Streeck, Wolfgang and Kathleen Thelen (2005) 'Introduction: Institutional Change in Advanced Political Economies', in Wolfgang Streeck and Kathleen Thelen (eds), *Beyond Continuity: Institutional Change in Advanced Political Economies*, Oxford: Oxford University Press.

Tarullo, Daniel K. (2008) 'Banking on Basel: The Future of International Financial Regulation', Peterson Institute for International Economics, Washington DC.

Thelen, Kathleen (2002) 'How Institutions Evolve: Insights from Comparative-Historical Analysis', in James Mahoney and Dietrich Rueschemeyer (eds), *Comparative Historical Analysis in the Social Sciences*, New York: Cambridge University Press, pp. 208–40.

UN (2011) 'Strengthening of International Arrangements to Promote International Cooperation in Tax Matters', Report of the Economic and Security Council: E/2011/76, United Nations Economic and Social Council, 18 March, available at http://www.un.org/esa/ffd/tax/SGR_InstitutionalArrangements_AUV.pdf (accessed July 2012).

Watt, Nicholas (2009) 'Brown Targets Switzerland in Global Tax Haven Crackdown', *Guardian*, 19 February, available at http://www.guardian.co.uk/business/2009/feb/19/gordon-brown-tax-avoidance-switzerland (accessed July 2012).

Watt, Nicholas, Larry Elliot, Julian Borger and Ian Black (2009) 'G20 Declares Door Shut on Tax Havens', *Guardian*, 19 February, available at http://www. guardian.co.uk/business/2009/feb/19/gordon-brown-tax-avoidance-switzerland (accessed July 2012)

WBG (2011) 'Policy on the Use of Offshore Financial Centers in World Bank Group Private Sector Operations *Application to IFC Operations*', International Finance Corporation: World Bank Group, 11 October, available at www1.ifc. org/wps/wcm/connect/.../IFC_OFC_Policy.docx?MOD=AJPERES (accessed July 2012).

Webb, Michael (2004) 'Defining the Boundaries of Legitimate State Practice: Norms, Transnational Actors and the OECD's Project on Harmful Tax Competition', *Review of International Political Economy*, **11** (4): 787–827.

Woods, Ngaire (2010) 'Global Governance after the Financial Crisis: A New Multilateralism or the Last Gasp of the Great Powers?' *Global Policy*, **1** (1), 51–63.

Woodward, Richard (2009) *The Organisation for Economic Co-Operation & Development*, London: Routledge.

Wouters, Jan, Steven Sterkx and Tim Corthaut (2010) 'The International Financial Crisis, Global Financial Governance and the European Union', Working Paper No. 52 – September, Leuven Centre for Global Governance Studies, Belgium.

5. The domestic politics of international tax cooperation in the United States and Switzerland

Effective global governance is critically dependent on the support of key states, or a coalition of leading powers, especially when the governance problem concerned resembles what in Chapter 2 was defined as a collaboration problem (Rixen 2008; Rosenzweig 2011). Given that international tax governance clearly exhibits these characteristics, together with the fact that political support for international tax cooperation among key actors in the regime has fluctuated in recent years, it is necessary to analyse the ways in which domestic political variables influence state interests and policy preferences in the international tax arena (Drezner 2007). This chapter provides important insights into the domestic politics of international tax cooperation through case studies of two of the most significant states in the international tax regime, the United States and Switzerland. These two cases have been selected on the basis of the historical analysis presented in Chapters 1 and 3. This analysis highlighted the fact that the United States frequently played a critical leadership role in international tax cooperation during the twentieth century by virtue of its position as the world's largest and most powerful economy, hosting the world's most significant capital markets, but also because it is the largest financial contributor to the OECD (Woodward 2009; Carroll and Kellow 2011, 128–33). Given this combination of structural power and historical leadership within the regime, Chapter 3 concluded that US support is best regarded as being a necessary but insufficient condition for effective international tax cooperation and, as such, it is important to assess the relationship between domestic politics and changing US international tax policy preferences.

As we turn to the question of regime compliance and effectiveness it is also important to assess the domestic political responses to the prospect of greater international tax transparency within what have traditionally been regarded as secrecy jurisdictions. For example, what are the domestic political and financial implications of any international commitment to increase transparency and to end bank secrecy? Do affected financial interests regard compliance as inevitable, or are they actively trying to undermine the regime at the domestic and/or international levels and with what effect? The second half of this chapter explores these questions in relation to the critical case of Switzerland, because of the size and sophistication of its private banking industry but also in response to the historical fact that failure to secure credible Swiss compliance with any international tax agreement has the potential to threaten the legitimacy of the entire regime. In short, the extent and durability of Swiss support for international tax cooperation is central to its long-term political viability.

THE DOMESTIC POLITICS OF INTERNATIONAL TAXATION IN THE UNITED STATES

The United States played a central leadership role in the development and implementation of the international economic architecture associated with the post-World War II Bretton Woods settlement. In the case of international taxation this role actually dates back to the 1920s when US commercial interests prompted the American government to take an active role in the League of Nations' attempt to develop a model bilateral tax treaty to prevent the double taxation of international business transactions (Picciotto 1992). However there was little interest in the potential risks associated with international tax avoidance until the 1960s (Eden and Kudrle 2005, 110). Indeed post-war US administrations actively used tax concessions to encourage their banks to establish offshore operations to increase the reach of American financial interests and as part of a broader reconstruction and development strategy (Picciotto 2011, 247).

This benign attitude towards the use of offshore jurisdictions for tax purposes started to change in the early 1960s as US tax officials began to appreciate the rapid growth in international tax evasion. As outlined in Chapter 1, early unilateral measures included Controlled Foreign Company (CFC) provisions introduced in 1962 which attempted to tax US-owned and controlled corporations registered in low tax jurisdictions as if they were resident in the United States for income tax purposes (Eden and Kudrle 2005, 110). Over the course of the 1960s and 1970s similar unilateral anti-avoidance measures relating to transfer pricing, thin capitalisation, treaty shopping and extending CFC provisions to trusts and other non-corporate entities were introduced (Picciotto 1992; Doggart 1997). Despite these initiatives, all the evidence suggested that these unilateral measures largely failed to address the growing problem of international tax evasion in the face of increased economic liberalisation and the exponential growth of transnational business and finance. For example, a US Treasury study published in 1981 found that bank-owned international deposits held in secrecy jurisdictions increased by 30-fold between 1968 and 1978 (cited in Picciotto 2011, 239).

This growing concern about the impact of offshore tax evasion, combined with the deteriorating fiscal conditions within the United States over the course of the 1970s, promoted the first comprehensive review of secrecy jurisdictions and their impact on the US tax system, which was published by the IRS in 1981 (IRS 1981). The so-called 'Gordon Report' (after author Richard Gordon) clearly described the extent of the 'offshore problem' and provided a series of recommendations in order to address it (for a summary see Eden and Kudrle 2005, Table 3). The most significant recommendation contained within the report so far as this study is concerned was a conclusion that the integrity of the United States tax system was critically dependent on the IRS being able to access information regarding the offshore assets of US residents and that this could only be achieved through the inclusion of robust information exchange provisions in all future tax treaties. At the level of process, the report tacitly accepted that unilateral actions were unlikely to be as effective as coordinated international action, and as a consequence, the United States gradually started promoting its anti-evasion provisions in the international arena through both the OECD and other forums. In the short term, and like the waning commitment of the United States to the HTC initiative in the 2001, the publication of the Gordon Report (commissioned by the Carter Administration) coincided with the incoming Reagan Administration which had little interest in implementing its recommendations (Shaxon 2011, 117).

There may be a deep-seated opposition in the United States to expanding the fiscal powers of the state (Ring 2009, 170), but historically it is important to recognise that insofar as international taxation is concerned, the United States has traditionally taken a lead role in the development of anti-avoidance provisions and promoting them internationally. In contrast, the United Kingdom has been more reluctant to regulate secrecy jurisdictions owing to the City of London's reliance on Britain's offshore dependencies as a tax effective way of attracting and managing capital (Shaxon 2011, 68–9). Yet beneath these national-level generalisations the domestic politics of international taxation is more nuanced and complex. Successive US administrations might have demonstrated a commitment to preventing the most egregious forms of international tax evasion and avoidance, but this belies deep-seated interests and tensions within the United States policy community and government itself. While the IRS and federal prosecutors have a long held interest in improving offshore compliance, the same could not be said for Wall Street and the financial sector or the corporations and wealthy clients they service, who have a symbiotic relationship with Caribbean secrecy jurisdictions such as the Cayman Islands and the Bahamas (Palan 1998). Given these divisions and the fragmented nature of the US political system, it is perhaps more accurate to portray the international tax policy arena as consisting of competing coalitions of government agencies, Congressional actors, and supporters from business and civil society groups, each trying to influence executive government and US policy (Heclo 1978).

These domestic cleavages and their impact on international tax policy in the United States became apparent after the publication of the Gordon Report when domestic business interests successfully argued that features of the United States tax code were inhibiting the ability of US firms to attract foreign investment. A critical development, which highlighted the competitive dimension of international tax policy, was the United Kingdom government's decision to abolish withholding taxes on payments to non-resident investors. Fearing that this would give the City of London a competitive advantage, the United States government followed suit in 1984, resulting in a situation where the United States and the United Kingdom were emulating some of the strategies associated with more traditional tax havens in order to attract capital (Picciotto 2011, 14). At a theoretical level this highlights the claims originally made by Gourevitch (1978, chapter 2) that changing circumstances in the international economy can shape domestic political interests and policy priorities.

As we shall see in the pages that follow, competing needs and interests within the United States tax policy community continue to drive a 'two-track' strategy whereby revenue raising agencies try to maximise the tax paid on the offshore assets of United States residents, while the Treasury and Wall Street resist any measures that undermine the ability of US banks and investment managers to attract foreign capital. This fundamental tension is at the core of many of the inconsistencies and variations in United States policy over the past 25 years. For example, the United States was the fourth country to sign the OECD-EU Multilateral Convention on Mutual Administrative Assistance in Tax Matters in 1984 which provides for information exchange and joint investigation on a wide range of tax matters (Tanzi 1995, 85). Despite this apparent commitment to international tax cooperation, by the late 1980s the refusal to tax non-resident aliens with investments in the United States 'had become the single largest loophole in the international tax system which cost Latin American Governments billions of dollars in revenues' (McLure 1988). This desire to attract capital was taken a step further when the Clinton Administration introduced the Qualified Intermediary Program (QI) in 2000. The QI scheme required participating offshore banks (the 'Qualified Intermediaries') to report only the investments held by United States citizens. The logic of this outsourcing operation was that United States revenue authorities wanted information on their citizens' offshore investments but not on those of foreigners because if the IRS held information relating to foreign investments in the United States then the IRS may be obliged to provide this information to the foreign investor's country of residence under treaty obligations (Spencer 2010a). Naturally banks that complied with the scheme were allowed to invest funds in the United States without incurring any withholding taxes, leading one former senior tax official to conclude 'The program was aimed at protecting the identity of foreigners while allowing them to invest in the US' (as quoted in Shaxon 2011, 120).

These competing interests, and the political tensions they created, were most clearly apparent in the domestic debate concerning United States support for the OECD's HTC initiative in late 1990s and early 2000s (described in Chapter 3). In this case the financial interests and allied groups such as the Centre for Freedom and Prosperity used the changing domestic political environment to mount a successful campaign to change United States international tax policy. While this was a decisive victory and brought the HTC initiative to its knees, it was by no means the end of the vigorous debate which has been ongoing in United States policy circles. Indeed the 9/11 terrorist attacks and the spectacular collapse of Enron in 2002, the United States' largest corporate failure at the time, would once again highlight the security, corporate governance and revenue risks associated with secrecy jurisdictions. The political pendulum was starting to turn.

The Rise of International Taxation as a Domestic Policy Issue

Security and corporate crises in the form of the 9/11 terrorist attacks and the collapse of Enron elevated international tax regulation from being a technical diplomatic issue to a point where policy concerning 'tax haven abuse' gained prominence on the overt political agenda (Wood 2005). Many commentators argue that the current push (2012) within the United States to improve international tax transparency can be traced back to the 2006 Senate Permanent Subcommittee on Investigations hearings on Tax Haven Abuse (United States Senate 2006), yet, as noted above, it is important to acknowledge that the Senate inquiry itself was motivated by concerns about the role of secrecy jurisdictions in terrorist financing and the 2002 collapse of the Enron corporation which had pioneered the use of offshore 'special purpose entities' to conceal debts and liabilities (Healy and Palepu 2003; Bingham 2008, 117).

The Senate hearings and subsequent investigation may have been triggered by the Enron collapse, but it soon evolved into a broader study of international tax abuse and the estimated $100 billion in revenue lost by the United States government through the non-disclosure of income earned each year in secrecy jurisdictions (US Senate 2008, 1). In addition to putting international taxation on the domestic policy agenda, the inquiry precipitated two significant developments which preceded the onset of the financial crisis.

First, in July 2008, as a consequence of increased surveillance and enforcement efforts over the previous two years, the Senate inquiry found evidence of major international banks based in secrecy jurisdictions directly marketing schemes to assist United States citizens evade their domestic tax obligations. Swiss bank UBS was initially singled out (although a major investigation into Credit Suisse was launched in July 2011) and was subject to a US grand jury investigation which identified 19 000 accounts holding an estimated US$17.9 billion in assets which had not been disclosed to the IRS (Bonzom 2011). When UBS executive Raoul Weil was finally indicted by a US court in late 2008 and the UBS management agreed to pay the United States government US$780 million in fines, the role of international banks and secrecy jurisdictions in international tax evasion had become a mainstream political issue in the United States, commanding headlines in the *New York Times* and other national media outlets (Browning 2008; Clark 2008). We will return to the Swiss response to the UBS case later in the chapter but now it is important to note the legislative responses that the Senate investigation prompted and their political consequences.

The findings of the Senate Permanent Subcommittee on Investigations have triggered a range of legislative proposals which have further enhanced awareness of offshore tax abuse. Advocates of improved tax and financial transparency had introduced legislative proposals with mixed success through most of the 1990s. Democratic Senator Carl Levin was a leading advocate of these causes having (largely unsuccessfully) proposed numerous anti-money laundering and tax haven bills and amendments in the Senate Banking Committee of which he was a member. Congressional support for anti-money laundering bills, including outlawing shell companies, was bolstered after 9/11 when the International Money Laundering Abatement and Anti-Terrorist Financing Act, together with the Patriot Act, was hastily signed into law on 21 October 2001 (Baker 2010). Yet despite this progress, as was outlined in Chapter 3, the Bush Administration had little interest in implementing more far-reaching anti-tax avoidance measures.

It was not until after the Senate Committee's 2006 report on offshore tax abuse was published that a small group of Congressional representatives sought to enshrine many of the committee's recommendations in legislation in the form of the Stop Tax Haven Abuse Act. While the bill, first introduced in February 2007 (S.681) and now in its third iteration, is yet to pass the House, its real significance lies in the fact that it was sponsored by long-time advocate of improved financial transparency, Senator Carl Levin (Dem-Michigan) and the then junior Illinois Senator Barack Obama. This legislative initiative ensured both that Obama was personally committed to ending the abuse of secrecy jurisdictions and that the issue received unprecedented publicity over the course of the 2008 Presidential campaign. The role of the Cayman Islands in international tax avoidance and evasion was subject to particular scrutiny, with Obama often citing the case of Ugland House, the registered address of some 19 000 companies which he described as 'Either this is the world's largest building or the world's largest tax scam' (Obama 2009). Since the 2008 Presidential election the Obama Administration has remained committed to the goal of improving tax transparency with Treasury Secretary Geithner (United States Senate 2009) affirming his 'Commitment to aggressively addressing the problem of offshore tax abuse' during his confirmation hearing, stating that 'If confirmed, this issue will be a high priority for the Treasury Department.' Perhaps the best evidence of the impact of President Obama's advocacy on the issue, at least among the Democratic caucus, is that the sponsorship of the second iteration of the End Tax Haven Abuse Act (HR-1265 – reintroduced in March 2009) increased from four members of the House in 2007 to 76 members in 2009. While HR-1265 did not progress beyond committee, a third version of the bill was introduced to the Senate in July 2011 (S-1346) to highlight the need to end offshore tax abuse as a part of a bi-partisan deficit reduction strategy.

The second element of the pre-crisis political mobilisation in relation to international tax issues has been the formation of a small number of public interest groups promoting a 'tax justice' agenda, whose profile has increased significantly since the early 2000s. While groups such as Tax Justice Network – USA, Citizens for Tax Justice and Global Financial Integrity have relatively meagre resources and capacity compared to the Centre for Freedom and Prosperity and the Heritage Foundation, they have been successful in highlighting the broader policy and financial consequences of international tax issues as well as building coalitions with a range of more established interest groups such as AFL-CIO and Public Citizen (author interview). The international tax policy arena may, as the academic literature suggests, still be dominated by financial actors, but the formation of nascent public interest groups in recent years has enhanced the viability of reform in American domestic politics (Eccleston 2000).

The Financial Crisis, the Obama Administration and United States Support for the International Tax Regime

Thus far we have noted how the renewed political commitment to enhanced tax transparency resulting from the Senate Permanent Subcommittee on Investigations and Barack Obama's rise to the Presidency largely preceded the acute phase of the financial crisis. Improving international tax transparency may have been on the policy agenda within the international tax policy community at this time, but the financial crisis transformed the politics of international tax reform in the United States in several significant ways.

Despite a growing awareness – prior to the financial crisis – among regulators, academics and some politicians of the increasingly significant, and potentially problematic, role of secrecy jurisdictions in the global economy, debate about how to regulate offshore finance was largely absent from the overt political agenda. This changed over the course of 2008 when it became increasingly apparent that the United States government's capacity to assess and regulate major financial institutions and the securities they issued and traded was being impeded by the opacity and lax regulatory standards of many secrecy jurisdictions (Levin and Coburn 2011). While most of the debate concerned the financial risks posed by the offshore 'shadow banking' system (Mosley 2009), at the level of domestic politics, American voters were coming to realise that secrecy jurisdictions were part of the problem that had precipitated the financial crisis and demanded that their elected representatives try to do something about it.

Not only did the poor financial regulation in secrecy jurisdictions contribute to the financial crisis, but this, combined with the ruthless exploitation by banks and other financial actors of the commercial advantages that could be achieved offshore, did a good deal to undermine the legitimacy of secrecy jurisdictions and global finance more generally. In 2001 and 2002 groups such as the Centre for Freedom and Prosperity were able to frame arguments against increased international tax cooperation which resonated with the American public. They argued that cooperation posed a threat to 'American sovereignty' and would 'limit tax competition' which in turn would lead to an expansion in the size of the state, threatening economic efficiency (Mitchell 2000). However, in the light of the financial crisis many of these arguments lost legitimacy among key segments of American voters, enhancing the political viability of proposed reforms. While there are no reliable longitudinal surveys to systematically assess the changes in United States public opinion in relation to offshore tax evasion over time, there is survey evidence to support the claim that awareness of the issues has increased since the onset of the financial crisis. For example, a June 2011 Pew Research survey found that 62 per cent of respondents believed 'that tax deductions to large corporations should be limited' in order to reduce the federal budget deficit (Pew 2011). Also, as noted in Chapter 1, the finding of a United States Government Accountability Office report published in late 2008 (GAO 2008a) that 83 of the 100 largest United States-listed firms operated subsidiaries in tax havens to reduce their United States income tax liability attracted significant media and political attention. This included articles in national broadsheets, such as the *New York Times*, highlighting the ways in which US corporate giants, such as GE, used offshore strategies to avoid paying any United States taxes at all, despite reporting multi-billion dollar profits (Kocieniewski 2011). Most recently President Obama has alluded to the aggressive use of offshore tax planning by many large US corporations, proposing a deficit reduction plan that seeks to 'eliminate tax loopholes that primarily go to the wealthiest taxpayers and biggest corporations – tax breaks that small businesses and middle-class families don't get' (Obama 2011). By the autumn of 2011 these sentiments were fuelling the grass-roots 'Occupy Wall Street' campaign, which seeks to 'stand against corporate greed, social inequality and other disparities between rich and poor' (Stelter 2011). Taken together this evidence suggests that the financial crisis has increased public awareness of the 'offshore problem' as well as undermining the legitimacy of offshore strategies among the American voting public. This is an example of the way in which an economic crisis can transform public sentiments, or the attitudes and beliefs held by ordinary citizens: 'the politicization of financial policies in the wake of the crisis has created societal pressures for far-reaching reform' (Zimmermann 2010, 172).

The impact of the financial crisis on prevailing norms and public sentiments relating to the offshore world has also been complemented by more instrumental concerns relating to the significant deterioration in United States public finances and the associated need to increase revenues without compromising economic growth. The combination of declining revenues and expensive fiscal stimulus packages and financial bailouts has resulted in almost unprecedented budget deficits and spiralling public debt. As has been noted previously, in the United States the federal deficit peaked at 12.8 per cent of GDP in 2009 while general government gross debt is expected to reach 85 per cent of GDP by 2014 (IMF 2011, 71). Similarly, in the United Kingdom an equally bleak deficit of £175 billion (10.3 per cent of GDP) was recorded in the 2009–10 financial year while other EU states such as Greece, Portugal, Spain and by late 2011 Italy, face fully fledged sovereign debt crises (Reinhart and Rogoff 2009). In an attempt to return public finances to a more sustainable footing, governments have been forced to impose new taxes, and have generally invested increased resources in tax enforcement and compliance (although the UK has been a notable exception). In this context initiatives designed to limit revenue losses through international tax evasion have been highlighted by the President's National Commission on Fiscal Responsibility and Reform as an efficient and politically palatable way of increasing revenue (Fiscal Commission 2010).

The financial crisis has not only undermined the legitimacy of offshore finance in the minds of the American public, but the subsequent rise in federal debt as a result of it has become a central issue in national politics following the debt ceiling crisis of mid-2011. The debt ceiling crisis was only resolved with the eleventh-hour passage of the Budget Control Act (2011) which outlines approximately US$900 billion in budget cuts over the next decade and established a Congressional 'Super Committee' charged with identifying a further US$1.5 trillion in budget savings through a combination of spending cuts and revenue increases over the next decade (*The Economist* 2011a). Such ideational and structural conditions are broadly supportive of proposals to promote international tax cooperation and offshore enforcement, but the political challenges associated with restoring United States public finances have been complicated by the political rise of the Tea Party faction within the Republican Party. By 2010 the Tea Party's libertarian and anti-state rhetoric and policies, including demands to limit government spending and to reduce and simplify taxes had become a central feature of Republican politics (Zernike 2010). Since the success of Tea Party endorsed candidates in 2010 Congressional mid-term elections and their subsequent influence in the Republican controlled House of Representatives, the views of the movement have had a significant impact on negotiations concerning the United States debt ceiling and subsequent deficit reduction strategies. For example, Republican House Leader John Boehner has consistently refused to support any proposals that involve 'job-killing tax increases' (Boehner 2011). Given the need to increase revenues without increasing domestic taxes or derailing the faltering recovery of the United States economy lawmakers have shown a good deal of interest in the Fiscal Commission's recommendation to review international tax arrangements with a view to increasing revenues (Kelechava 2010). Other initiatives consistent with this broad strategy include the IRS's move to improve international cooperation in relation to tax administration through assuming the chair of the OECD's Forum on Tax Administration as well as promoting voluntary disclosure schemes (discussed in Chapter 6) and the potentially revolutionary Foreign Account Tax Compliance Act which was passed by Congress in 2010 and is described in more detail below.

The financial crisis has put the issue of improved offshore regulation on the domestic political agenda in the United States and has enhanced the political viability of domestic measures or international agreements designed to achieve this objective. However, it is perhaps best to regard the period immediately following the crisis as a unique window of opportunity that may soon close. The legitimacy of financial interests may well have been eroded by the crisis but perversely, as the politics of financial reform associated with the Dodd-Frank Wall Street Reform Act (2010) demonstrated, the structural political power of finance may actually have increased as a result of the increasingly acute need to promote private investment to support both employment and the growing budget deficit. Indeed in early 2011 Washington insiders conceded that any international tax measures that were likely to have a detrimental effect on United States competitiveness or on US-based firms were off the political agenda for fear that such measures may compromise investment or employment (author interviews). These political constraints have driven a number of related developments over the course of 2009 and 2010. For example, almost all enforcement and anti-evasion measures designed to increase revenues have been aimed at individuals rather than firms because of an assumption that increasing effective tax rates for US-based firms would be detrimental to the economy. To this end, the IRS is aggressively promoting voluntary disclosure schemes designed to encourage individuals to disclose offshore investments (described in Chapter 6), while at the level of firms, consideration is being given to granting a 'deferral holiday' for United States firms who wish to repatriate profits from offshore (Gilleard 2011). While such a scheme may provide some short-term economic stimulus, critics argue that regular deferral holidays simply encourage firms to use aggressive offshore structures so that they periodically repatriate profits tax free (GAO 2008b, 13–14).

The most significant consequence of the ailing economic recovery in the United States and the associated imperative to encourage economic growth at all costs, is that it risks promoting a more instrumental and unilateral approach to international tax policy whereby the United States government is willing to pursue aggressive measures to maximise the tax paid by United States citizens with offshore assets while remaining reluctant to reciprocate by providing information on non-residents with assets in the United States for fear of deterring foreign investment. Reverting to this type of mercantilism is a perennial risk for any major economy struggling to recover from an economic crisis and while it may have short-term economic and political appeal, such a strategy seriously undermines the prospects for effective international cooperation. Indeed, given its central role in the international tax regime, a failure on the part of the United

States to fully comply with the Global Forum's new global standard on tax information exchange by refusing to provide information on the investments of non-residents held within the United States perhaps represents the greatest threat to enhanced international tax cooperation. In this regard it is important to note that the Foreign Account Tax Compliance Act 2010 (FATCA), the most significant American legislation in this arena over the last decade, has been developed outside the Global Forum framework. Given its potential impact on both United States offshore tax enforcement and its broader consequences for the politics of international tax cooperation, it is necessary to examine FATCA in more detail.

The Foreign Account Tax Compliance Act

In July 2010 President Obama signed the Foreign Account Tax Compliance Act (FATCA) into law after Congress passed the legislation with no hearing and little fanfare (Michel and Rosenbloom 2011). Following the Congressional investigations into offshore tax abuse described above and the high profile UBS case, there was a growing consensus in Washington that broad-based statutory measures were required to complement existing enforcement efforts. When combined with the fact that FATCA was presented as a revenue-raising provision within a broader job creation bill (the Unemployment Compensation Extension Act 2010 – HR 4213) the legislation attracted remarkably little attention (Quinn 2011; US Congress 2011). In contrast to these humble beginnings, FATCA is increasingly being described by lawyers and accountants as the 'The most extensive extraterritorial reach of US tax enforcement in history' (Scott and Rosenbloom 2011, 709), while being hailed by advocates in favour of enhanced offshore regulation as 'A major step toward encouraging foreign governments to implement automatic exchange, thereby transforming the international financial architecture' (Spencer 2010b, 64). Given that the phased implementation of the FATCA legislation will not commence until 2013, a good deal of uncertainty remains about its precise impact and effectiveness (Browning 2011). Despite this uncertainty there is a broad consensus that the current legislation has the potential to transform international tax compliance and potentially undermine the existing tax information exchange regime being developed and implemented by the Global Forum.

FATCA has many unique features which are a product of the domestic political and policy tensions that are shaping United States international tax policy in the aftermath of the financial crisis. In common with most international enforcement policies FATCA aims to assist the IRS to obtain information relating to the offshore investments and savings of

United States tax residents. In contrast to most regimes, the legislation does not seek to create international agreements or treaties between states, but seeks to force foreign financial institutions to reveal information concerning accounts held by United States tax residents. Requiring financial institutions rather than foreign tax authorities to provide tax and financial information amounts to an extension of the existing Qualified Intermediary Program introduced in 2001 (discussed above) and has a number of consequences (Tax Justice Network 2010). The legislation, which requires financial institutions automatically to provide information relating to United States citizens has a number of advantages for the US tax authorities. First, it effectively transfers the administrative costs associated with requesting and gathering tax information on US citizens on to financial institutions as part of the price of doing business in the United States. Second, and more controversially, critics of both the QI regime and of FATCA argue that the approach is designed to ensure that financial institutions only provide financial information relating to United States (as opposed to foreign) tax residents to the United States government. This, so it is argued, is to protect the identity of non-resident investors by ensuring that the United States government does not hold financial information pertaining to foreigners who hold assets in the United States and therefore is not obliged to exchange this tax information with foreign tax authorities under the ever expanding treaty and TIEA network. If these fears are realised and the US fails to reciprocate effectively by providing adequate information pertaining to non-resident investors in the United States then this clearly represents a major risk to international tax cooperation.

Before exploring the potential political risks associated with FATCA it is first necessary to assess whether international financial institutions are likely to comply with the legislation and its likely effectiveness. The United States enforcement strategy is based on imposing a 30 per cent withholding tax on all United States sourced income generated by foreign financial institutions which do not provide tax and income data on the offshore assets of United States citizens (Michel and Rosenbloom 2011, 710). Despite industry estimates that large banks will incur start up compliance costs of between US$100 and $200 million per institution, most commentators expect major international banks to comply with the standard because their business is so critically dependent on access to US financial markets (Meek 2011; author interview). While this strategy is likely to be effective in the case of the United States, it is only available to leading financial powers as firms would not acquiesce to the governments of non-core economies making such demands (Shambaugh 1999; Drezner 2002). So while global banks and investment houses will comply with FATCA it is arguably a coercive strategy that cannot be replicated by small jurisdictions and is therefore unlikely to serve as the foundation for a global standard.

Perhaps the greatest risk associated with FATCA is that it has the potential to undermine the reciprocity and cooperation associated with the Global Forum process (Spencer 2010b, 63). If the United States pursues the FATCA without supporting similar initiatives from other jurisdictions then there is a real risk that cooperation will give way to conflict and rival standards, seriously undermining the progress that has been achieved in recent years. Already there is growing concern that FATCA perpetuates and perhaps exacerbates the double standards in United States international tax policy by seeking to provide United States authorities with information about its citizens while still providing de facto bank secrecy for foreigners who invest in the United States (Tax Justice Network 2010). Indeed opposition to FATCA both in the international banking community and among non-US tax authorities has been growing, with FATCA being described by one commentator as another 'example of strong-armed American law enforcement imposing its will on other countries without their consent'. Beyond its impact on United States offshore enforcement efforts, the critical test for FATCA will be the way in which foreign governments respond to the legislation; there is growing speculation that some jurisdictions may retaliate by enacting their own versions of the regime while some Asian commentators believe that the Chinese government and by implication Chinese firms and financial institutions may simply ignore the legislation: 'Daring the US to invoke a 30% withholding tax on the principle financiers of the US deficit' (Michel and Rosenbloom 2011, 711).

Despite these concerns about the implications of FATCA for international tax enforcement and cooperation, developments in early 2012 concerning the formation of an intergovernmental agreement on expanding the FATCA framework to additional jurisdictions provide some cause for optimism (UK Treasury 2012). If implemented the proposed intergovernmental agreement announced between the United States, France, Germany, Italy, Spain and the United Kingdom would involve the United States reciprocating by providing European signatories with tax and financial information pertaining to their tax residents' offshore holdings. This proposed expansion of the FATCA framework is a significant development for the international tax regime and has the potential to serve as the basis for the automatic exchange of tax and financial information that tax justice NGOs have long been seeking. On the other hand, it is important to note that for a host of practical and political reasons the United States and other key European states may not be willing to extend this regime to smaller secrecy jurisdictions and other developing states, potentially undermining its potential as an international standard.

A New Unilateralism?

The sustainability and effectiveness of the international tax regime is critically dependent on United States support and leadership. Indeed since the 1960s the broad contours of international tax cooperation have been defined by changing US policy preferences. The analysis of US domestic politics concerning international taxation presented above provides some cause for optimism, with the financial crisis reinforcing and legitimising the Obama Administration's established agenda of addressing offshore tax abuse. However, it is also important to note that there are increasingly powerful countervailing forces acting against international cooperation. At the level of electoral politics, the rise of the Tea Party movement and the success of Tea Party aligned Republican candidates at the 2010 mid-term elections represents a major constraint on the Obama Administration's fiscal strategy, with Republicans maintaining their majority in the House of Representatives after the 2012 Congressional elections there is likely to be ongoing opposition to any proposals to increase the tax burden on US citizens and firms. Less obvious, but perhaps more significant, is the way in which the faltering US economic recovery and the associated determination of United States policymakers to promote employment and investment has increased the structural power of American business. In the current political environment there is very little support from either Republicans or Democrats for increasing the tax burden on business for fear that it may undermine the fragile economic recovery. In historical terms, we seem to be entering a phase where corporate interests once again enjoy a privileged position in the international tax debate, yet both financial need and public sentiments are supportive of enhanced cooperation and transparency.

One interpretation of these competing political imperatives is that they are contributing to a continuation of what Braithwaite and Drahos (2000, 131) describe as a 'double game' whereby 'From time to time they talk up the need to be tough on wealthy individuals and the need for more aggressive enforcement of the rules. [Yet] Covertly, they play the tax haven game . . . in effect offering arrangements facilitating the evasion of laws of other countries.' In the current context US authorities remain committed to improving offshore compliance for United States citizens, while also attempting to maintain and enhance the tax competitiveness of the United States as a financial centre and investment destination. One example of this 'double game' to date can be found in the structure and rationale of the FATCA, depending on whether there is genuine commitment to expand the regime, similarly the reluctance to end onshore bank secrecy in a number of US states is also consistent with this approach (Sharman 2011). The risk associated with this 'double game' strategy is that if US policy is motivated by an instrumental concern with improving offshore tax compliance without a commitment to reciprocity and sharing tax information with foreign tax administrations this may undermine the fragile commitment to enhanced tax cooperation and to 'establishing a level playing field' which is central to the Global Forum process. It is difficult to make a definitive assessment of the factors driving contemporary US international tax policy but the evidence suggests that the United States is only willing to support the Global Forum and other multilateral initiatives to the extent that they are congruent with their own immediate policy interests, such as improving the IRS's capacity to tax US residents' offshore holdings. In this sense the international tax regime is at a critical juncture. A great deal has been achieved in terms of promoting and institutionalising international tax cooperation since the onset of the financial crisis. On the other hand, the political and economic consequences of the crisis are also fostering a new unilateralism informed by a mercantilist logic and motivated by domestic political imperatives. As a joint OECD, UN and WTO report on trade and investment concluded in November 2010 there are 'signs of intensifying protectionist pressures, dark clouds that are being driven by persistent high levels of unemployment in many G20 countries, macroeconomic imbalances between them, and tensions over foreign exchange rates' (OECD 2010, 4; Wolf 2010).

THE DOMESTIC POLITICS OF INTERNATIONAL TAXATION IN SWITZERLAND

Thus far we have argued that the effectiveness and sustainability of international tax cooperation is critically dependent on the support of key states in the international tax regime such as the United States (Drezner 2007). Moreover, given that the governance of international tax avoidance is akin to a collaboration problem, in which individual secrecy jurisdictions have an incentive to refuse to exchange information which in turn may undermine the entire regime (Chapter 2), it is also important to evaluate the domestic politics of international taxation within key secrecy jurisdictions. For example, what are the domestic political and financial implications of any international commitment to increased transparency and ending bank secrecy? Do affected financial interests regard compliance as inevitable, or are they actively trying to undermine the regime at the domestic and/or international levels and with what effect? The answers to these questions will vary both between secrecy jurisdictions and across time, however the remainder of this chapter focuses specifically on the Swiss case for three reasons.

First, the Swiss case is critical to the effectiveness of any attempt to control international tax evasion because of the size and sophistication of its private banking industry. It is estimated that Swiss banks manage between US$2 and US$5 trillion, or up to one third of the world's private wealth (Swiss Bankers Association 2009; Mathiason 2009; OECD 2011, 15; Boston Consulting Group 2011). Second, not only is Switzerland arguably the world's largest and most important secrecy jurisdiction, but the size and maturity of the financial sector means there is a high likelihood of staunch and effective domestic political resistance to any international attempts to undermine Swiss financial interests. Indeed, as the literature on global governance suggests, controversial international policies tend to meet with more political resistance at the domestic level than in the international arena (Underdal 1998; Hooghe and Marks 2009).

Finally, the Swiss case is also critical because not only is there likely to be staunch political resistance from the banking sector, but, as was demonstrated in Chapter 3, given Switzerland's membership of the OECD, a lack of credible Swiss compliance with any international agreement has the potential to threaten the legitimacy of the entire regime. In the words of one senior tax official from an OECD member state 'Swiss compliance is the key to the success or otherwise of the Global Forum process. Not only would any agreement lack legitimacy without Swiss support but the Swiss will also push to make sure that other haven jurisdictions also comply to ensure that they are not at a competitive disadvantage' (author interview 2010). In short, the extent and durability of Swiss support for international tax cooperation is central to its long-term political viability.

The Evolution of Swiss Banking

Chapter 1 described how the Swiss pioneered bank secrecy in the late nineteenth century, noting the successful strategy of providing a safe haven for wealthy Europeans seeking to avoid growing tax obligations and other financial risks in their home countries (Palan 2003, 115; Chaikin 2005). By 1934 the Swiss Banking Act provided a statutory basis for bank secrecy at a national level, raising concerns at the League of Nations that the Swiss were profiting at the expense of tax authorities in neighbouring countries (Palan et al. 2010, 119–21; Rixen 2008, 120). The success of the Swiss model of providing discreet yet reliable private banking services designed to allow wealthy investors to hold their wealth and income-earning assets offshore and effectively hidden from tax authorities was soon emulated by

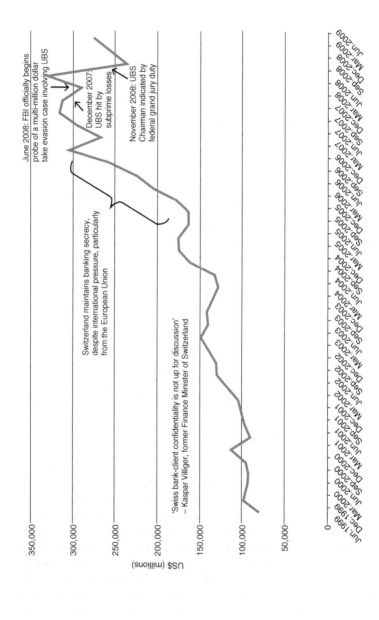

Source: Hollingshead (2010).

Figure 5.1 Foreign funds held in Swiss Banks, 1999–2009

other jurisdictions both in Europe and beyond in the second half of the twentieth century.

The threat that Switzerland posed and continues to pose to tax enforcement in neighbouring countries has led in more recent years to increasing diplomatic pressure by the EU and the United States. Yet the significance of the industry to the Swiss economy has ensured that successive governments have remained fiercely protective of bank secrecy. Not only has the banking sector accounted for between 7 per cent and 10 per cent of GDP in recent years but the sustained foreign inflow into Swiss banks has resulted in lower domestic interest rates, making borrowing cheaper for other businesses and households (Logutenkova 2012). When combined with currency stability and an unsurpassed reputation as an expert, well regulated and reliable financial services provider, Switzerland has continued to attract offshore funds despite growing competition from rival jurisdictions such as Luxembourg and the Netherlands. Indeed Swiss bankers have forged innovative partnerships with jurisdictions such as the Channel Islands and Liechtenstein to provide clients with extra layers of protection from tax authorities (Palan 2003, 136–7). When forced to comply with international agreements designed to stamp out illegal money laundering and terrorist financing the Swiss allowed criminal investigations into such illicit activities to pierce the veil of bank secrecy while continuing to maintain that tax evasion and avoidance was an administrative, rather than a criminal, matter and should remain subject to strict bank secrecy provisions. This reputation for providing private banking services, combined with a fierce determination to protect bank secrecy, resulted in offshore deposits held by Swiss banks increasing by an estimated 250 per cent between March 2001 and March 2008 (Hollingshead 2010, 24; see Figure 5.1).

The Financial Crisis, UBS and Growing International Pressure

In Chapter 3 it was shown how Swiss authorities successfully resisted the OECD HTC regime and were fighting a determined battle to minimise the impact of the EU Savings Directive which aimed to establish a system of automatic exchange of tax information relating to savings income derived from bank accounts held in both EU member states and neighbouring jurisdictions such as Switzerland (European Commission 2011). Faced with the prospect of EU sanctions, in late 2004 the Swiss agreed to impose a 15 per cent withholding tax (to be transferred to the foreign investors' 'home' tax administration) on interest income earned by residents of EU member states in return for maintaining the veil of bank secrecy. Despite this strident and largely effective defence of bank secrecy, by 2008 the political tide had turned to the extent that established Swiss banking practices were under direct threat. The main catalyst for this unprecedented scrutiny of Swiss bank secrecy was the so-called UBS case.

UBS, or the Union Bank of Switzerland as it was known until the late 1990s, was founded in the 1860s and by the 1990s had become the second largest bank in Switzerland, offering a full range of retail, commercial and investment banking and wealth management services (Ipsen 1996). When UBS merged with the Swiss Bank Corporation in 1998 not only did it create the world's largest bank outside Japan, but the newly merged entity also embarked on an aggressive expansion into the United States market (Tagliabue 1997). As part of this strategy UBS spent an estimated US$700 million hiring established United States bankers and wooing their wealthy clients and by 2004 had 'become the world's biggest money manager for the rich' (*New York Times* 2004). What was less well appreciated at the time was the extent to which the newly established US-based wealth management division was trading off its ability to offer bank secrecy to assist wealthy Americans evade their United States tax obligations (US Senate 2008).

The UBS case broke in July 2008 when the US Senate Permanent Subcommittee on Investigations released a report which not only estimated that offshore abuses were costing American taxpayers over $100 billion per year, but also claimed that Swiss and Liechtenstein-based banks were actively promoting tax evasion schemes. According to the report 'UBS Swiss bankers targeted United States clients and . . . aggressively marketed their services to United States taxpayers who might otherwise have never opened Swiss accounts'. In the specific case of UBS, it was estimated that United States residents held approximately 20000 Swiss-based accounts of which 95 per cent were undeclared. In terms of value, these 19000 undeclared accounts held an estimated US$17.9 billion (US Senate 2008). Given the magnitude of these revelations and the publicity they received, it was not long before more aggressive enforcement measures were implemented, including a US Justice Department summons for UBS to provide detailed information on all US taxpayers who held UBS accounts (Klapper 2008). Swiss bank secrecy was under unprecedented threat.

After over 12 months of legal proceedings and diplomatic negotiations the United States court case between UBS and the IRS was resolved when UBS agreed to hand over files relating to more than 4450 clients and pay a fine of $780 million to US authorities (Allan 2011). At the time this was regarded as a reprieve for both UBS and bank secrecy in Switzerland more generally given that the settlement involved only a quarter of the UBS accounts held by United States citizens (Stephens 2009). However, the

UBS case only served as the first round in a broader legal attack on Swiss bank secrecy, with civil action against UBS superseding the initial criminal case described above and as United States authorities launched investigations against other Swiss banks including Credit Suisse (Allen 2011; *The Economist* 2012). However, the greater significance of these legal proceedings was the fact that the UBS case put the issue of Swiss bank secrecy on the diplomatic agenda, ultimately forcing the Swiss government to comply with the international standard for tax information exchange.

Domestic Political Constraints and Resistance

The evidence emerging from the UBS case, combined with the financial crisis and the response it triggered from the international community, forced a fundamental shift in Swiss international tax policy. While Switzerland had been exempt from the OECD HTC initiative during the early 2000s under the organisation's 'mutual agreement' provisions (Chapter 3), the G20 at its April 2009 meeting in London committed to take action against all secrecy jurisdictions to ensure that 'the era of bank secrecy is over' (G20 2009; see also Chapter 3 above). As a consequence, and for the first time, Switzerland appeared on a 'grey list' published by the OECD in April 2009, indicating that while Switzerland had committed to the OECD standard for tax information exchange, it had not yet fully implemented the regime. This blunt assessment prompted an immediate commitment from the Swiss government to renegotiate its existing DTAs in such a way that its own bank secrecy laws could no longer be used as a basis for denying information exchange requests (Danzinger 2009). The requisite 12 treaties to meet what in 2009 was the international standard for information exchange were negotiated within six months, with the Swiss national assembly ratifying these agreements shortly thereafter. These actions resulted in Switzerland being transferred to the OECD's white list of states that were compliant with the international standard as it stood at the time.

The Swiss government's decision to comply with Article 26 of the OECD model convention and its provision to exchange tax information in non-criminal matters may have been a watershed for the international tax regime, but it is was by no means the end of the domestic political battle within Switzerland, with the finance industry and the popular Swiss People's Party opposing the reforms. The ensuing political debate, which has played out within the Swiss National Assembly since 2009, has focused on how broadly Article 26 of the OECD model convention should be interpreted. The first tranche of revised treaties negotiated and ratified in 2009 provided for administrative assistance and tax information exchange only in cases where individuals' names, addresses and account information could be identified by the requesting authority (OECD 2011). However the Global Forum Phase 1 Peer Review report on Switzerland published in February 2011 criticised this narrow interpretation, arguing that accounts only need be identified by the unique IBAN, or International Bank Account Number assigned to each account (Keiser and Kobler 2011). Somewhat reluctantly the Swiss government agreed to amend existing DTAs to address this deficiency in the face of growing political resistance (OECD 2011).

The Swiss Bankers Association (SBA) have perhaps been the most vocal opponents of the increasingly broad interpretation of Article 26, maintaining that the provision is designed to ensure that 'countries are not at liberty to engage in fishing expeditions or to request information that is unlikely to be relevant to the tax affairs of a given taxpayer' (Stephens 2011). When in July 2011 the Global Forum suggested that information exchange requests could target groups of account holders rather than individuals, the debate intensified, with SBA arguing that the Swiss government 'should not give into the OECD again' while the Swiss People's Party, who then held the largest block of seats in the National Assembly, argued that the request regarding groups' accounts was a breach 'of all the promises that had been given' (Allen 2011). What most commentators agree on is that the real battle is to ensure that the Swiss government does not concede to EU demands for automatic information exchange concerning all bank accounts and other financial assets held in Switzerland (Allen 2010). The question of whether international pressure to end Swiss bank secrecy will prevail over the interests of the powerful financial sector is far from resolved. Those determined to end Swiss bank secrecy will take heart from national elections held in October 2009 in which support for the Swiss People's Party fell for the first time since the mid-1990s (from 29 per cent of the national vote to 26 per cent) (*The Economist* 2011c). On the other hand, recent bilateral treaties negotiated with both the United Kingdom and Germany may allow the Swiss to preserve their cherished bank secrecy.

The Emerging Compromise

In the aftermath of the financial crisis Switzerland's European neighbours have become increasingly unwilling to allow their citizens to use Swiss accounts to evade their tax obligations. On the other hand, in Switzerland there is significant political resistance both within the finance sector and among the wider electorate to any change to Swiss banking practices, given it has been estimated that up to half of all funds managed by Swiss banks on behalf of private foreign clients may be at risk (Logutenkova 2012). By mid-2011 these competing pressures on Swiss international tax policy yielded a distinctive compromise which will inevitably have significant implications for the international tax regime. In August 2011 the Swiss government signed new tax treaties with Germany and the United Kingdom which seek to tax residents' income derived from Swiss accounts while preserving core elements of bank secrecy (UK Treasury 2011; MacDonald 2011). In the British case, existing accounts held by UK tax residents will be subjected to a one-off deduction of between 19 per cent and 34 per cent to settle past tax liabilities and from 2013 these accounts will be subject to withholding taxes of 48 per cent on investment incomes and 27 per cent on capital gains, approximately 2 per cent less than the comparable rates for onshore investments (UK Treasury 2011). Significantly the regime is designed to protect the identity of account holders, thus preserving Switzerland's reputation for bank secrecy (MacDonald 2011).

In financial terms both the British and German treaties are likely to deliver their respective tax authorities significant revenues. In the British case HM Revenue and Customs estimates the new treaty may yield as much as £5 billion, either through the proposed withholding arrangements or because UK tax residents elect to disclose their offshore income and settle unpaid tax and penalty obligations (UK Treasury 2011). Despite the fact that the new regime is clearly dependent on the capacity and willingness of Swiss authorities and banks to identify and collect the taxes owed by UK or German taxpayers, commentators believe that Swiss integrity and compliance is such that the regime should be effective, but caution that there are few other jurisdictions that could be trusted to collect and transfer the taxes of unknown account holders. In this sense the new Swiss treaties are hardly a template for a universal model (author interview).

Of greater concern is that while the treaties should increase the tax paid by UK and German taxpayers this will be achieved at the price of diminished transparency. The success of the Swiss campaign is remarkable given the political pressure bank secrecy has been under since 2007. Simonian (2011) attributes the UK and German deals to the combination of an unprecedented diplomatic effort on the part of Swiss authorities headed by a special unit in the finance ministry and the growing financial vulnerability of most European governments. Whereas prior to the ongoing European sovereign debt crisis EU members were determined to end Swiss bank secrecy, now they are much more willing to consider a sufficiently generous financial settlement.In the words of tax justice campaigner Nicholas Shaxson, the treaty represents a 'Swiss tax Swizz – the country will pay a fat fee to avoid revealing clients' names' (*The Economist*

2011b). The real concern is that other jurisdictions will use the treaties as a precedent for preserving secrecy, as was the case in the early 2000s, or that the Swiss will negotiate similar agreements with other countries but with less onerous withholding provisions. It has been reported that the United States government considered establishing a similar agreement but was of the view that 'it completely failed to tackle the perceived cause of tax evasion – bank secrecy' and instead used its unrivalled economic and political power to force Swiss banks (via FATCA) to provide information concerning United States taxpayers, rather than relying on the Swiss government to provide both the identity and account information relating to United States taxpayers (Eversheds 2011).

CONCLUSION

The analysis provided in this chapter has highlighted the varied ways in which domestic political considerations influence the politics of international tax cooperation. Despite significant domestic differences in Switzerland and the United States there were common elements and considerations. In both jurisdictions there is evidence of the mutually constitutive role of domestic and international considerations in shaping international tax policy, largely affirming Kingsbury's (2005) observation that the politics of domestic and international financial regulation are largely intertwined. In the United States the acute need to attract foreign investment and capital to promote the post-crisis recovery has underpinned the structural power and apparent success of corporate efforts to preserve the United States' ability to tax foreign capital concessionally. In Switzerland, the UBS case, followed by the decision of the G20 and the resulting commitment from the international community to establish and enforce a new international standard of tax information exchange, undermined the political viability of trying to preserve bank secrecy as it had been historically practised.

Despite these broad similarities, there have also been stark contrasts in the ways in which domestic politics have influenced international tax policy, highlighting the significant role that domestic institutions, electoral politics and ideas play in shaping international policy preferences (Underdal 1998; Young 1999). In the United States, Barack Obama's victory in the 2008 Presidential election certainly consolidated United States support for international tax cooperation, although the Democrats' subsequent defeat in the 2010 Congressional mid-term elections has constrained the prospects of further legislative action. In Switzerland, the multi-party system and the central role of banking in the national economy has ensured a robust parliamentary debate in relation to the ratification of treaty commitments made in the aftermath of the financial crisis.

Perhaps the most significant conclusion that can be drawn from the case studies is the enduring structural power wielded by financial interests over the domestic politics of international taxation, a theme to which we will return in the concluding chapter. While the financial crisis has clearly undermined the legitimacy of financial interests in the eyes of the mass public, since the onset of the crisis corporate interests seem to have gradually reasserted their control over the agenda as national governments have engaged in desperate attempts to promote the economic recovery (Zimmermann 2010). In contrast to the prominent role of corporate interests identified in the cases of either the United States or Switzerland there was limited evidence of institutional socialisation (Chapter 3) wherein domestic policymakers adopt and promote preferences advocated by international organisations. While there has been near universal acceptance of the OECD standard for tax information exchange since 2009, the evidence presented in the previous chapter suggests that this was more the product of instrumental concerns relating to the political need to agree on an existing standard at the height of the crisis. However, with the passage of time the standard is being subjected to changes and, as argued above, both the United States (through FATCA) and Switzerland (through their new bilateral agreements with Germany and the UK) are effectively proposing alternative standards which are more consistent with their national interests. In defence of the institutional socialisation hypothesis, evidence of bureaucratic engagement contributing to the convergence of state interests is more likely during 'normal' times than at moments of crisis and in relation to technical rather than contested issues.

A final conclusion that can be drawn from the domestic case studies is how the United States' leading role in the international tax regime continues to have an impact on the strategies it is able to pursue in terms of proposing and promoting a regime such as that of FATCA, which rivals and perhaps undermines the work conducted by the Global Forum. As Drezner has argued (2002; 2007), great powers have the unique capacity to either remake existing regimes or create rival regimes that are congruent with the interests of dominant domestic actors. In contrast, Switzerland, as a middle power, had overtly to accede to the demands of the international community to end bank secrecy, with resistance focusing on the interpretation and implementation of these international commitments (Underdal 1998). This highlights the critical issues of enforcement and implementation in shaping regime effectiveness, questions which are the focus of the following chapter.

REFERENCES

Allan, Matthew (2010) 'Has Switzerland Saved Bank Secrecy', *Swissinfo*, 29 October.

Allan, Matthew (2011) 'Eyebrows Raised at US Tax Deal Rumours', *Swissinfo*, 19 June.

Baker, Raymond (2010) 'Transparency First', *American Interest*, July/August.

Bingham, Simone (2008) 'Regulating Corporate Governance', in Peter Carroll and Richard Eccleston (eds), *Regulating International Business*, Sydney: Pearson International, pp. 111–38.

Boehner, John (2011) 'Cutting Taxes and Creating Jobs', available at http://john boehner.house.gov/Issues/Issue/?IssueID=3944 (accessed September 2011).

Bonzom, Marie-Christine (2011) 'Credit Suisse "Worse Off" than UBS in US', *Swissinfo*, 27 July.

Boston Consulting Group (2011) 'Global Wealth 2011: Shaping a New Tomorrow', available at https://www.bcgperspectives.com/content/articles/financial_institut ions_pricing_global_wealth_2011_shaping_new_tomorrow/ (accessed January 2012).

Braithwaite, John and Peter Drahos (2000) *Global Business Regulation*, Cambridge: Cambridge University Press.

Browning, Lynnley (2008) 'UBS Executive Indicted in U.S. Inquiry', *New York Times*, 12 November.

Browning, Lynnley (2011) 'Critics Say New Laws Make them Tax Agents', *Reuters*, 19 August.

Carroll, Peter and Aynsley Kellow (2011) *OECD: A Study of Organisational Adaption*, Cheltenham, UK and Northampton, MA, USA: Edward Elgar.

Chaikin, David (2005) 'Policy and Fiscal Effects of Swiss Bank Secrecy', *Revenue Law Journal*, **15** (1), 90–110.

Clark, Andrew (2008) 'UBS Executive Charged with Helping 20,000 Americans Avoid Tax', *Guardian*, 12 November.

Danzinger, Monique (2009) 'Swiss Tax Deal a Tiny Step Forward, at Best', Global Financial Integrity, available at http://www.gfip.org/index.php?option=com_con tent&task=view&id=263&Itemid=70 (accessed December 2010).

Doggart Caroline (1997) *Tax Havens and Their Uses*, London: The Economist Intelligence Unit.

Drezner, Daniel (2002) 'Who Rules? The Regulation of Globalization', Working Paper, available at http://danieldrezner.com/research/whorules.pdf (accessed March 2010).

Drezner, Daniel (2007) *All Politics is Global: Explaining International Regulatory Regimes*, Princeton, NJ: Princeton University Press.

Eccleston, Richard (2000) 'The Significance of Business Interest Associations in Economic Policy Reform: The Case of Australian Taxation Policy', *Business and Politics*, **2** (3), 309–25.

The Economist (2011a) 'The Debt Ceiling: Glum and Glummer', 30 July.

The Economist (2011b) 'Trouble Island', 15 October.

The Economist (2011c) 'The Swiss National Election', 29 October.

The Economist (2012) 'Don't Ask, Won't Tell', 11 February.

Eden, Lorraine and Robert T. Kudrle (2005) 'Tax Havens: Renegade States in the International Tax Regime?' *Law & Policy*, **27** (1), January, 100–127.

European Commission (2011), 'The Taxation of Savings: The EU Directive', available at http://ec.europa.eu/taxation_customs/taxation/personal_tax/savings _tax/rules_applicable/index_en.htm (accessed May 2011).

Eversheds, Ben (2011) 'Swiss Say "Hard Cheese" to Tax Transparency', *Accountancy Age*, 19 October.

Fiscal Commission (2010) 'The National Commission on Fiscal Responsibility and Reform', The White House, Washington DC, available at http://www.fiscal commission.gov/sites/fiscalcommission.gov/files/documents/TheMomentofTruth 12_1_2010.pdf (accessed May 2011).

G20 (2009) G20, *London Communiqué*, G20, London, available at http://www.g20. org/Documents/final-communique.pdf (accessed June 2010).

GAO (2008a) 'US Multinational Corporations: Effective Tax Rates are Correlated with Where Income is Reported', GAO-08-950, available at http://www.gao.gov/ new.items/d08950.pdf (accessed June 2010).

GAO (2008b) 'International Taxation: Large U.S. Corporations and Federal Contractors with Subsidiaries in Jurisdictions Listed as Tax Havens or Financial Privacy Jurisdictions' GAO-09-157, http://www.gao.gov/products/GAO-09-157 Accessed January 201.

Gilleard, Matthew (2011) 'Bipartisan Agreement in the US on Repatriation Relief', *International Tax Review*, 18 October.

Gourevitch, Peter (1978) 'The Second Image Reversed', *International Organization*, **32** (4), 881–912.

Healy, Paul and Krishna Palepu (2003) 'The Fall of Enron', *Journal of Economic Perspectives*, **17** (2), 3–26.

Heclo, Hugh (1978) 'Issue Networks and the Executive Establishment', in A. King (ed.), *The New American Political System*, Washington DC: AEI, pp. 46–57.

Hollingshead, Ann (2010) *Privately Held, Non-Resident Deposits in Secrecy Jurisdictions*, Global Financial Integrity, available at http://www.gfintegrity. org/storage/gfip/documents/reports/gfi_privatelyheld_web.pdf (accessed March 2011).

Hooghe, Liesbet and Gary Marks (2009) 'A Postfunctionalist Theory of European Integration: From Permissive Consensus to Constraining Dissensus', *British Journal of Political Science*, **39** (1), 1–23.

International Monetary Fund (2011) *Fiscal Monitor, September 2011*, available at http://www.imf.org/external/pubs/ft/fm/2011/02/fmindex.htm (accessed October 2011).

Internal Revenue Service (IRS) (1981) *Tax Havens and Their Use by United States Taxpayers*, The Gordon Report, Washington DC, IRS.

Ipsen, Erik (1996) 'Switzerland's Top Bank Spurns Merger Bid', *New York Times*, 12 April.

Kelechava, Erin (2010) 'Congress Looks to International Tax to Raise Revenue', *International Tax Review*, **21** (5), 11–12.

Keiser, Andreas and Eveline Kobler (2011) 'Switzerland Aims to Extend Cooperation' *Swissinfo*, 16 February.

Klapper, Bradley (2008) 'Senate: UBS Liechtenstein Aided US Tax Cheats', *USA Today*, 17 July.

Kingsbury, Benedict, Nico Krisch and Richard B. Stewart (2005) 'The Emergence of Global Administrative Law', New York University Public Law and Legal

Theory Working Papers 17, available at http://lsr.nellco.org/nyu_plltwp/17 (accessed July 2012).

Kocieniewski, David (2011) 'GE's Strategies Let it Avoid Tax Altogether', *New York Times*, 24 March.

Levin, Carl and Tom Coburn (2011) *US Senate Permanent Subcommittee on Investigations Report on the Financial Crisis*, 13 April, available at http://hsgac. senate.gov/public/index.cfm?FuseAction=Press.MajorityNews&ContentRecord _id=51bf2c79-5056-8059-76a0-6674916e133d (accessed May 2011).

Logutenkova, Elena (2012) 'Swiss Secrecy Besieged Makes Banks Fret', *Bloomberg*, available at http://www.bloomberg.com/news/2012-03-19/swiss-secrecy-besiege d-makes-banks-fret-world-money-lure-fading.html (accessed March 2012).

MacDonald, Andrew (2011) 'Revolutionary New UK-Swiss Tax Deal', *Wall Street Journal*, 25 August.

Mathiason, Nick (2009) 'New Threat for UK's Offshore Havens', *Guardian*, 28 October.

Meek, Jessica (2011) 'Banks Fear that FACTA Raises Operational and Systematic Risks', *Financial Risk Management*, 26 September, available at http://www.risk. net/operational-risk-and-regulation/feature/2109648/banks-fear-fatca-raises-op erational-systemic-risks (accessed July 2012) .

McLure, Charles (1988) 'US Tax Laws and Capital Flight from America', Hoover Institution and Stanford University Working Papers in Economics, E-88-21, Palo Alto, California.

Michel, Scott and David Rosenbloom (2011) 'FATCA and Foreign Bank Accounts: Has the US Overreached?' *Tax Analysis*, 30 May, 709–13.

Mitchell, Dan (2000) 'An OECD Proposal to Eliminate Tax Competition Would Mean Higher Taxes and Less Privacy', Economic Policy Series Research Paper, Heritage Foundation, Washington DC.

Mosley, Layna (2009) 'An End to Global Standards and Codes?' *Global Governance*, **15** (1), 9–14.

New York Times (2004) 'Higher Fees and Trading Help Double UBS income', 5 May.

Obama, Barack (2009) 'Remarks by the President on International Tax Policy Reform', 4 May, available at http://www.whitehouse.gov/the_press_office/ Remarks-By-The-President-On-International-Tax-Policy-Reform   (accessed July 2012).

OECD (2010) *Report on Trade and Investment Measures: Mid-May to Mid-October 2010*, Paris, OECD, available at http://www.oecd.org/dataoecd/20/56/46318551. pdf (accessed February 2011).

OECD (2011) *Global Forum Peer Review Report – Switzerland, Phase* 1, Paris: OECD, available at http://eoi-tax.org/jurisdictions/CH#peerreview (accessed July 2012).

Obama, Barack (2011) 'Remarks by the President on Economic Growth and Deficit Reduction – September 19th 2011', available at http://www.whitehouse. gov/the-press-office/2011/09/19/remarks-president-economic-growth-and-deficit-reduction (accessed July 2012).

Palan, Ronen (1998) 'Trying to Have Your Cake and Eating It: How and Why the State System has Created Offshore', *International Studies Quarterly*, **44**, 625–43.

Palan, Ronen (2003), *The Offshore World: Sovereign Markets, Virtual Places, and Nomad Millionaires*, Ithaca: Cornell University Press.

Palan, Ronen, Richard Murphy and Christian Chavagneux (2010) *Tax Havens: How Globalization Really Works*, Ithaca: Cornell University Press.

Pew (2011) 'More Blame Wars than Domestic Spending or Tax Cuts for Nation's Debt', Pew Research Centre, available at http://people-press.org/2011/06/07/more-blame-wars-than-domestic-spending-or-tax-cuts-for-nations-debt/ (accessed July 2012).

Picciotto, Sol (1992) *International Business Taxation: A Study in the Internationalization of Business Regulation*, London: Weidenfeld and Nicolson.

Picciotto, Sol (2011) *Regulating Global Corporate Capitalism*, Cambridge: Cambridge University Press.

Quinn, Greg (2011) 'Canada Wants Special Treatment from US Bank Law', *Bloomberg*, 26 February.

Reinhart, Carmen M. and Kenneth S. Rogoff (2009) *This Time is Different: Eight Centuries of Financial Folly*, Princeton, NJ: Princeton University Press.

Ring, Diane (2009) 'What's at Stake in the Sovereignty Debate? International Tax and the Nation-State', *Virginia Journal of International Law*, **49** (1), 154–233.

Rixen, Thomas (2008) *The Political Economy of International Tax Governance: Transformations of the State*, New York: Palgrave Macmillan.

Rosenzweig, Adam (2011) 'Thinking Outside the (Tax) Treaty', Paper presented to the New York University School of Law Colloquium on Tax Policy and Public Finance, Spring.

Scott, Michel and David Rosenbloom (2011) 'FATCA and Foreign Bank Accounts: Has the U.S. Overreached?' *Tax Analysis*, 30 May, 609–703.

Shambaugh, George (1999) *States, Firms and Power: Successful Sanctions in United States Foreign Policy*, Albany: State University of New York Press.

Sharman, Jason (2011) *The Money Laundry: Regulating Criminal Finance in the Global Economy*, Ithaca: Cornell University Press.

Shaxon, Nicholas (2011) *Treasure Islands: Uncovering the Damage of Offshore Banking and Tax Havens*, New York: Palgrave Macmillan.

Simonian, Haig (2011) 'Confidentiality: Switzerland Moves to Avert Threat to Privacy', *Financial Times*, 20 November.

Spencer, David (2010a) 'Atmosphere is Changing for Information Exchange', *International Tax Review*, **25** (5), n.p.

Spencer, David (2010b) 'FATCA and Automatic Exchange of Tax Information', *Journal of International Taxation*, September, 62–4.

Stelter, Brian (2011) 'Occupy Wall Street Occupies the Headlines', *New York Times*, 12 October.

Stephens, Thomas (2009) 'UBS off the Hook, but is Swiss Banking?' *Swissinfo*, 12 August.

Stephens, Thomas (2011) 'Tax Assistance Move Wins Few Friends', *Swissinfo*, 7 July, available at http://www.swissinfo.ch/eng/business/Tax_assistance_move_wins_few_friends.html?cid=30629274 (accessed July 2012).

Swiss Bankers Association (2009), *Wealth Management in Switzerland*, Basel, January.

Tagliabue, John (1997) 'Two of Three Swiss Banks to Join to Seek Global Heft', *New York Times*, 9 December.

Tanzi, Vito (1995) *Taxation in an Integrating World*, Washington, DC: Brookings Institution.

Tax Justice Network (2010) 'FATCA: New Automatic Exchange Tool', available at http://taxjustice.blogspot.com.au/2010/05/fatca-new-automatic-info-exchange-tool.html (accessed July 2012).

Wood, Duncan (2005) *Governing Global Banking: The Basel Committee and the Politics of Financial Globalisation*, Aldershot: Ashgate.

UK Treasury (2011) 'Agreement with Switzerland to Secure Billions in Unpaid Tax', Media Release, 24 August, available at http://www.hm-treasury.gov.uk/pr ess_98_11.htm (accessed July 2012).

UK Treasury (2012) 'Joint Statement Regarding an Intergovernmental Approach to Improving International Tax Compliance and Implementing FATCA', Statement Release, 8 February, available at http://www.hm-treasury.gov.uk/joi nt_intl_statement_fatca.htm (accessed July 2012).

Underdal, Arild (1998) 'Explaining Compliance and Defection: Three Models', *European Journal of International Relations*, **4** (1), 5–30.

United States Congress (2011) HR 4213: Unemployment Compensation Extension Act, available at http://www.govtrack.us/congress/bill.xpd?bill=h111-4213 (accessed June 2011).

United States Senate (2006) 'Hearings on Tax Haven Abuses: The Enablers, The Tools and Secrecy', S.Hrg. 109–797 (8/1/06).

United States Senate (2008) 'Tax Haven Banks and US Tax Compliance', Permanent Subcommittee on Investgations, available at http://hsgac.senate.gov /public/_files/071708PSIReport.pdf (accessed June 2011).

United States Senate (2009) 'Finance Committee Questions for the Record: Hearing on Confirmation of Mr Timothy F. Geithner to be Secretary of the U.S. Department of Treasury, January 21, 2009', available at http://www.finance .senate.gov/imo/media/doc/012209%20TFG%20Questions1.pdf (accessed July 2012).

Wolf, Martin (2010) 'Currencies Clash in a New Age of Beggar-My-Neighbour', *Financial Times*, 29 September.

Woodward, Richard (2009) *The Organisation for Economic Co-operation & Development*, London: Routledge.

Young, Oran R. (1999) *Governance in World Affairs*, Ithaca: Cornell University Press.

Zernike, Kate (2010) *Boiling Mad: Inside Tea Party America*, New York: Times Books.

Zimmermann, Hubert (2010) 'Conclusion – Whither Global Financial Regulation?' in Eric Helleiner Stefano Pagliari and Hubert Zimmermann (eds), *Global Finance in Crisis: The Politics of International Regulatory Change*, Oxford: Routledge.

6. Beyond the financial crisis: regime implementation and effectiveness

The Organisation for Economic Cooperation and Development claims to have presided over a 'revolution' in tax transparency since the financial crisis. We have noted that the sheer number of tax information agreements negotiated since 2007 broadly supports such claims. Yet the more important question is whether the enhanced legal structures for tax information exchange combined with the unilateral measures described in previous chapters have had a significant impact on international tax evasion? It is particularly important to focus on the implementation and efficacy of the evolving international tax regime owing to widely held theoretical and practical concerns (Meinzer 2012). The implementation and enforcement of international agreements is the least researched yet arguably the most important aspect of global economic governance, with the established literature suggesting that implementation has long been regarded as the Achilles heel of global governance (Young 1999; Keohane 2001; Joachim et al. 2008). Liberal institutionalists and realists alike highlight both the lack of incentives to comply with international agreements and the ability of powerful domestic interests to persuade national governments to ignore their international commitments (North 1990; Raustiala and Victor 2004). While recent research in the sociological tradition is more optimistic in arguing that international engagement and deliberation through forums such as the OECD can promote compliance through persuasion, there is also a good deal of evidence to the contrary (Barnett and Finnemore 2004).

In addition to these general barriers to effective implementation it is argued that the structure of the governance problem in question will influence the prospects of effective implementation. Ominously for international tax agreements, in the case of *collaboration* problems, where there are net benefits from cooperation, there are also strong incentives to defect or free-ride (such as a Prisoner's Dilemma). The established literature suggests that in such situations formal rules-based enforcement regimes with the capacity to invoke credible sanctions for non-compliance are required (Zagaris 2005; Downs et al. 1996). Yet more recent research (Joachim et al. 2008) highlights the increasing difficulty of promoting implementation through coercion and enforcement because of the lack of formal authority in emerging global governance structures. Given the sovereignty-preserving nature of the international tax regime and the OECD's lack of formal political authority this chapter will provide an assessment of the extent to which compliance has been achieved in the absence of direct enforcement measures.

A final cause for scepticism in so far as implementation and compliance are concerned has been the poor historical record in relation to international tax matters. As was noted in Chapter 4, most analysts agree that the original OECD Harmful Tax Competition initiative of the late 1990s and early 2000s was largely ineffective in terms of combating the use of secrecy jurisdictions for international tax evasion. Despite the real progress that has been made in terms of improving the legal framework for international tax cooperation and information exchange since the financial crisis, NGOs and various tax justice activists remain extremely sceptical as to whether these developments will have any material impact on the international tax evasion, with commentators such as Nicholas Shaxon (2011, 169) describing the OECD's initial 2009 blacklist provided to the G20 as 'a sad joke' and 'a whitewash'. These concerns are well founded, but tend to conflate the implementation of the OECD standard and very legitimate concerns about its effectiveness. Given the need to establish a conceptual distinction between implementation, enforcement and regime effectiveness this chapter will begin by sketching a framework for assessing the implementation and effectiveness of recent regulatory and policy initiatives in the international tax arena before presenting some preliminary evidence for assessing regime efficacy.

IMPLEMENTATION, ENFORCEMENT AND EFFECTIVENESS: SOME CONCEPTUAL FOUNDATIONS

In their seminal study of implementation at an international level Joachim et al. (2008, 6–7) establish a useful demarcation between implementation, compliance and effectiveness as well as a framework for analysing the distinctive contributions that implementation and compliance make to regime effectiveness. Drawing on implementation studies at a domestic level (see Victor et al. 1998) implementation is defined as 'the translation of agreed-upon international agreements into concrete policies which manifests itself in the adoption of rules or regulations, the passage of legislation or the creation of institutions'. In terms of the revised Global Forum process described in Chapter 4, this narrow legalistic definition of implementation is the central focus of the forum's 'Phase 1' peer reviews, with their emphasis on assessing the extent to which a jurisdiction 'had established an appropriate legal and regulatory framework to support information exchange' (OECD 2010a).

However Joachim et al. (2008, 6) argue that formal legal implementation is only the first, albeit necessary, step towards creating an effective regime, one that 'improves the underlying problem or the degree to which it achieves its stated policy objectives'. The critical link between implementation and regime effectiveness is the extent to which the legal and regulatory structures central to the implementation phase result in the behavioural changes that the regime is trying to achieve (Young 1979; Victor et al. 1998). As the established literature on compliance highlights, there are a number of processes that may lead to changed behaviour either on the part of states or at the level of individuals. As mentioned above, rationalist theories of international relations suggest that compliance is best achieved through the provision of tangible incentives to promote desired behaviour or through imposing sanctions on those who are unwilling to comply. In contrast, sociological theories suggest that compliance can be promoted through engagement and persuasion, the inference being that a 'management approach' to implementation and compliance may be the most effective and desirable (Chayes and Chayes 1995, 303; Risse 2000). In reality many of the most effective regimes use a combination of these approaches in order to change behaviour, depending on the nature of the governance problem at hand. According to Young (1999), this complexity suggests that 'The most useful contributions to implementation analysis . . . will take the form of interpretive accounts based on efforts to join general knowledge with an in-depth understanding of individual cases in contrast to the applications of simple recipes to complex problems of governance in world affairs.'

Such complexity is clearly evident in the case of international tax information exchange. This manifests itself not only in terms of the combination of persuasion, incentives and possible sanctions that characterise the Global Forum process and the associated use of forum assessments by national tax authorities in their various enforcement strategies, but also in the way that the regime seeks to influence behaviour and promote compliance at a number of different levels. First, the aim of the Global Forum (and the design of its 'Phase 2' assessments in particular) is to assess and promote compliance with the OECD standard among forum members. While this is a significant objective in itself the effectiveness of the regime in terms of reducing the extent of international tax evasion will ultimately depend on the way in which improved tax information exchange, combined with other administrative cooperation and unilateral enforcement measures, affect both the compliance behaviour of taxpayers and the supply of aggressive tax planning schemes designed to exploit offshore opacity. Given that the ultimate effectiveness of anti-evasion measures depends on the extent to which they can influence both the underlying demand for aggressive tax planning schemes and their supply by financial services providers, it is important to try and assess the extent to which the developments described in previous chapters have influenced behaviour at the micro level. Reflecting this objective the chapter will, based on preliminary evidence, evaluate the extent to which the Global Forum process has influenced state behaviour before attempting to assess how individual taxpayer compliance has changed in recent years. While it is extremely difficult to assess this in precise terms the success or otherwise of various 'voluntary disclosure' schemes introduced by national tax authorities represents a reasonable proxy and for this reason they will be examined in the final section of the chapter.

The above discussion also highlights the possibility that while the implementation of the OECD's tax information exchange standard via the Global Forum process may be a success, it may still prove to be ineffective in terms of its stated goals of 'ending international tax evasion' and 'outlawing tax havens' because the standard itself is flawed and is unable to create the desired behaviour change (Brown 2009). This is precisely the concern held by those experts who advocate the automatic exchange of information and 'country by country' reporting of taxable income and liabilities. We will return to this theme in the concluding chapter, with an evaluation of the political sustainability of the existing regime and the prospects for achieving international agreement on a more rigorous international standard.

THE GLOBAL FORUM: A PRELIMINARY ASSESSMENT

Chapter 4 described how the financial crisis not only transformed the political and economic context in which international tax negotiations occur but also resulted in the creation of new institutional structures designed to promote international tax cooperation. Of these developments the creation of the revised Global Forum on Transparency and Information Exchange for Tax Purposes under the auspices of the OECD is perhaps the most significant. The G20 mandate for the Global Forum's tax transparency agenda has had a number of significant consequences, such as increasing participation in the forum and ensuring it has adequate financial resources to implement its mandate. At a procedural level significant developments include an enhanced peer review process which assesses both the formal implementation with the OECD standard (Phase 1 assessments) and the extent of compliance with the standard in practice (Phase 2). However, as noted above, these Phase 2 assessments are particularly significant given the gap between the political commitments that states make to meeting international obligations and their compliance in practice.

Given that the revised Global Forum first met in September 2009, and published its first assessments in September 2010, it is too early to make a definitive judgement about the effectiveness of the forum process and the extent to which it has promoted compliance with the OECD standard on information exchange. However, based on a combination of the published peer review reports and a series of interviews conducted with a range of stakeholders directly involved in the peer review process, it is possible to make some assessments about the extent to which the forum process is promoting compliance with the OECD standard as well as the likely vulnerabilities of the new regime. For the purposes of this initial analysis it is important to focus on three sets of issues central to the forum process:

1. The peer review process in practice, including the involvement of non-OECD states and democratic participation in the peer review process;
2. The integrity of published reviews including whether they have been rigorous and consistent; and
3. The extent of financial and technical support available to assist smaller forum members to improve compliance with the OECD standard.

The Practice of Peer Review

One of the main criticisms levelled against the OECD's HTC initiative of the late 1990s and early 2000s was that it was undemocratic and inconsistent in that non-OECD member states were being assessed through a process in which they were unable to participate (Chapter 3). The legitimacy of the HTC process was further compromised by its inconsistency in that key OECD member states, such as Switzerland and Luxembourg, refused to participate in or be bound by the project, leading to charges that the OECD was hypocritical in demanding that small and relatively powerless non-member states comply with a standard which its own members ignored (Sharman 2006, 86–93). Given these shortcomings and their ultimate consequences there has been a determination that the revised Global Forum would be more democratic, with the equal participation of all members in the forum's deliberations and reviews.

The commitment to broadening participation in the forum process has a number of dimensions. In terms of organisational structure there has been a concerted effort to expand the Global Forum's membership and to establish a degree of independence from the OECD. On the membership front, efforts to increase participation in the forum's activities have been successful, with 91 jurisdictions committing to the process in 2009, a number that had increased to 101 by the June 2011 Global Forum meeting in Bermuda (OECD 2011a). More importantly, all major financial centres were committed to the process. This broadening of the forum's membership not only enhances its legitimacy but is essential in order to conduct detailed Phase 2 reviews. In the words of a key actor in the forum process 'you can conduct a desk-based Phase 1 assessment based on published information without active cooperation but to assess how it works in practice (as per Phase 2) you really do need the jurisdiction to help out' (author interview). How then can we explain the increased willingness of non-OECD jurisdictions to both participate in and fund the forum process? The consensus view among smaller jurisdictions, which perhaps had most at stake in the forum process, was that the G20 London declaration of 2009, combined with the international response to the financial crisis more generally, demonstrated that the international community was serious about improving international tax transparency and information exchange and that irrespective of misgivings about this agenda they would be best served by engaging with the process (author interview).

A second set of organisational reforms that enhanced participation within the regime concerns the determination to establish the Global Forum at arms length from the OECD and to promote the involvement of non-OECD members in the forum's management and activities. This institutional separation was formally established by the OECD Council's 2009 decision not only to sponsor and provide secretarial support to the Global Forum but also to grant it formal autonomy from the organisation's governance structures (OECD 2009a; Porter and Rubio-Vega 2012). In practical terms, this is designed to formalise the position of OECD members and non-members on an equal footing in the Forum's Steering Committee (which establishes the work programme) and in the Peer Review Group (which conducts assessments) as well as on the forum's secretariat. Given non-OECD members' lack of participation in the failed HTC initiative, improving the inclusiveness and legitimacy of the forum is central to its ongoing success (Porter and Rubio-Vega 2012, 63). While critics argue that the forum's agenda, work programme and aspects of the assessments it conducts continue to be dominated by the interests of powerful member states, these critics acknowledge that this is inevitable in any international forum and that the current regime represents a significant improvement on past practice (author interview). There is also a consensus that a critical test as to whether the revised forum process is inclusive and equitable will be the extent of preferential treatment in the review of OECD member states relative to non-members. In terms of participation, the fact that non-member states Bermuda and China have been elected to positions as vice-chairs of the Forum Steering Committee while India and Jersey have been elected as vice-chairs of the Forum Peer Review Group represents significant progress (OECD 2011a).

The revised Global Forum has clearly created a more democratic process for developing standards and procedures as well as for conducting peer review assessments, but this does not mean that the process is without criticism. A concern raised by a handful of jurisdictions is that non-member states who were quick to embrace the forum process were rewarded with membership of the abovementioned peer review and steering committees, while those who failed to gain membership of these groups and the executive control that they confer remain as vulnerable as ever. For example, one jurisdiction claims that it was subjected to an early peer review despite a request to delay its assessment so that it could 'get its house in order' leading to a belief that it was being 'made an example of to demonstrate the Forum's effectiveness' (author interview). However, it must be stressed that this is an isolated claim and that all peer review reports are ultimately approved by the forum's general membership.

Despite significant progress in terms of institutionalising more democratic practices within the Global Forum there remains a risk that core states will establish a privileged position within the regime and that small states may be marginalised. While this may be inevitable to an extent, if discrimination becomes too entrenched and it becomes apparent that the Global Forum is not promoting a level playing field in international tax affairs then this will have significant consequences for the forum's sustainability. At an instrumental level, secrecy jurisdictions will be less likely to comply with forum assessments and directives if there is a perception that rival jurisdictions are not being subjected to similar treatment. Under this scenario more robust enforcement measures, such as sanctions, would be required to achieve compliance. Further, as was demonstrated by the original HTC initiative in the late 1990s and early 2000s (Chapter 3), if the consistency and political legitimacy of the regime is called into question this allows non-compliant states to defy the regime without incurring reputational costs. While there are claims of discrimination within the Global Forum, with the representative of one jurisdiction describing it as 'a two-level table', such concerns remain isolated. Perhaps the test of the legitimacy of forum practices among smaller jurisdictions will be the extent to which these countries build a coalition and mobilise a caucus to express their concerns. Thus far, and unlike the early 2000s, no such political activity has occurred.

The Integrity and Rigour of the Peer Review Process

The second critical test for the revised Global Forum concerns the rigour and integrity of the peer review assessments which have been conducted to date. As of early June 2012, 59 peer review assessments had been published including 16 combined Phase 1 and 2 reports (OECD 2012; Sawyer 2011). Given that half of the Global Forum's membership has now been subjected to a Phase 1 review it is possible to draw some conclusions concerning the process. It is obviously more difficult to draw firm conclusions in relation to Phase 2 reviews given that only 16 jurisdictions have been subjected to such an assessment, with this sample being dominated by OECD member countries with a history of tax information exchange. Despite these qualifications there is some preliminary evidence of jurisdictions responding to and addressing regulatory and legislative deficiencies identified in their Phase 1 assessments. On the critical question of whether the assessment process has been equitable and whether the peer review regime will enhance international tax information exchange and transparency, the preliminary evidence is more ambiguous.

Based on the 59 Phase 1 reports conducted to date it is clear that the Global Forum review process and assessment regime has progressed beyond the earlier 'white' and 'grey' lists that determined compliance with the international standard. This progress is especially significant given the criticisms that have been levelled against the old standard which was based solely on whether a jurisdiction had entered into 12 or more agreements irrespective of whether they were capable of or actually supported effective information exchange. More specifically 49 of the 59 peer review reports published at the time of writing identified legislative and administrative deficiencies that were likely to hinder the effective exchange of tax information and, in a classic example of a 'management' approach to implementation, requested that the jurisdictions concerned report back to the Global Forum within 12 months, outlining how they have responded to the problems identified (see Figure 6.1; Sawyer 2011, 10).

In the cases of Panama (which was on the OECD's 'grey list' as of November 2010; Yates et al. 2011) and Botswana, the deficiencies were sufficiently serious that they were not permitted to proceed to a full Phase 2 review until they had acted on the recommendations outlined in the Phase 1 assessment (OECD 2010b; OECD 2011b). Both countries have committed to providing a progress report to the Global Forum within 12 months.

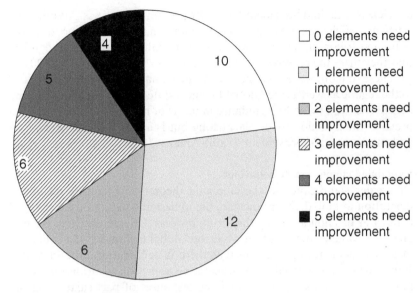

Source: OECD (2012, 22).

Figure 6.1   Number of recommendations for improvement per jurisdiction identified in Phase 1 reviews as of early 2012

Despite lingering concerns about whether powerful OECD member states have received preferential treatment in their Global Forum assessments, even analysts who have been critical of the OECD's approach to improving tax transparency concede that most of the peer review reports which have been published to date have been thorough and have exceeded expectations. For example, Richard Murphy (2011a), a long-time researcher and activist on tax justice issues notes that 'although reservations still exist about this process and tax information exchange agreements themselves remain fundamentally flawed ... the actual peer review process itself seems to be delivering, so credit is given where credit is due, and I offer it on this occasion, as I know others in Tax Justice Network do as well.'

The most important evidence of the effectiveness of the peer review reports published to date has been the extent to which jurisdictions that have undergone Phase 1 assessments have responded by making tangible legislative changes. For example, 13 of the jurisdictions that completed a Phase 1 assessment prior to May 2011 reported to the third Global Forum meeting in Bermuda that they had made progress addressing the deficiencies that had been identified in the peer review process. Additionally Barbados, Belgium, Cayman Islands, Qatar and San Marino formally requested follow-up assessments so that the Global Forum can confirm that they meet the required legal and regulatory standards (OECD 2011c, 3). These outcomes are consistent with the management approach central to the regime as well as the Global Forum's stated objective of 'identifying deficiencies and providing guidance in terms of how to address them' in a process which 'is not about blacklisting but is about measuring progress and encouraging improvement' (Saint-Amans 2011).

Explaining changed state behaviour
Of greater significance to the emerging theoretical literature on implementation in global governance are the underlying causes of the changed behaviour brought about by the forum process (Chapter 2). Here the preliminary evidence suggests that while the Global Forum has the hallmarks of a management approach, in that there is deliberation around setting standards complemented by a cooperative approach to promoting compliance, there is also evidence that the responses of particular states are shaped by both reputational and instrumental concerns. Taken together this evidence supports the claim that distinct sociological and instrumental explanations of compliance behaviour in the extant literature may be overstated (Joachim et al. 2008, 12; Tallberg 2002). While the OECD clearly states that it has neither the capacity nor the intention of trying to impose sanctions for non-compliance with the agreed standard (OECD 2011a), there is widespread recognition that non-compliance poses real reputational risks and threats of other unilateral or collective measures. For example, the Panamanian government have stated their intention to meet the recommendations outlined in their peer review in part because of the reputational damage associated with a negative assessment which in turn can impact on their ability to attract foreign capital and participate in international markets. One tangible example of how a negative Global Forum assessment can be used by a third party with real economic implications was that Panama's poor performance on tax transparency compromised the World Economic Forum's assessment of Panama's economic competitiveness (World Economic Forum). While tax transparency is only one small component of the index (Switzerland typically tops the ranking) the issue was seen to be sufficiently significant to influence the Panamanian government's response to the Global Forum's advice (author interview).

As was noted in Chapter 4, Global Forum assessments are also being used by national governments to target enforcement strategies and other aspects of international tax policy. In March 2010 the French government, frustrated by the reluctance of various Caribbean financial centres to enter into and honour TIEAs, unveiled a list of 18 uncooperative jurisdictions and announced that dividends paid by French corporations to these jurisdictions would be subjected to a 50 per cent withholding tax on interest and dividend payments (the standard rate is 15 per cent) until the jurisdictions complied with French demands (International Tax Review 2010). The UK government has also announced a variation on this approach with a new policy under which tax authorities impose higher penalties on jurisdictions regarded as lacking transparency (HMRC 2011). The logic is that this will act as a disincentive to concealing savings and income in jurisdictions that do not exchange tax information with UK authorities and may prompt these offshore centres to improve their transparency in order to attract investment from the UK.

Beyond these examples of unilateral action, there is already evidence of forum assessments being used by third parties on a broader scale. Perhaps the best example of this is the Financial Stability Board's (FSB) *Framework for Strengthening Adherence to International Standards* which was established in March 2010 and is designed to promote international cooperation and adherence to information exchange standards in relation to financial data as well as encouraging compliance with international standards more broadly (FSB 2010, 1–2). It can be argued that this initiative may be seen as an attempt to implement the OECD enhanced peer review framework in other regulatory arenas, but it is also important to acknowledge some important differences with the emerging process. In particular the FSB is more willing to evoke the threat of possible sanctions administered by member states in the event of blatant non-compliance:

> If, one year after the approval of the evaluation report by the Plenary, a jurisdiction has not made sufficient progress, the FSB may call upon its members to take stronger measures, including sanctions, to promote the jurisdiction's adherence to international standards and reduce risks to the global financial system. (FSB 2010, 12)

According to smaller jurisdictions who have completed the Phase 1 peer review process, the greatest incentive to comply with the Global Forum standard is the clear potential for the G20 to take punitive action against states and territories who fail to come up to scratch. Whether the G20 will take action against non-compliant states is far from certain, but communiqués following the G20 leaders' summits in both April and September 2009 made it clear that the G20 stood ready to direct its members to impose sanctions or 'countermeasures' against non-cooperative jurisdictions (G20 2009a; G20 2009b). The G20 rhetoric in relation to sanctions may have softened since the height of the crisis, but Global Forum participants are acutely aware of the forum's obligation to report progress to the G20 on a regular basis. Indeed this reporting process is so significant that discussions concerning the final recommendations to be reported back to the G20 prior to the November 2011 meeting in Cannes became the most significant item on the forum's agenda during its June 2011 meeting in Bermuda (author interview). Concerns among secrecy jurisdictions about the possibility of sanctions for non-compliance being announced at the G20 meeting in Cannes were particularly acute given France's traditionally aggressive posture on the issue. In the words of one representative from a small secrecy jurisdiction: 'After Cannes we will all have a much clearer idea of the G20's role in the process and whether it is likely to wield a big stick' (author interview). This suggests a process in which behaviour is being shaped by the possibility (albeit vague) of future sanctions. To paraphrase Fritz Scharpf (1997) this is best understood as 'voluntary compliance in the shadow of enforcement'.

Capacity Building, Cooperation and Compliance

The evidence outlined above suggests that the Global Forum has been largely successful in terms of promoting the implementation of the legal and regulatory structures necessary to facilitate the OECD standard of information exchange on request, but as the implementation literature highlights this is only the first step towards achieving the tangible outcomes that are central to the critical issue of regime effectiveness (Young 1979; Victor et al. 1998). Notwithstanding the Global Forum's success in terms of promoting regulatory change, potential barriers remain that may prevent the forum achieving its stated aims. One such constraint on the effective exchange of tax information is whether the jurisdiction which is the subject of an EOI request has the administrative capacity to collect and provide accurate information in a timely manner. Domestic capacity constraints are a well documented barrier to the effective implementation of international agreements (Haas et al. 1993) and represent an acute challenge for the Global Forum given that its membership has expanded to include many smaller jurisdictions which have underdeveloped tax administrations and corporate governance frameworks. Take the case of the TIEA agreed between Australia and Vanuatu in April 2010. Based on long-standing concerns held by Australian tax authorities that resident taxpayers were holding undeclared funds in Vanuatu the Australian Tax Office lodged a request for the details of 14000 accounts held by Australian tax residents in the Pacific island state (Gluyas 2011). Yet the Vanuatu government has not complied with the request, largely because it lacks the administrative capacity to collect the data required under the TIEA request. Given such cases, the Global Forum acknowledged in its first meeting that small financial centres may need assistance in building administrative capacity and consequently made a commitment to develop concrete proposals for providing technical assistance by late 2009 (OECD 2009b, 3).

The forum's subsequent response has been three-fold. First there has been a concerted effort to improve coordination between the key international organisations engaged in promoting better governance in the developing world. As one official close to the Global Forum process explains:

> You can have as much transparency as you like, but if 'they' don't have the capacity to obtain the information or to know what they are looking for, it can be very difficult. There are a lot of people and international organisations involved in improving tax administration in non-OECD countries, not only the OECD, but the IMF and World Bank and the regional development banks are all involved and provide technical assistance. So one of the tasks that needs addressing is mapping what is being done with a view to understanding who is doing what. (Author interview)

The need for better organisational coordination was also highlighted by the G20 which has established a joint OECD, WB, IMF and UN working group to map existing capacity-building programmes with a view to developing strategies for improving coordination between agencies. In a similar vein the Global Forum itself has established formal relations with the World Bank, IMF, UN and Caribbean Community and the African Tax Administration Forum (Qureshi 2011; OECD 2011a).

The second dimension of the Global Forum's strategy has been to provide targeted technical assistance to small jurisdictions preparing for a peer review assessment as well as providing regional training sessions and workshops for tax administrators (OECD 2011a). These initiatives have been complemented by the resurrection of the OECD's Multilateral Convention on Mutual Administrative Assistance in Tax Matters (OECD 1988). This convention was established jointly with the Council of Europe and the OECD to reduce jurisdictional barriers to international administrative cooperation in tax investigations including allowing joint audits and cross-border tax investigations. At the time the convention was vigorously opposed by Switzerland, a host of international business groups including the OECD's own BIAC, and the financial press. As a consequence the convention was only ratified by a handful of European states and failed in its ambition to establish a widely accepted rules-based regime for administrative cooperation (Radaelli 1997; Picciotto 1992, 305). Despite these inauspicious beginnings the current drive to promote international administrative cooperation has resulted in the revival of the multilateral convention, including its endorsement by the G20 Finance Ministers meeting in Paris in February 2011 (G20 2011). As a result the convention was modified in mid-2010 so that states outside Europe can participate in the regime and by June 2011, 21 jurisdictions had become signatories (OECD 2011d). In theory this should allow tax authorities in requesting countries to provide direct assistance to the governments of poorer states in investigations in which they hold a direct interest.

Despite this clear recognition of the need to build the capacity of tax administrations in developing countries, the inability of small jurisdictions to obtain and transfer appropriate information remains a real risk to the effectiveness of the Global Forum's work. Smaller states certainly appreciate the modest technical assistance and training opportunities that have been provided to date; they also argue that much more serious investment is required to build tax administrations with the capacity to provide effective information exchange (author interview). As one interviewee from a developing state commented, 'we are committed to information exchange but what "they" fail to appreciate is that for every TIEA that we sign we require one or two additional staff in our tax office, trained tax officials which we don't have'. Despite the resource imposts associated with servicing TIEAs, small states also acknowledged that neither the Global Forum nor the OECD possess the financial resources to fund the development of tax administrations in non-OECD member states, which highlights the abovementioned need for improved coordination between the Global Forum and those agencies with significant development mandates. Allocating a greater portion of the UN and WB development budget to tax administration may be one viable approach, but given that building the capacity and effectiveness of tax administrations in non-OECD states amounts to providing a global public good then it could be argued that wealthy states – as potentially the greatest beneficiaries of the regime – have an obligation to fund such development (Picciotto 1992, 255). One controversial option that has been mooted by smaller Global Forum members is a 'fee for service' funding system whereby jurisdictions pay a fee for making an EOI request.

The third element of the response relates to the extent to which the Global Forum can establish and sustain a culture of cooperation sufficient to facilitate effective information exchange. Both the wider literature on implementation in global governance and that on international tax administration highlight the fact that the effectiveness of international cooperation depends on creating both an effective legal framework and a willingness to comply with the specific obligations set out in an international agreement. As was described in Chapter 2, the implementation of international commitments often runs into difficulties when they have adverse consequences for powerful domestic interests, leading to what Underdal (1998) has described as the 'vertical disintegration' of global public policy (see also Drezner 2007; Ikenberry et al. 1988; Risse-Kappen 1995). In the case of the tax information exchange this type of domestic veto needn't take the form of overt dissent, but can be manifest as a reluctance to cooperate with a requesting country at an administrative level. This is because the effectiveness of international tax governance rests to a high degree on informal administrative cooperation between national tax authorities (Picciotto 1992; Eccleston 2010).

The challenge for the Global Forum is that when EOI requests extend beyond like-minded and compliant tax authorities there is significant scope for an uncooperative jurisdiction to obfuscate and stonewall while still complying with their obligations under a TIEA (Walter 2008). In the words of one senior official from an OECD member state:

> While some argue that TIEAs on request are a narrow and ineffective instrument the reality is that there is a significant degree of information exchange and cooperation on tax investigations between many OECD member states which is based on informal cooperation and assistance within the confines of international agreements. The challenge will be extracting useful information from jurisdictions who have committed to the Global Forum process but may not be as willing to help. (Author interview)

These concerns have taken tangible form in the context of Switzerland's adoption of the Global Forum standard. As described in Chapter 5, in March 2009 Switzerland withdrew its reservations in relation to the OECD standard for tax information exchange. However there was widespread concern that the TIEAs and amended DTAs that the Swiss have subsequently negotiated adopted a prohibitively narrow interpretation of the identity requirements for the subject of an EOI request (OECD 2011e). This, combined with the fact that Swiss tax authorities do not hold (but have the power to obtain) all relevant information which may be subject of an EOI led to a perception that Swiss tax authorities, in the face of strong domestic political pressure, were trying to obstruct the effective exchange of information. In fairness to the Swiss, as of February 2011 the Swiss government agreed to interpret the definition of a person who is subject to a request 'in a wider sense' . . . 'Provided that it is otherwise demonstrated that the request does not represent a fishing expedition' (OECD 2011e, 96). Whether this willingness to meet the legal and regulatory requirements associated with the Global Forum standard for information exchange also translates into the level of informal administrative cooperation necessary to sustain effective information exchange remains to be seen. However it must be noted that a strength of the revised Global Forum process is that if there are organisational or cultural barriers to effective exchange of information on request in Switzerland or any other jurisdiction then such deficiencies should be identified in the relevant Phase 2 report.

Impact on Taxpayer Compliance Behaviour

The scope and effectiveness of exchange of information provisions is one aspect of a broader collection of factors which ultimately determine the extent of international tax avoidance and evasion. Perhaps the most significant factor in terms of influencing the effectiveness of the regime is the extent to which perceptions that tax authorities are willing and able to exchange tax and financial information will influence the compliance behaviour of taxpayers who had hitherto used secrecy jurisdictions to evade tax. While a detailed assessment of how improvements in tax transparency achieved in recent years have influenced taxpayer compliance is beyond the scope of this study, there is some anecdotal evidence and preliminary data which suggest that rhetorical commitments from world leaders to end tax haven abuse, enhanced information exchange, unilateral anti-avoidance measures and specific high-profile international tax evasion case such as those concerning UBS and the Liechtenstein Group Trust (Chapter 5) have together resulted in improved compliance behaviour.

The most concrete evidence of improved compliance behaviour with reference to offshore investments and income is the proliferation and effectiveness of voluntary disclosure schemes (VDSs). Broadly speaking, VDSs are amnesty schemes that offer non-compliant taxpayers incentives in the form of reduced or waived tax liabilities and penalties to declare previously undisclosed offshore investments or income streams on the condition that they either repatriate or declare these investments in the future (OECD 2010c). Not only do VDSs aim to tax previously undeclared offshore income, but more importantly they allow previously non-compliant taxpayers to start afresh and establish a legitimate relationship with tax authorities which, if well managed should improve the integrity of the tax base in the future (Braithwaite 2005, ch. 5).

The renewed commitment of the international community to ending bank secrecy and improving tax transparency has provided clear motivation for taxpayers to declare assets and income previously hidden in offshore jurisdictions (OECD 2010c, 9). While many elements of the regime are still to be implemented there is a consensus that the risks associated with non-disclosure are growing and the prospects of detection and prosecution are increasingly real. Under these circumstances taxpayer compliance would be expected to improve and VDS schemes should be able to capitalise on this. Indeed since the height of the financial crisis tax authorities of almost all OECD member states have been actively promoting their general voluntary disclosure provisions while 12 countries, including the UK, USA, France and Australia, have developed special programmes designed to capitalise on the changing international tax environment (OECD 2010c). In the case of the United Kingdom a special Liechtenstein Disclosure Facility (LDF) has been created to capitalise on the disclosure of offshore accounts arising from the Liechtenstein Group Trust case.

The UK's LDF has arguably been one of the most successful VDSs introduced in the aftermath of the financial crisis and between its establishment in March 2009 and January 2011 has attracted 1500 disclosures from high-wealth UK tax residents, which will yield an estimated £3 billion in undisclosed taxes, or almost three times the amount anticipated when the scheme was established (Wilkinson 2011). Indeed the scheme has been so successful that other unidentified jurisdictions have approached the UK government to establish similar arrangements, fearing that UK investors would move assets into Liechtenstein to benefit from the arrangement, which runs until 2015 (Wilkinson 2011). Yet as with all VDSs, the success of the scheme depends on the ability of tax authorities to identify taxpayers who fail to disclose offshore assets and to subject them to harsher penalties than those who have used the LDF because, as the OECD (2010c, 11) rightly notes, such schemes 'must walk a fine line between providing sufficient incentives for those engaged in non-compliance to come forward and not rewarding or encouraging such conduct'. Indeed even in the case of the LDF critics argue that while declarations of offshore funds are welcome, the terms of the amnesty are too generous, with assessment liabilities being limited to the past 10 years and with penalties limited to 10 per cent of unpaid taxes (Murphy 2011b).

The Australian government has also run a successful VDS in conjunction with its own high-profile offshore enforcement initiative and a more general commitment to tax information exchange. The Australian Tax Office's (ATO) 'Project Wickenby', designed to prevent people promoting or participating in the abusive use of secrecy jurisdictions was launched in 2006 and to date has gathered information on 32 000 offshore bank accounts held by Australian tax residents and has increased tax liabilities by over A$1 billion (although some assessments are in dispute) (ATO 2011). Beyond increasing revenues from offshore investment and in combination with improved information exchange the scheme seems to have had a deterrent effect, with capital flows between Australia and secrecy jurisdictions that have historically been popular with Australian investors diminishing in recent years. For example, the ATO notes that flows to Liechtenstein, Vanuatu and Switzerland have fallen by 80, 50 and 22 per cent respectively in recent years (Walsh 2011). In line with such evidence, tax attorneys in Australia concede that the combination of targeted enforcement and improved information exchange and data matching has diminished demand for aggressive offshore schemes.

The success of these VDSs not only boosts revenues but in combination suggests that improved tax information exchange and greater enforcement efforts from national tax authorities is actually changing taxpayer behaviour and improving compliance, which in turn is the only way to effectively regulate international tax evasion (Braithwaite 2005). However, despite this cautious optimism there are very real risks that recent progress may not be sustainable because as the OECD (2010c) notes, it is not known whether even well designed and administered schemes will be effective over the longer term. The risk is that with time taxpayers will become better informed about the risks and rewards of non-compliance under a VDS and as a result they may revert to non-compliant behaviour. For example, in the United States there is evidence that the second round of the IRS's Offshore Voluntary Disclosure Initiative (OVDI) launched in March 2009 has been less successful than expected, largely because of the perceived harsh treatment of those who had disclosed offshore income in the first round of the scheme (Matthews and Michel 2010). Ultimately only time will tell if improving compliance behaviour can be sustained as world leaders' rhetoric 'to end tax secrecy and tax havens' abates and taxpayers become more familiar with enforcement initiatives introduced in the immediate aftermath of the crisis.

CONCLUSIONS

This chapter has provided a preliminary assessment of the implementation and effectiveness of the Global Forum and various associated initiatives aimed at enhancing international tax transparency. The broad aim is to shed light on the critical question of whether the growing international commitment to end offshore tax evasion that was triggered by the financial crisis is likely to yield tangible results. Overall the evidence suggests that there is cause for cautious optimism, albeit with a number of significant caveats. Of particular significance is whether the very high levels of success in formally implementing the OECD's tax information exchange standard will actually result in reducing international tax evasion. This issue reflects a broader concern in the emerging literature on implementation in global governance that in many instances a lack of enforcement capacity and domestic political will may prevent international agreements and obligations from achieving their stated objectives.

Despite lingering concerns about the longer term efficacy of the post-crisis changes in the international tax regime, the progress that has been made on a number of fronts since the height of the crisis has exceeded the expectations of most analysts. Translating the international community's stated determination at the height of the financial crisis to address international tax evasion into a commitment to the rejuvenated Global Forum represents a major achievement. As has been argued both in Chapter 4 and above, the revised forum is both more inclusive and more democratic and promises a more robust peer review process. The international community's commitment to the Global Forum together with its reformed processes have led to unprecedented participation in the regime and implementation of the standard. As of early 2012 the vast majority of the 59 jurisdictions who had completed a Phase 1 Global Forum peer review indicated that they would be addressing the deficiencies identified in their assessment (Sawyer 2011). This evidence suggests that the Global Forum is highly likely to achieve its stated objective of ensuring the implementation of the OECD standard for tax information exchange among international financial centres.

The second and more important question is whether the formal implementation of the OECD's standard actually facilities the effective exchange of relevant tax information in practice. Here too some progress has been made but the chapter has also argued that challenges remain. For example, there are widespread concerns that smaller jurisdictions will lack the administrative capacity and access to sufficient tax and financial data to effectively exchange tax information in practice. A related issue is that the OECD standard of tax information exchange on request can only work effectively if there are high level of administrative cooperation between tax authorities and could easily be undermined by a national government determined to preserve opacity. While these are legitimate criticisms and real barriers to effective exchange of tax information, we can take some consolation that the new Phase 2 stage of the peer review process should be able to identify these deficiencies and promote an agenda for further reform.

The final and most important dimension of the international tax regime's effectiveness is whether the various measures to improve tax transparency and information exchange between states has had a discernable impact on the compliance behaviour of financial service providers and taxpayers. Clearly a good deal more research needs to be done to assess the impact of developments described in this book on patterns of taxpayer behaviour, both in the form of large-scale quantitative analyses of capital and investment flows to secrecy jurisdictions and through more sociological and ethnographic studies designed to provide insights into individual taxpayer behaviour. However this chapter has argued that the success of many VDS schemes gives cause for short-term optimism and suggests that a significant percentage of taxpayers who had used offshore investment strategies to conceal income from tax authorities are having second thoughts about this strategy in the light of improved tax information exchange.

Despite these improvements in terms of international commitment to tax transparency and institutional reforms in international tax governance which are promoting improved tax cooperation between national tax authorities, history suggests that the real political challenge may be consolidating these reforms. Previous chapters highlighted how the financial crisis played a critical role in galvanising political will behind an ambitious international reform agenda, including tax transparency, which in turn gave rise to the creation of the G20 Leaders' Forum. Just as these developments played a critical role in the reform of the international tax regime there is an attendant risk that as the acute phase of the financial crisis passes into history, the resolve of world leaders to tackle politically contested governance issues may start to wane. Yet as Braithwaite (2008, chapter 2) argues, effective governance requires eternal vigilance, as some jurisdictions attempt to subvert new standards while newly regulated actors mobilise against them. Perhaps the greatest threat of all is the capacity for commercial actors to develop innovative strategies and financial products to avoid regulation completely.

Even if the political commitment from world leaders to the regime remains strong, this chapter has identified a number of practical factors that could undermine the efficacy of the regime. These include a lack of administrative capacity to implement the standard or a simple realisation among non-compliant taxpayers that exchange of information on request is an ineffective instrument for detecting sophisticated international evasion strategies. This would result in a return to the pre-financial crisis scenario for many wealthy residents of high-tax jurisdictions where the rewards of investing offshore exceeded the risks for detection by tax authorities. Despite these real risks, and others besides, there is also a prospect that the events describes in this volume may prove to be a watershed in international tax regulation and a significant step towards the institutionalisation of a governance framework capable of supporting international tax cooperation. This theme of regime stability and consolidation is the focus of the concluding chapter.

REFERENCES

ATO (2011) 'Project Wickenby: Getting Results', Australian Tax Office, available at http://www.ato.gov.au/corporate/distributor.aspx?menuid=0&doc=/content/00220075.htm&page=16#P532_21116 (accessed September 2011).

Barnett, Michael and Martha Finnemore (2004) *Rules for the World: International Organizations in Global Politics*, Ithaca: Cornell University Press.

Braithwaite, John (2005) *Markets in Vice, Markets in Virtue*, Sydney: Federation Press.

Braithwaite, John (2008) *Regulatory Capitalism: How it Works, Ideas for Making it Work Better*, Cheltenham, UK and Northampton, MA, USA: Edward Elgar.

Brown, Gordon (2009) as quoted in Nick Mathiason, 'Obama Bid To Stamp Out Tax Havens', *Guardian*, 4 March.

Chayes, Abram and Antonia Chayes (1995) *The New Sovereignty: Compliance with International Regulatory Agreements*, Cambridge, MA: Harvard University Press.

Downs, George, David Rocke and Peter Barsoom (1996) 'Is the News about Compliance Good News about Cooperation?' *International Organization*, **50** (3), 379–406.

Drezner, Daniel (2007) *All Politics is Global: Explaining International Regulatory Regimes*, Princeton, NJ: Princeton University Press.

Eccleston, Richard (2010) 'Institutionalising International Cooperation in Tax Administration: The Evolution and Effectiveness of the OECD Forum on Tax Administration', Paper presented at the Australian School of Taxation International Tax Administration Conference, University of New South Wales, Sydney, available at http://ecite.utas.edu.au/73526/ (accessed September 2011).

FSB (2010) *Framework for Strengthening Adherence to International Standard*, Financial Stability Board, available at http://www.financialstabilityboard.org/publications/r_100109a.pdf (accessed July 2011).

G20 (2009a) 'Declaration on Strengthening the Financial System – London, 2 April 2009', available at http://www.g20.org/Documents/Fin_Deps_Fin_Reg_Annex_020409_-_1615_final.pdf (accessed June 2010).

G20 (2009b) 'Leaders' Statement: The Pittsburgh Summit September 24–25 2009', available at http://www.g20.org/Documents/pittsburgh_summit_leaders_statement_250909.pdf (accessed June 2010).

G20 (2011) 'Communiqué: Meeting of Finance Ministers and Central Bank Governors, Paris, 18–19 February 2011', available at http://www.g20.org/Documents2011/02/COMMUNIQUE-G20_MGM%20_18-19_February_2011.pdf (accessed September 2011).

Gluyas, Richard (2011) 'Australian Tax Office on a Fishing Expedition, Says Vanuatu', *Australian*, 24 February, available at http://www.theaustralian.com.au/business/australian-tax-office-on-a-fishing-expedition-says-vanuatu/story-e6frg8zx-1226010981573 (accessed July 2012).

Haas, Peter M., Robert Keohane and Marc A. Levy (eds) (1993) *Institutions for the Earth: Sources of Effective Environmental Protection*, Cambridge, MA: MIT Press.

HMRC (2011) 'How Territories are Categorised for Offshore Penalties', Her Majesty's Revenue and Customs, available at http://www.hmrc.gov.uk/news/territories-category.htm (accessed July 2011).

Ikenberry, John, David A. Lake and Michael Mastanduno (1988) *The State and American Foreign Economic Policy*, Ithaca: Cornell University Press.

International Tax Review (2010) 'A Time for Tax Transparency and Clarity', *International Tax Review*, **21** (3), 13–15.

Joachim, Jutta, Bob Reinalda and Bertjan Verbeek (eds) (2008) *International Organizations and Implementation, Enforcers, Managers, Authorities?* Oxford: Routledge.

Keohane, Robert (2001) 'Governance in a Partly Globalized World', *American Political Science Review*, **95** (1), 1–13.

Matthews, Mark and Scott Michel (2010) 'IRS's Voluntary Disclosure Program for Offshore Accounts: A Critical Assessment After One Year', *Daily Tax Report*, 21 September.

Meinzer, Markus (2012) 'The Creeping Futility of the Global Forum's Peer Reviews', Tax Justice Network, Tax Justice Briefing – March, available at http://www.taxjustice.net/cms/upload/GlobalForum2012-TJN-Briefing.pdf (accessed March 2012).

Murphy, Richard (2011a) 'The OECD Peer Review Process: Praise Where it is Due', *Tax Research UK,* 11 July, available at http://www.taxresearch.org.uk/Blog/2011/07/11/the-oecd-peer-review-process-%e2%80%93-praise-where-it-is-due/ (accessed July 2012).

Murphy, Richard (2011b) 'Do You Remember When They Said the Liechtenstein Deal Wouldn't Work?' *Tax Research UK*, 13 June, available at http://www.tax research.org.uk/Blog/2011/06/13/do-you-remember-when-they-said-the-liechten stein-deal-wouldnt-work/ (accessed July 2012).

North, Douglass C. (1990) *Institutions, Institutional Change and Economic Performance*, New York: Cambridge University Press.

OECD (1988) *Multilateral Convention on Mutual Administrative Assistance in Tax Matters*, Paris: OECD.

OECD (2009a) 'Decision of the Council Establishing The Global Forum on Transparency and Exchange of Information for Tax Purposes', available at ww w.olis.oecd.org/olis/2009doc.nsf/ENGDATCORPLOOK/NT00004F8E/$FILE /JT03270334.PDF (accessed September 2011).

OECD (2009b) 'Summary of Outcomes of the Mexico Meeting, September 1–2 2009', available at http://eoi-tax.org/keydocs/64b16f519e656fc34a7fe299bf9b41 d9 (accessed June 2010).

OECD (2010a) *Tax Cooperation 2010: Towards a Level Playing Field*, Paris: OECD.

OECD (2010b) *Peer Review Report of Panama – Phase 1: Legal and Regulatory Framework*, available at http://www.oecd.org/document/16/0,3746,en_21571361 _43854757_46099152_1_1_1_1,00.html (accessed September 2011).

OECD (2010c) *Offshore Voluntary Disclosure: Comparative Analysis, Guidance and Policy Advice*, Paris: OECD.

OECD (2011a) *The Global Forum on Transparency and Exchange of Information for Tax Purposes: Information Brief June 2011*, available at http://www.oecd.org /dataoecd/32/45/43757434.pdf (accessed September 2011).

OECD (2011b) *Peer Review Report of Botswana – Phase 1: Legal and Regulatory Framework*, available at http://www.oecd.org/document/25/0,3746,en_2649_201 185_46498457_1_1_1_1,00.html (accessed September 2011).

OECD (2011c) 'Bermuda Statement of Outcomes', available at http://www.oecd.o rg/dataoecd/50/11/48083609.pdf (accessed September 2011).

OECD (2011d) 'Convention on Mutual Administrative Assistance in Tax Matters – November 2011 Update', available at http://www.oecd.org/document/14/0,374 6,en_2649_33767_2489998_1_1_1_1,00.html (accessed November 2011).

OECD (2011e) *Peer Review Report of Switzerland – Phase 1: Legal and Regulatory Framework*, available at http://www.oecd.org/document/47/0,3746,en_21571361 _43854757_48079087_1_1_1,00.html (accessed September 2011).

OECD (2012) *The Global Forum on Transparency and Exchange of Information for Tax Purposes: Information Brief 16 April 2012*, available at http://www.oecd.org /dataoecd/32/45/43757434.pdf (accessed April 2012).

Picciotto, Sol (1992) *International Business Taxation*, London: Quorum.

Porter, Tony and Veronica Rubio-Vega (2012) 'Global Forum on Transparency and Exchange of Information for Tax Purposes', in Thomas N. Hale and David Held (eds), *Handbook of Innovations in Transnational Governance*, Cambridge: Polity Press, pp. 61–5.

Qureshi, Zia (2011) 'International Institutions and G20 Growth and Development Agenda', Presentation at HSE Conference Moscow, 20 April, available at http:/ /transcend-global.org/sites/default/files/IOs%20and%20G20-zq_0.pdf (accessed July 2012).

Radaelli, Claudio M. (1997) *The Politics of Corporate Taxation in the European Union*, London: Routledge.

Raustiala, Kal and David Victor (2004) 'The Regime Complex for Plant Genetic Resources', *International Organization*, **58** (2), 277–309.

Risse, Thomas (2000) 'Let's Argue: Communicative Action in World Politics', *International Organization*, **54** (1), 1–35.

Risse-Kapen, Thomas (1995) (ed.) *Bringing Transnational Relations Back In*, Cambridge: Cambridge University Press.

Saint-Amans, Pascal (2011) 'Remarks Made at the Closing Press Conference', Global Forum 2011, Bermuda, 1 June, available at http://www.oecd.org/docum ent/2/0,3746,en_21571361_43854757_48075778_1_1_1_1,00.html (accessed July 2011).

Sawyer, Adrian J. (2011) 'The OECD's Tax Information Exchange Agreements: An Example of (In)effective Global Governance', *Journal of Applied Law and Policy*, **4** (1), 41–54.

Scharpf, Fritz (1997) *Games Real Actors Play. Actor-Centered Institutionalism in Policy Research*, Boulder, CO: Westview.

Sharman, Jason (2006) *Havens in the Storm*, Ithaca: Cornell University Press.

Shaxon, Nicholas (2011) *Treasure Islands: Uncovering the Damage of Offshore Banking and Tax Havens*, New York: Palgrave Macmillan.

Tallberg, Jonas (2002) 'Paths to Compliance: Enforcement, Management and the European Union', *International Organization*, **56** (3), 609–43.

Underdal, Arild (1998) 'Explaining Compliance and Defection: Three Models', *European Journal of International Relations*, **4** (1), 5–30.

Victor, David, Kal Raustiala and Edward Skolinkoff (eds) (1998) *The Implementation and Effectiveness of Environmental Commitments*, Cambridge, MA: MIT Press.

Walsh, Katie (2011) 'Inquiry Windfall for ATO', *Australian Financial Review*, 13 July.

Walter, Andrew (2008) *Governing Finance: East Asia's Adoption of International Standards*, Ithaca: Cornell University Press.

Wilkinson, Thomas (2011) 'Tax Evaders Admit to Liechtenstein Accounts', Dow

Jones News, 3 February, available at http://www.efinancialnews.com/story/2011 -02-03/liechtenstein-disclosure-facilty-kaiser (accessed September 2011).

World Economic Forum (Various Years) *Global Competitiveness Index*, available at http://www.weforum.org/issues/global-competitiveness (accessed October 2011).

Yates, Marie Thérèse, Amber Hoffman, Kyle Bishop and Marnin Michaels (2011) 'The Death of Information Exchange Agreements? Part Three', *Journal of International Taxation*, **22** (4), 48–62.

Young, Oran (1979) *Compliance and Public Authority*, Baltimore: Johns Hopkins University Press.

Young, Oran R. (1999) *Governance in World Affairs*, Ithaca: Cornell University Press

Zagaris, Bruce (2005) 'The United Nations Role in International Tax Cooperation', *Tax Notes International*, April.

Conclusion: regime dynamics and the sustainability of international tax cooperation

The financial crisis that engulfed global markets in late 2007 continues to represent both a challenge and an opportunity for global economic governance. As of early 2012 the global economic outlook was far from certain and the prospects of restoring the 30 million jobs or the estimated 45 per cent of global wealth that have been destroyed since 2007 seem remote, as advanced industrial economies struggle under the weight of spiralling public debt and political malaise (ILO 2011; Davies 2009). Yet on a more optimistic note the severity of the crisis has acted as a catalyst for unprecedented international cooperation in developing and implementing a collective response to the severe challenges facing the global economy.

At the broadest level this book assesses the prospects for achieving effective and sustainable global economic governance in the aftermath of the financial crisis. Using international taxation as a case study, the book has described and evaluated how the acute challenges facing the global economy since the financial crisis began in 2007 and the resultant political and financial pressures that have been exerted on national governments have influenced patterns of global governance and international co-operation. Given the ongoing and rapidly evolving nature of the financial crisis our conclusions must be qualified, yet there is some evidence that the international community has responded to the call for 'all countries to join together to develop a global solution to . . . the greatest challenge the world economy has faced in modern times' (G20 2011). In the international tax arena the financial crisis has precipitated rapid, and in some ways unprecedented change, yet the processes through which this change has been achieved are complex and progress is far from assured. The following pages provide a summary of the analysis presented in the preceding chapters with an emphasis on the three central objectives of the study. First we summarise the theoretical insights that can be drawn from the empirical analysis presented in the volume. How significant was the financial crisis in shaping new patterns of international cooperation? To what extent have recent changes in the international tax regime relied on established international organisations and associated forums and the ideas they promote? How significant were domestic political factors in mediating such processes? Second, and perhaps more significantly, the chapter assesses the sustainability and likely effectiveness of recent initiatives in the international tax arena, such as the Global Forum, asking the critical question of whether such governance structures are capable of limiting international tax evasion on a sustainable basis. Finally the study concludes with an assessment of the outlook for global economic governance in the twenty-first century.

THE DYNAMICS OF REGIME CHANGE

The primary theoretical goal of this book is to make a contribution to the active debate concerning the dynamics of global economic governance and the complex array of variables that shape the nature of international regimes and the extent and effectiveness of international cooperation. The analysis presented in the preceding pages may have focused on the politics of international tax cooperation but this case study arguably provides important insights into the wider debate concerning cooperation in contemporary global governance.

Specifically, the literature summarised in Chapter 2 identified a number of causal processes that have the potential to influence patterns of international cooperation. For the purposes of this synopsis we revisit the three levels of analysis that were proposed to differentiate between the complex combinations of variables that have influenced patterns of international tax cooperation in recent years. The first concerns the impact of structural and international developments on patterns of international cooperation. Such variables may include changing geopolitical or international economic interests but also include the causal role of ideas, their development, proliferation and influence on the preferences of actors in the international tax arena. The second, organisational level concerns the changing institutional structure of the international tax regime including the changing roles of key international organisations, such as the OECD, and the development and impact of new inter-organisational networks such as that established between the OECD and the G20 at the height of the financial crisis. Finally, at the domestic level, we consider the enduring impact of the interests of key actors in the international tax regime. This analysis includes the capacity of financial interests to use their structural power to influence domestic policy preferences concerning international tax matters as well as the increasingly significant role of countervailing NGOs and tax justice activists.

Ideas and Regime Dynamics

Arguably the most significant trend in international political economy and global governance scholarship over the past decade has been the renewed focus on the causal role of ideas on patterns of international economic relations (Abdelal et al. 2010). The evidence presented in this book has highlighted some of the varied ways in which ideas and sociological variables can influence patterns of international cooperation. Arguably the most definitive way in which ideas shape international behaviour is consistent with liberal institutionalist claims concerning the significance of 'focal points' in international regimes which in turn enhance certainty and shape expectations concerning future behaviour. To recap, this literature argues that state behaviour and preparedness to comply with international agreements is influenced by engagement with and negotiation through forums (Keohane 1984; Checkel 2005). Central to this convergence process is the ability of international organisations to provide credible information, to reduce uncertainty and transaction costs, and to provide focal points amid regulatory uncertainty (Martin and Simmons 1998). Political expectations can also play a role in compliance, and if the vast majority of states believe that a regulatory agenda has momentum and is likely to persist as a dominant standard then compliance is likely, owing to the 'shadow of the future' (North 1990; Axelrod and Keohane 1993; Dal Bo 2005).

The evidence presented in Chapter 6 supports this hypothesis to the extent that the OECD's ability to provide a credible (albeit still contested) standard for information exchange provided a firm foundation for the proliferation of bilateral information exchange agreements from 2009 onwards. Significantly, interview-based data gathered for this study suggest that the OECD standard endorsed by the G20 and adopted by the Global Forum was, by and large, implemented by forum members not because it was regarded as appropriate and legitimate (many secrecy jurisdictions still have significant concerns on this account), but because (unlike the HTC regime in the early 2000s) their expectations were that compliance would be enforced and that rival jurisdictions would not be able to win market share by failing to implement the standard. In terms of Checkel's framework outlined in Chapter 2, this is a clear example of *Type 1* socialisation in which rational actors accept institutionally appropriate rules, behaviours and incentives through their participation in the regime. In contrast there was much less evidence of deeper 'constitutive' *Type 2* socialisation which occurs when actors adopt new norms and assume new interests as a result of prolonged participation in a regime, although it is also important to note that this form of deep socialisation takes time and the operations of the revised Global Forum are in their infancy. On the other hand, the preparedness of the UK, Germany and the US to develop alternative standards that may undermine the Global Forum's work (Chapter 5) suggests that their commitment to the forum process may be more instrumental than normative.

At the macro level of 'policy paradigms', or the broad cognitive frameworks used to interpret the political world, there is an established literature that suggests that a political or economic crisis of the magnitude of the present crisis has the potential to undermine the intellectual credibility and political viability of the prevailing policy order, leading to its displacement (Hall 1993; Kay 2006; Widmaier et al. 2007; Chapter 5). Despite credible claims that excessive financial liberalisation was a central cause of the financial crisis it is remarkable that, to date at least, the intellectual and political viability of the liberal order that has defined the global political economy since the mid-1970s has gone largely unchallenged (Gill 2010; Crouch 2011). Even at the more applied level of specific policy instruments, proposals such as developing new and more robust approaches to taxing capital income through a financial transaction tax or even allocating the corporate and capital income tax base on a country-by-country basis via a formula apportionment system still only enjoy limited political support (Kudrle 2010, 84; Clausing and Avi-Yonah 2007). Despite its severity, the financial crisis has not led to a fundamental shift in thinking about how either the global economy or the international tax regime ought to be regulated.

One particular area in which there is evidence that the financial crisis has had an impact on the ideational construction of international tax governance has been in promoting awareness of the problems associated with international tax evasion among the mass public. This greater awareness of the problem, combined with a popular backlash against banks and international financial organisations more generally has greatly enhanced electoral support for the introduction of more robust anti-evasion measures and enhanced international tax cooperation. This shift in public sentiments explains world leaders' preparedness to endorse the OECD's tax transparency measures at G20 meetings over the course of 2009 (Chapter 4) and the Obama campaign and the administration's commitment to the issue since 2008 (Chapter 5). As will be discussed in greater detail below, this shift in popular awareness of and support for international tax transparency may have contributed to the viability of the reform agenda which has evolved since 2008, but there is also evidence that the prolonged crisis has enhanced the structural power of financial interests opposed to enhanced tax transparency. In many ways the policy and political conflict over the merits of enhanced tax transparency versus international tax competitiveness remains unresolved.

Institutions and Inter-Organisational Networks and Regime Dynamics

The second important set of theoretical questions outlined in Chapter 2 concerns the ways in which the institutional structure of a regime influences patterns of international cooperation. The first aspect of this debate relates to the potentially independent impact of international organisations, such as the OECD, on the extent and effectiveness of international tax cooperation. Whereas realist scholars argue that international organisations largely reflect and promote the interest of the states that create them (Waltz 2000), liberals argue that they can have an independent impact in terms of regime dynamics by providing certainty and incentives to engage in mutually beneficial behaviour (Keohane 2005). The argument that international organisations have a significant and autonomous impact on patterns of global governance is taken further in the constructivist literature, with its emphasis on their potential to generate and disseminate policy ideas and norms (Barnett and Finnemore 1999, 2004). We have already noted the role that organisations such as the OECD have played in reshaping the preferences of member states through a process of *Type 1* socialisation, but there is also a good deal of evidence to suggest they have had an independent impact on promoting tax issues on the international policy agenda. The revisionist literature on international organisations highlights their potential to create, promote and enforce their own agendas in global politics (Abbott and Snidal 2001; Barnett and Finnemore 2004), and this study clearly identified the OECD's central role in actively promoting its established tax transparency agenda, which resulted in its endorsement by the G20 in 2009 (Chapter 4). The nature and impact of the relationship between the G20 and the OECD concerning international tax matters since the onset of the financial crisis also highlights the significance of relationships and network structures between organisations and other stakeholders in global governance. As scholars of networks in both global governance and public policy have argued, patterns of engagement between actors and the nature of their mutual dependence has a significant bearing on the nature of political outcomes. The evidence presented in Chapter 4 highlighted how the OECD actively engaged with the G20, promoting its capacity to provide a refined and credible regulatory reform agenda. This advocacy resulted in the G20 endorsing the OECD tax transparency regime which in turn mobilised political support for the agenda. This development may have been a fillip for the campaign to enhance international tax transparency, but it also highlights the need to assess the longer-term viability of the G20-OECD relationship forged during the height of the financial crisis (see below). A final conclusion that can be drawn from this analysis is the need for more

theoretical work and detailed empirical analysis on the extent and consequences of inter-organisational networks in global governance (Eccleston
et al. 2010).

Domestic Politics, Structural Power and Regime Dynamics

In contested and financially sensitive international policy arenas, such as
international trade and taxation, domestic politics clearly matters. If international commitments run contrary to powerful interests then national
governments will be pressured to withdraw from agreements (if they are
entered into) or, at the very least, will fail to implement them in a mean-
ingful way (Drezner 2007). If powerful states are particularly concerned
about the impact of a specific regime they may attempt to undermine it
by creating alternative standards and regulatory frameworks in a process
referred to as 'forum shifting' (Braithwaite and Drahos 2000, ch. 24).
Often, as Underdal (1998) highlights, well intentioned commitments made
by national governments in the international arena will unravel in the
face of staunch domestic resistance, leading to the 'vertical disintegration
of global public policy'. This dynamic has a number of causes including
international negotiators' lack of awareness of domestic political sensitivi-
ties; it is also particularly vulnerable to business interests, which are better
organised and more able to exert political influence at the domestic level
(Kellow 2002).

Not only do domestic politics and, more specifically, domestic political
resistance have a significant impact on international taxation but as this
study has clearly demonstrated, changing domestic preferences and priorities influence regime dynamics (Chapters 3 and 5). This evidence affirms
the need to further develop and refine our theoretical understanding of
the complex and interdependent relationship between domestic politics
and international affairs. One of the most important conclusions that
can be drawn from this study is the need to place a much greater emphasis on business power; how it varies and how it is exerted at a domestic
level. This is not to say domestic institutions, governing coalitions and
ideas (Katzenstein 1978) are unimportant, but rather that this focus on
institutional and ideational variables needs to be supplemented with more
sophisticated theories of business power and why it fluctuates across
time. To this end, we need to follow Vogel's lead (1989) and move beyond
static conceptions of structural power to develop theoretically informed
accounts of why the structural power of business varies. This study has
argued that the structural power of financial interests has increased in
most advanced democracies since 2009 as governments have become
increasingly desperate to promote private investment, employment and

economic growth, which in turn threatens to have a profound impact on international tax policy. However, as constructivists such as Barnett and Duvall (2005) argue, structural power is not simply a product of the business cycle; it is also the product of social relations and the inter-subjective assessments of prevailing economic conditions and appropriate policy responses. Bell's (2012) recent call to focus on state actors and the changing ways in which they interpret the demands being made of them by powerful business interests represents the most sophisticated contribution to the debate thus far and could usefully be incorporated into a more comprehensive account of how changing domestic political and economic conditions can influence both national policy preferences and the prospects for international cooperation.

The complex array of factors and processes that have influenced the nature of the international tax regime and the changing patterns of international cooperation identified in this study affirm the need to adopt an empirically grounded research method and then draw connections from detailed to case studies to broader theories of international regime change (Young 1999, 132). More specifically, this study has applied extant theories of international regime change to an analysis of recent developments in the international tax arena. While the theoretical findings of the study outlined above are, by necessity, largely contingent on the historical circumstances prevailing in the international tax arena in the aftermath of the financial crisis, more robust analytical claims could be made if this analysis of international taxation is supplemented with similar studies of post-crisis politics in other regulatory arenas. Such a comparative study of post-crisis international regime change is an important agenda for future research.

THE SUSTAINABILITY OF INTERNATIONAL TAX COOPERATION AND ITS IMPLICATIONS FOR GLOBAL GOVERNANCE

This book argues that the progress that has been made in relation to international tax cooperation since 2007 remains vulnerable and that there are still many challenges to be overcome. Given that high levels of public debt and associated fiscal and political problems are threatening to engulf many advanced industrial economies it is important to assess the sustainability of international tax cooperation and the prospects for establishing an efficient and equitable international taxation regime in the twenty-first century.

A central theme in the literature on the political economy of economic regulation is the cyclical nature of the relationship between regulators and the regulated. A crisis or a lesser incident that highlights an acute regulatory failure will momentarily politicise an issue and spur regulatory action (Zimmermann 2010; Braithwaite 2008, ch. 2). Yet, with the passage of time the political agenda moves on, providing an opportunity for countervailing groups to erode regulatory standards or develop new practices to circumvent established rules. This study clearly provides some evidence to support the notion that international tax cooperation has fallen into what Downs (1972) described as 'the issue attention cycle'. The communiqué arising from the G20 Leaders' Forum held in Cannes in November 2011 both 'welcome(d) the progress made' in relation to international tax matters and 'encouraged further work and cooperation', but clearly lacked the solidarity and resolve that was a feature of the London 2009 communiqué (G20 2011). As was argued in Chapters 5 and 6, there is still broad-based commitment to improving offshore tax enforcement, but increasingly this is being pursued through unilateral rather than collective initiatives.

At the level of institutions, this study has argued that the rise of the G20 Leaders' Forum and its endorsement of the OECD's tax transparency agenda can explain a good deal of the recent progress that has been made in relation to international tax cooperation. As a consequence, the sustainability of the regime in part depends on the ongoing support and ongoing viability of the G20 Leaders' Forum. This is especially true given the possible gradual decline in US power and influence in global economic affairs in coming decades, which may limit the extent and effectiveness of American leadership on international tax matters. It is difficult to make definitive predictions, but it is important to note the growing uncertainty in relation to the G20's longer-term role, regulatory reform agenda and influence. A critical issue here is that the rise of the G20 was born out of the political need to exercise solidarity and act decisively at the height of the crisis. The increasingly apparent concern is that with the passage of time tensions between G20 members will increase and the forum will be less willing and able to endorse the programmes of partner organisations. A particular risk insofar as the OECD is concerned is that the developing states within the G20, and China in particular, may be unwilling to endorse and promote the activities of an organisation so closely associated with Western economic interests (Malloch-Brown 2010; Garrett 2010).

The outlook for the G20 may be less than certain, but even if its influence wanes over time it has left an important institutional legacy in the form of the revised Global Forum. As was argued in Chapter 6, the revised forum does represent significant progress in terms of its expanded membership and more robust processes, but its effectiveness and sustainability are also critically dependent on its successful implementation and reasonably broad-based compliance. As Levi (1989) has argued, compliance with many international agreements is 'semi-voluntary' in nature and states are more likely to meet their international obligations if they are confident that other jurisdictions are also going to be bound by the same commitments. This is why members' perceptions of the integrity of the Global Forum's peer review process (Chapter 6) is so important; it also highlights a more general need for a greater focus on implementation in global governance research (Young 1999; Keohane 2005; Joachim et al. 2008).

Despite this progress towards establishing a more universal and rigorous approach to tax transparency, including the OECD's recent commitment to automatic information exchange, the governance challenges still facing such a regime make it necessary to consider practical alternatives. The Achilles heel of the evolving regime is that states are unwilling to cede sufficient sovereignty to ensure ongoing and universal compliance. The theoretical basis of this argument is now well understood, with scholars such as Rixen (2008) arguing that national governments should cede formal 'de jure sovereignty' to a more formal international tax organisation in order to enhance their 'de facto sovereignty', or a government's ability to achieve policy objectives in practice. Despite the compelling logic of such arguments the political reality is that even at the height of the crisis there was little enthusiasm for a more formal, multilateral form of international tax governance.

What may ultimately be required are innovative approaches that both preserve sovereignty and address the challenges of international tax evasion. One such proposal is a system of 'formula apportionment' whereby tax liabilities would reflect the underlying realities of where commercial activity actually occurred. Under such a regime a firm's, or an international investor's worldwide income would be allocated to jurisdictions according to the proportion of economic activity they actually hosted (Clausing and Avi-Yonah 2007; Picciotto 2011). Firms would have little incentive to shift income through various legal structures to low-tax jurisdictions for bookkeeping purposes because in the absence of significant economic activity little tax would be paid offshore. Such an approach could help end the artificial separation of legal and economic aspects of commerce which underpins the current offshore system and which provides fertile ground for international tax evasion (Chapter 1; Palan et al. 2010).

Despite the intuitive appeal of formula apportionment, many practical and political barriers stand in the way of its adoption, including reaching international agreement on an appropriate formula and basis for sharing international tax income and on establishing a standard for what constitutes real economic activity. Given these formidable barriers to formal implementation an important intermediate step is to encourage multinational corporations to report their profits, tax paid and activities on a country-by-country basis. As tax justice campaigners have rightly argued, the current requirements for firms to publish one set of consolidated accounts allows them to obscure the full extent and geographic spread of their commercial activities and tax contributions (Murphy 2004). If activists, customers and other stakeholders can mobilise and encourage multinational firms to engage in country-by-country reporting then this will enhance awareness of the extent and consequences of aggressive tax planning, which will serve as a foundation for more substantial reform.

Whatever the merits of alternative systems of international tax governance, they all rely on high levels of international cooperation and transparency. For example, a robust system of formula apportionment would rely on all members of the international community providing appropriate information concerning the commercial activities of all firms operating in their territory. Even if such a system was implemented and was successful in terms of effectively taxing publicly listed multinational corporations, it would arguably have much less impact on the ability of private investors to evade tax offshore. If, in the coming years the international community is unable to agree on and implement effective rules for governing international taxation then it is perhaps inevitable that all but the most powerful governments may be forced to abandon the taxation of capital and corporate income, leaving middle and lower income earners to shoulder a significantly greater share of the tax burden. Such an outcome would not only be inequitable but would also further undermine the legitimacy and sustainability of democratic governance.

This study has largely focused on the politics of international tax cooperation and information exchange in the aftermath of the financial crisis but it has also highlighted some of the fundamental challenges in global governance which are likely to dominate world politics in the twenty-first century. The dilemma facing the international community is that the need for effective global governance is as acute now as at any time in recent history, given ever increasing economic integration, global environmental and development challenges, not to mention the specific coordination challenges arising from the financial crisis itself. Despite this acute need, the capacity of the international system to develop and deliver effective governance is arguably lower today than during the immediate post-war period. Not only is the United States less willing and able to provide global leadership in the way that it did in the second half of the twentieth century, but many of the rules-based multilateral institutions that were created as part of the Bretton Woods settlement are also in decline. Overall these broader historical trends have generally intensified as a result of the financial crisis. The acute phase of the crisis may have necessitated greater levels of cooperation but it also highlighted the limits of existing international financial institutions and the structural problems and declining power of Western economies. As the acute phase of the crisis passes and many developed nations enter a sustained period of slow economic growth, debt reduction and politically unpopular restructuring, protectionist instincts and mercantilist politics are on the rise. When this is combined with a lack of leadership from emerging 'growth' economies, it is arguable that the political and economic conditions for effective global governance have never been more challenging.

REFERENCES

Abbot, Kenneth and Duncan Snidal (2001) 'Why do States Act through Formal Organizations', in Paul Diehl (ed.), *The Politics of Global Governance*, Boulder, CO: Lynne Reinner, pp. 25–59.

Abdelal, Rawi, Mark Blyth and Craig Parsons (eds) (2010) *Constructing the World Economy*, Ithaca: Cornell University Press.

Axelrod, Robert and Robert Keohane (1993) 'Achieving Cooperation under Anarchy', in David Baldwin (ed.), *Neorealism and Neoloberalism: The Contemporary Debate*, New York: Columbia University Press, pp. 85–115.

Barnett, Michael and Raymond Duvall (2005) 'Power in International Politics', *International Organization*, **59**, 39–75.

Barnett, Michael and Martha Finnemore (1999) 'The Politics, Power and Pathologies of International Organizations', *International Organization*, **43** (4), 699–732.

Barnett, Michael and Martha Finnemore (2004), *Rules for the World: International Organizations in World Politics*, Ithaca: Cornell University Press.

Bell, Stephen (2012) 'The Power of Ideas: The Ideational Shaping of the Structural Power of Business', *International Studies Quarterly*, **26** (3), forthcoming.

Braithwaite, John (2008) *Regulatory Capitalism: How it Works, Ideas for Making it Work Better*, Cheltenham, UK and Northampton, MA, USA: Edward Elgar.

Braithwaite, John and Peter Drahos (2000) *Global Business Regulation*, Cambridge: Cambridge University Press.

Checkel, Jeffrey T. (2005) 'International Institutions and Socialization in Europe: Introduction and Framework', *International Organization*, **59** (4), 801–26.

Clausing, Kimberly and Reuven Avi-Yonah (2007) 'Reforming Corporate Taxation in a Global Economy: A Proposal to Adopt Formulary Apportionment, in Path to Prosperity', Brookings Institution, Washington DC, available at http://www.brookings.edu/papers/2007/06corporatetaxes_clausing.aspx (accessed July 2012).

Crouch, Colin (2011) *The Strange Non-Death of Neo-Liberalism*, Cambridge: Polity Press.

Dal Bo, Pedro (2005) 'Cooperation under the Shadow of the Future', *American Economic Review*, **95** (5), 1591–604.

Davies, Megan (2009) '45 percent of world's wealth destroyed', *Reuters*, 10 March.

Downs, Anthony (1972) 'The Issues-Attention Cycle', *Public Interest*, **28**, 38–50.

Drezner, Daniel. (2007) *All Politics is Global: Explaining International Regulatory Regimes*, Princeton, NJ: Princeton University Press.

Eccleston, Richard, Peter Carroll and Aynsley Kellow (2010) 'Handmaiden to the G20? The OECD's Evolving Role in Global Governance', Paper presented at the Australian Political Science Association Conference 2010, University of Melbourne, Melbourne, 27 September.

G20 (2011) 'Cannes Summit Final Declaration – November 2011', available at htt p://www.g20.org/Documents2011/11/Cannes%20Declaration%204%20Novemb er%202011.pdf (accessed November 2011).

Garrett, Geoffrey (2010) 'G2 in G20: The United States and the World after the Global Financial Crisis', *Global Policy*, **1** (1), 29–39.

Gill, Stephen (2010) 'The Global Organic Crisis: Paradoxes, Dangers, Opportunities', *Monthly Review*, available at http://mrzine.monthlyreview.org /2010/gill150210.html (accessed July 2012).

Hall, Peter (1993) 'Policy Paradigms, Social Learning and the State: The Case of Economic Policymaking in Britain', *Comparative Politics*, **25** (3), 275–96.

International Labour Office (2011) *Global Employment Trends 2011: The Challenges of a Jobs Recovery*, Geneva: ILO.

Joachim, Jutta, Bob Reinalda and Bertjan Verbeek (eds) (2008) *International Organizations and Implementation: Enforcers, Managers, Authorities?* Abingdon and New York: Routledge.

Katzenstein, Peter (1978) *Between Power and Plenty: Foreign Economic Policies of Advanced Industrial States*, Madison: University of Wisconsin Press.

Kay, Adrian (2006) *The Dynamics of Public Policy: Theory and Evidence*, Cheltenham, UK and Northampton, MA, USA: Edward Elgar.

Kellow, Aynsley (2002) 'Comparing Business and Public Interest Associability at the International Level', *International Political Science Review*, **23** (2), 175–86.

Keohane, Robert (1984) *After Hegemony: Cooperation and Discord in the World Political Economy*, Princeton, NJ: Princeton University Press

Keohane, Robert (2005) *After Hegemony: Cooperation and Discord in the World Political Economy*, Princeton, NJ: Princeton University Press.

Kudrle, Robert (2010) 'Tax Policy in the OECD: Soft Governance Gets Harder', in Kerstin Martins and Anja Jakobi (eds), *Mechanisms of OECD Governance: International Incentives for National Policy-Making?* Oxford: Oxford University Press, pp. 75–95.

Levi, Margaret (1989) *Of Revenue and Rule*, Los Angeles: University of California Press.

Malloch-Brown, Mark (2010) 'How the G20 is under Attack', *Financial Times*, 11 November.

Martin, Lisa and Beth Simmons (1998) 'Theories and Empirical Studies of International Institutions', *International Organization*, **52** (4), 729–57.

Murphy, Richard (2004) 'Location, Location', *Accountancy Magazine*, March.

North, Douglass (1990) *Institutions, Institutional Change and Economic Performance*, Cambridge: Cambridge University Press.

Palan, Ronen (2003), *The Offshore World: Sovereign Markets, Virtual Places, and Nomad Millionaires*, Ithaca: Cornell University Press.

Palan, Ronen, Richard Murphy and Christian Chavagneux (2010) *Tax Havens: How Globalization Really Works*, Ithaca: Cornell University Press.

Picciotto, Sol (2011) *Regulating Global Corporate Capitalism*, Cambridge: Cambridge University Press.

Rixen, Thomas (2008) *The Political Economy of International Tax Governance: Transformations of the State*, New York: Palgrave Macmillan.

Underdal, Arild (1998) 'Explaining Compliance and Defection: Three Models', *European Journal of International Relations*, 4 (1), 5–30.

Vogel, David (1989) *Fluctuating Fortunes: The Political Power of Business in America*, New York: Basic Books.

Waltz, Kenneth N. (2000) 'Structural Realism after the Cold War', *International Security*, 25 (1), 5–41.

Widmaier, Wes, Mark Blyth and Len Seabrooke (2007) 'The Social Construction of Wars and Crises as Openings for Change', *International Studies Quarterly*, 52, 747–59.

Young, Oran R. (1999) *Governance in World Affairs*, Ithaca: Cornell University Press.

Zimmermann, Herman (2010) 'Whither International Financial Regulation?', in Eric Helleiner, Stefano Pagliari and Herman Zimmermann (eds), *Global Finance in Crisis: The Politics of International Regulatory Change*, Oxford: Routledge, pp. 170–75.

Index